Praise for
THE LANGUAGE

"[Jurafsky's] brilliant achievement is t̶ ̶̶̶̶̶̶̶̶ ̶̶̶̶̶̶̶̶ ̶̶̶̶̶̶̶̶ ̶̶̶̶̶ journey food makes through culture with the journey its name makes through language."　　　—Peter Sokolowski, *New York Times Book Review*

"Fascinating."　　　　　　　　　　　　　—Ezra Klein, *Vox*

"Readers will leave the table with their taste buds tempted and their intellects fully nourished."　　　—Kristin Baird Rattini, *American Way*

"You'll never look at 'chef's choice' the same way again."
　　　　　　　　　—Ruth Walker, *Christian Science Monitor*

"People may swoon over colorful expressions and interesting etymologies. And Mr. Jurafsky's book offers plenty of that. . . . But for linguists, the less obviously colorful aspects of our food talk reveal much about the deeper structures of our language and psychology."
　　　　　　　　　—Jennifer Schuessler, *New York Times*

"The complexities of language, intertwined with the endless combinations of ingredients and the rich history of eating, make for a rich and rewarding read."　　　—Matthew Tiffany, *Minneapolis Star Tribune*

"Spectacular."　　　　　—Joshua David Stein, *New York Observer*

"A panoramic window onto everything from the modern descendants of ancient recipes to the covert persuasion on restaurant menus."
　　　　　　　　　　　　　　　　　—*Jewish Book World*

"Hugely entertaining."　　　—Clint Witchalls, *Independent* (UK)

"Engrossing. . . . [W]eaves history, language, psychology and cultural studies together in a series of deeply informed, highly entertaining gastro-etymological quests."   —*Passport Magazine*

"Ever since I heard the phrase 'fresh frozen' I have been wondering about food language. Now Dan Jurafsky has taken on the subject with scholarship, wit, and charm, making *The Language of Food* a very engaging book."   —Mark Kurlansky, author of *Cod*

"Writing with knowledge and wit, Dan Jurafsky shows that the language of food reflects our desires and aspirations, whether it's on a fancy French menu or a bag of potato chips."   —Bee Wilson, author of
Consider the Fork: A History of How We Cook and Eat

"*The Language of Food* is excellent, a fascinating read from beginning to end. From pastas to pastries, you can't resist Dan Jurafsky's insights into what we say about food."   —Tyler Cowen, professor of economics,
George Mason University, and author of *Average Is Over*

"Mix equal parts fascinating history, surprising etymology, and brilliant linguistic analysis, add a generous dollop of humor, and savor *The Language of Food*. You'll never think of ketchup, French fries, fish and chips, or toast in the same way."
—Deborah Tannen, author of the #1 bestseller
You Just Don't Understand: Women and Men in Conversation

"Delightful. The distinguished linguist Dan Jurafsky brings a battery of skills to reveal the far-flung links of many of our dishes, to reveal how potato chip advertisements work, and to give an insider's guide to reading menus. I couldn't put this book down."
—Rachel Laudan, author of
Cuisine and Empire: Cooking in World History

THE
LANGUAGE
OF FOOD

A Linguist Reads the Menu

Dan Jurafsky

W. W. NORTON & COMPANY

Independent Publishers Since 1923

New York · London

Lime Syrup recipe (page 149) reproduced with permission from *Food of Life:
Ancient Persian and Modern Iranian Cooking and Ceremonies*, by Najmieh Batmanglij,
Mage Publishers, www.mage.com

For information about permission to reproduce selections from this book,
write to Permissions, W. W. Norton & Company, Inc.,
500 Fifth Avenue, New York, NY 10110

For information about special discounts for bulk purchases, please contact
W. W. Norton Special Sales at specialsales@wwnorton.com or 800-233-4830

Manufacturing by LSC Harrisonburg
Book design by Kristen Bearse
Production manager: Anna Oler

Library of Congress Cataloging-in-Publication Data

Jurafsky, Dan, 1962–
The language of food : a linguist reads the menu / Dan Jurafsky.
pages cm
Includes bibliographical references and index.
ISBN 978-0-393-24083-2 (hardcover)
1. Food—History. 2. Food—Terms and phrases.
3. Dinners and dining—Terms and phrases. 4. Food habits—History.
5. English language—Etymology. I. Title.
TX353J78 2014
641.32009—dc23

2014020202

ISBN 978-0-393-35162-0 pbk.

W. W. Norton & Company, Inc.
500 Fifth Avenue, New York, N.Y. 10110
www.wwnorton.com

W. W. Norton & Company Ltd.
15 Carlisle Street, London W1D 3BS

2 3 4 5 6 7 8 9 0

For Janet

Contents

Introduction   1

1   How to Read a Menu   7

2   Entrée   21

3   From Sikbāj to Fish and Chips   35

4   Ketchup, Cocktails, and Pirates   49

5   A Toast to Toast   64

6   Who Are You Calling a Turkey?   78

7   Sex, Drugs, and Sushi Rolls   92

8   Potato Chips and the Nature of the Self   107

9   Salad, Salsa, and the Flour of Chivalry   117

10   Macaroon, Macaron, Macaroni   130

11   Sherbet, Fireworks, and Mint Juleps   144

12   Does This Name Make Me Sound Fat?
Why Ice Cream and Crackers Have Different Names   159

13   Why the Chinese Don't Have Dessert   171

Epilogue   187
Notes   191
References   211
Acknowledgments   229
Image Credits   231
Index   233

THE LANGUAGE
OF FOOD

Introduction

THIS BOOK BEGAN WITH two questions. The first came from Katie, the very observant seven-year-old daughter of my old friends Jim and Linda. Katie asked why the label of a ketchup bottle read "tomato ketchup." (Go look: most of them do.) Isn't that redundant, she asked? It was a sensible question. After all, if I go into a bar and order a margarita, I don't order a "tequila margarita." A margarita is made of tequila. (Otherwise, it would be a daiquiri. Or a gimlet. Or even, God forbid, a cosmopolitan.) The tequila is understood.

So why do we mention the tomatoes in ketchup?

The second question came from Shirley, a friend from Hong Kong. Back when I was a young linguist studying Cantonese there, everyone assured me that the word ketchup came from Chinese—the second part of ketchup, *tchup*, is identical to the word for "sauce" in Cantonese, and the first part, *ke*, is part of the Cantonese word for "tomato." Shirley was so convinced that ketchup was a Chinese word that when she went to a McDonald's in the United States she confused her friends by asking what the English word for *ke-tchup* was. But how could ketchup be Chinese?

It turns out Katie's question and Shirley's question have the same answer. The ketchup we eat today is nothing like the original version created many centuries ago. Few people today would recognize the link with the original *ke-tchup*, a Chinese fermented fish sauce first made in Fujian province (an area that also gave us the word *tea*). From the fourteenth to the eighteenth centuries, Chinese traders settled in ports throughout Southeast Asia and brought Chinese fermentation methods. They fermented local fish into ke-tchup—a fish sauce like the modern Vietnamese fish sauce *nuoc mam*—they fermented soybeans into soy sauce, and they fermented rice with a red ferment, molasses, and palm sugar and distilled it into an ancestor of rum called *arrack*. Arrack was the first widely produced liquor, long before rum or gin had been invented, so when English and Dutch sailors and merchants came to Asia around 1650 to trade for silk, porcelain, and tea, they bought vast quantities of arrack and used it to invent the world's first cocktail ("punch") for their navies. (And punch led eventually to modern cocktails like daiquiris and gimlets and margaritas.). Along the way, they also acquired a taste for the pungent fish sauce.

The traders brought ke-tchup back to Europe and over the next 400 years this dish evolved to fit Western tastes, losing its original ingredient, the fermented fish. Early recipes replaced the fish with English mushroom or, as in Jane Austen's household, walnuts. By the nineteenth century in England, there were many recipes for ketchup; eventually the most popular one added tomatoes and then came to America where it acquired sugar. Then it acquired even more sugar. This version eventually became America's national condiment, and was then exported to Hong Kong and the rest of the world.

The story of ketchup is a fascinating window onto the great meetings of East and West that created foods we eat every day, telling us how sailors and merchants spent a thousand years melding the food preferences of the West and the East to form our modern cuisines. But this great process produced more than just ketchup, as we can tell from linguistic evidence scattered through modern languages. Fish and chips, England's national dish, began with Persian *sikbāj*, a sweet-and-sour stew with vinegar and onions loved by the Shahs of sixth-century Persia. The dish leaves its marks in the names descended from *sikbāj* in different languages—French dishes like *aspic*, Spanish dishes like *escabeche*, or Peruvian dishes like *ceviche*— and the story moves from the golden palaces of medieval Baghdad to the wooden ships of Mediterranean sailors, from the religious fasts of medieval Christians to the cold Sabbath fish of the Jews who left Spain in 1492.

Macaroons, *macarons*, and *macaroni* all descend from one sweet doughy predecessor, when a Persian food, the almond pastry called *lauzīnaj*, intermingled with the pastas of the Arab world and the durum wheat that the Romans had planted in Sicily, the breadbasket of the Roman Empire.

We'll look at the answers to questions of science, politics, and culture. Who came up with the idea of putting cream or juice into a bucket surrounded by salt and ice to make sorbet or ice cream, and how does it relate to the patent medicinal syrups that became our modern Cokes and Pepsis? The answers lie in the adventures of the words *sherbet*, *sorbet*, and *syrup*, and their descent from an Arabic word meaning drink or syrup.

Why is the *turkey*, a bird native to Mexico, named for a Muslim democracy of the eastern Mediterranean? It has to do with the fanatic secrecy of the Portuguese in the fifteenth and sixteenth centuries, whose attempt to keep other countries from finding their overseas sources of gold and spices and exotic birds led to the confusion of the turkey with an entirely different bird that was imported by the Mamluks.

Why do we give *toasts* at weddings? It is not related to the custom of toaster ovens as wedding presents, but the two do share a surprising history involving toasted bread.

Why do we fancy something sweet at the end of a meal—so much so that we have influenced Chinese restaurants in the United States to offer one when their own culture didn't even have a word for "dessert," let alone a fortune cookie? We'll see the history of dessert (rooted in Andalusia, Baghdad, and Persia), and we'll introduce the grammar of cuisine, the idea that eating sweets at the end of a meal (rather than, say, the beginning) is rooted in the implicit structures that define each modern cuisine in the same way grammar rules help define a language.

The language of food helps us understand the interconnectedness of civilizations and the vast globalization that happened, not recently, as we might think, but centuries or millennia ago, all brought together by the most basic human pursuit: finding something good to eat. You might call this aspect of the book "EATymology." But the language of food isn't just an etymological clue to the past. The words we use to talk about food are also a code that we can decipher to better understand the present.

In our lab at Stanford, we use linguistic tools to study online or digital texts of all kinds, with the goal of better understanding the human condition. We've studied recordings of speed dates to uncover the subconscious linguistic signs of a date going well or badly, showing that the advice from dating manuals is completely backward. We've tested pages on the online encyclopedia Wikipedia to uncover the subtle linguistic cues to an author's covert biases. We've used linguistic theories of politeness to automatically measure how polite different people are on the web, and show that, sadly, the more power and status people achieve, the less polite they become.

Throughout this book I'll apply these computational linguistic tools to the study of food, drawing on rich datasets now available due to the rise of the Internet and examining millions of online restaurant reviews, thousands of online menus, the linguistics of food advertising and food brands.

I'll use these tools and others from the intersection of linguistics and economics to uncover subtle linguistic cues hidden in the language of today's food advertisers, showing surprising ways that you are being targeted every time you read a menu or even look at the text on the back of a package of potato chips. You will even see how linguistic cues can predict the price of individual dishes on a menu, based not only on the words that appear but also on those purposely omitted.

The language of food also tells us about human psychology, who we are, from the nature of our perception and emotions to the social psychology of our attitudes toward others. By using software to investigate millions of online reviews of restaurants or beers, we discover evidence for the Pollyanna effect: a claim from psychology that human nature strongly tends toward the positive and optimistic. Hence our comparisons of good food to, say, sexual pleasure. We'll also look at how people talk about restaurants they really hate, the scathing 1-star reviews, discovering what people are most traumatized by, and we'll see that it's all about our connection to others.

Finally, we'll talk about health. Why were *flour* and *flower* once the same word and what does that suggest about our unhealthy obsession with refined food? What does the fact that *salad, salami, salsa, sauce,* and *soused* all originally meant the same thing tell us about the difficulty of reducing the sodium in our diets?

Like the incriminating evidence in Poe's *Purloined Letter*, the answers to each of these questions is hidden in plain sight in the words we use to talk about food.

The structure of the book follows the meal, starting with menus and then the fish course, replete with sailors and pirates, followed by a break for the punch course and toast that traditionally preceded the roast in formal dinners, then the roast itself, a brief interlude to talk about snacks and craving before finishing with dessert. (But the chapters can also be read independently in any order. My mom, whose love of consensus is legendary in our family, only read every other chapter of *War and Peace*, so we like to say she just read Tolstoy's *Peace*.)

All innovation happens at interstices. Great food is no exception, created at the intersection of cultures as each one modifies and enhances what is borrowed from its neighbors. The language of food is a window onto these "between" places, the ancient clash of civilizations, the modern clash of culture, the covert clues to human cognition, society, and evolution. Every time you roast a turkey for Thanksgiving, toast the bride and groom at a wedding, or decide what potato chips or ice cream to buy, you are having a conversation in the language of food.

San Francisco, California
April 2014

One

How to Read a Menu

SAN FRANCISCO'S MOST EXPENSIVE restaurant won't give you a menu. Well, that's not strictly true. The attentive staff will happily offer you a beautifully printed list of dishes ("trout roe, sea urchin, cardoon, brassicas . . .")—by email, after you get home, as a souvenir. Saison, this marvelous Michelin-starred restaurant, isn't alone. Expensive restaurants everywhere increasingly offer "blind" tasting menus in which you don't know what you're going to eat in each course until the plate is set down on your table. When it comes to high-status restaurants, it seems that the more you pay, the less choice you have.

Status used to be expressed a different way. If you ate out in the 1970s I'm sure you dined at one of those establishments that writer Calvin Trillin called *La Maison de la Casa House, Continental Cuisine*. Trillin, an early supporter of local and ethnic eating, mocked pretentious restaurants whose menus were as macaronic a mishmash of French and English as their names (*macaronic*: from a sixteenth-century verse style mixing Latin with Italian dialect originally named, as we'll see, after macaroni). Trillin complained of being led to a "purple palace that serves 'Continental cuisine' and has as its chief creative employee a menu-writer rather than a chef."

Menu writing manuals of the day advised restaurants to "continentalize your menu," and indeed they did, as we see from these examples, with French words mixed in randomly with English or Italian words;

sometimes even just the French article "Le" with an otherwise English sentence:

Flaming Coffee Diablo, Prepared en Vue of Guest
Ravioli parmigiana, en casserole
Le Crabmeat Cocktail

Menus full of macaronic French weren't just a fad. Through the wonder of the Internet, we can go back in time more than a century in the New York Public Library's online menu collection (donated by Miss Frank E. Buttolph [1850–1924], a "tiny, unostentatious, literary-looking lady" with an obsession for menus). The 10,000 menus start with the Astor House's breakfast menu for the Ladies Ordinary meeting of August 25, 1843 (clam soup, boiled cod, mutton cutlets "sauté, with champignons," calf's head, chicken pies, mashed potatoes, beets, squash, roast beef, lamb, snipe, squab, goose, and in case anyone was still hungry, blackberry pie, cream pie, peach ices, and macarons for dessert; we'll come back to those macarons). Menus from the early 1900s are full of interwoven bits of French, especially those from expensive and upper-middle-priced restaurants, which use it five times more than cheap restaurants:

Flounder sur le plat
Eggs au beurre noir
Fried chicken a la Maryland half
Green turtle a l'anglaise
Sirloin steak aux champignons

We're not in the 1970s any more (let alone the 1870s), and now this kind of fake French just seems amusing to us. But status and social class never really go away; modern expensive restaurants still have ways of signaling that they are high-status, fancy places, or aspire to be. In fact, every time you read a description of a dish on a menu you are looking at all sorts of latent linguistic clues, clues about how we think about wealth and social class, how our society views our food, even clues about all sorts of things that restaurant marketers might not want us to know.

What are the modern indicators of an expensive, high-class restaurant? Perhaps you'll recognize the marketing techniques in the descriptions of these three dishes from pricey places:

HERB ROASTED ELYSIAN FIELDS FARMS LAMB

Eggplant Porridge, Cherry Peppers,
Greenmarket Cucumbers and Pine Nut Jus

GRASS FED ANGUS BEEF CARPACCIO

Pan Roasted King Trumpet Mushrooms
Dirty Girl Farm Romano Bean Tempura
Persillade, Extra Virgin Olive Oil

BISON BURGER

8 oz. blue star farms, grass fed & pasture raised,
melted gorgonzola, grilled vegetables

You probably noticed the extraordinary attention the menu writers paid to the origins of the food, mentioning the names of farms ("Elysian Fields," "Dirty Girl," "blue star"), giving us images of the ranch ("grass fed," "pasture raised"), and alluding to the farmer's market ("Greenmarket Cucumbers").

And menu writers aren't the only ones to get carried away. In the first episode of the show *Portlandia* Fred Armisen and Carrie Brownstein, obsessive locavores, question the provenance of the chicken at a restaurant. The waitress tries to reassure them that the chicken is "a heritage breed, woodland raised chicken that has been fed a diet of sheep's milk, soy, and hazelnuts." Armisen and Brownstein, still unsatisfied ("The hazelnuts, these are local?") head out to visit the farm where the chicken was raised just to make sure.

I suppose linguists can be annoying dinner companions as well. All that reading of words on menus does tend to slow down dinner ordering. And yet studying menus one by one, while good for inspiration, is generally not sufficient for uncovering the subtle differences. For that you need larger amounts of data.

Luckily, these days restaurants digitize their menus and put them online, making it possible to look at a huge number of menus, and hence test hypotheses about restaurant language and price while controlling for the geographic location, the type of cuisine, and so on.

To find out how widespread this locavore trend really is, and to see what other subtle cues restaurant menus are hiding, I conducted a study with Victor Chahuneau, Noah Smith, and Bryan Routledge from Carnegie Mellon University. We used a very large dataset consisting of 6500 modern menus (describing a total of 650,000 dishes) culled from the web, covering restaurants in seven cities (New York, Boston, Chicago, Philadelphia, Washington DC, San Francisco, Los Angeles). This allowed us to control for the city, the neighborhood, the type of cuisine, and many other factors that economists control for when studying restaurant price (such as being on a main street versus a side street, a factor I learned from economist Tyler Cowen's *An Economist Gets Lunch*).

We then wrote software to count the number of references to farms, ranches, pastures, woodlands, gardens, farmer's markets, heritage pork, or heirloom tomatoes that occur on the menus of restaurants of different price classes—from cheap one-dollar-sign restaurants [$] to expensive four-dollar-sign restaurants [$$$$]. Across this very large dataset, very expensive ($$$$) restaurants mention the origins of the food *more than 15 times as often as inexpensive restaurants!* This obsession with provenance is a strong indicator that you are in an expensive, fancy restaurant. (Or that you are purchasing an expensive package of junk food, marketed with the exact same strategies, as we'll see.)

We discovered many other linguistic properties with economic implications in our study. For example, the tendency of expensive restaurants to choose what you're going to eat extends far beyond posh Michelin-star places like Saison. Even on a la carte menus, a more expensive restaurant is more likely to offer a prix fixe selection, or to describe an individual dish as being composed of a "chef's choice" or the "chef's selection," as we see in the following examples:

Sashimi Omakase: *ten kinds of chef's choice*
Antipasto Della Casa: *The chef's daily selection*

In cheaper restaurants, by contrast, the diner has a lot of choice, as linguist Robin Lakoff pointed out. First of all, inexpensive restaurants just have far more dishes. On average twice as many. Think about the menu at the last Chinese restaurant you went to, or the last diner, compared to the last fancy restaurant. Cheap restaurants are likely to give a choice of sizes (small, medium, or large), or a choice of proteins (chicken, shrimp, or tofu). Another linguistic cue on menus of cheap restaurants is that the word *you* appears much more often, in phrases like "your choice" or "your way." Here are some examples:

Baby lamb chops grilled to your liking
Marinated flank steak with eggs your way
Quiche with your choice *of either house salad or a cup of soup*
Biscuits and gravy with eggs anyway you like 'em

We found that expensive ($$$$) restaurants have half as many dishes as cheap ($) restaurants, are three times less likely to talk about the diner's choice, and are seven times more likely to talk about the chef's choice.

Fancy restaurants, not surprisingly, also use fancy words. In menus from 50 to 100 years ago this often meant long French words, but now lots of other foreign words are used on fancy menus. In our sample of expensive modern menus this means words like *tonnarelli, choclo, bastilla, kataifi, persillade,* and *oyako* (from Italian, Peruvian Spanish, Arabic, Greek, French, and Japanese, respectively).

But there are fancy words in English too—what my dad calls "two-dollar words," long multisyllabic words with 11 or 12 letters or more. Why would a word be fancy just because it is longer? Well, for one thing, many of our longer words came into English from French or Latin, historically high-status languages. For another: longer words are used less frequently; in fact, the longer, the rarer. This is obvious if you think about it; short words (words like *of, I, the, a*) are grammatical words that appear all over the place, while very long words (like *accompaniments*) appear in much fewer situations.

This relationship between word length and word frequency was first discovered by Sibawayhi, a Persian grammarian of the eighth century, in one of many scientific revolutions and inventions that come from the Muslim world. Sibawayhi came to what is now Iraq just after the construction of Baghdad, the fabled capital of the Abbasid Dynasty and perhaps the greatest center of learning and science in the medieval world. (As we'll see in later chapters, Baghdad was also where the fabulous foods of the caliphs were developed that became the source of many of our modern foods.)

Sibawayhi originally came from Persia to study law, but then one day when reciting out loud he made an embarrassing error in pronouncing an Arabic word. His fellow students shamed him in public for his bad language skills (I guess eighth-century law students were no less cutthroat than modern ones), and according to at least one story that's why Sibawayhi switched fields and spent the rest of his life studying linguistics. (Public humiliation is not a method that is normally recommended in modern universities to get students to choose a major. Unless, of course, it gets students interested in linguistics.)

Sibawayhi's theory was reinvented and formalized 1200 years later, in the 1930s, when linguist George Zipf suggested that frequently used words are shortened so as to make communication more efficient; you can pack more words in a smaller space and time for your listener if the ones that you use more often, the frequent ones, are shorter. Zipf's ideas helped lead to the brilliant work of Claude Shannon 10 years later at Bell Labs in creating information theory. Without these ideas, our modern digital collections of menus (or sound recordings, or photographs) would be impossible.

Anyhow, these rare, long, fancy words that appear more often in expensive restaurants are words like *decaffeinated, accompaniments, complements, traditionally, specifications, preparation, overflowing, magnificent, inspiration, exquisitely,* and *tenderness.* By contrast, cheaper restaurants use shorter forms: *decaf* instead of *decaffeinated, sides* instead of *accompaniments* or *complements.* Words on menus at expensive restaurants average about half a letter longer than those on menus at cheap ones.

Fancy words are thus an indicator that we are at a fancy restaurant. But using a fancy word in a dish description tells you something even more specific: it tells you about the actual price of the dish!

To study this, my colleagues and I looked at the price of all 650,000 dishes on the 6500 menus, and used statistical tools to find which words are associated with higher and lower prices. The most important factor that affects the price of a dish is the type of food; lobster costs more than chicken, which costs more than a side of toast. So we statistically controlled for the type of food, the cuisine of the restaurant (Chinese, Italian, steakhouses, diners, cafes) and how expensive the restaurant is, and which city and neighborhood the restaurant was in. After all these controls, we then studied the additional affect of individual words on the prices.

What we found is that when a restaurant uses longer words to describe a dish, it charges more for the dish. Every increase of one letter in the average length of words describing a dish is associated with an increase of 18 cents in the price of that dish! This means that if a restaurant uses words that are on average three letters longer, you'll be paying 54 cents extra for your roast chicken or pasta. I guess they're just "half-dollar words" rather than "two-dollar words," but you'll still be paying extra for them when the restaurant uses these long, fancy words on the menu!

Counting letters is one way to find out the hidden information that restaurateurs are sneaking onto your menu, but another is to check whether the restaurant emphasizes how exotic or spicy the food is. If so, watch out! Look for phrases like "exotic blend of Indian spices" or "exotic Ethiopian spices" or even just "tamarind fish soup with exotic vegetables." Our study found that every use of the word *exotic* or *spices* raises the price of a dish. Presumably the reason is that such foods would not be exotic to someone who is in fact Ethiopian or Indian: These restaurants are not advertising to native eaters of the cuisine, who eat it every day and are aware of the exact value. That "exotifying" or orientalist stance is instead directed at the nonnative eaters, food tourists like me who want something different and, fair is fair, get charged more for it.

Five Spices Duck: *Young duck boiled in exotic five spices broth, deboned and served with spicy vinaigrette.*

Bhindi Masala: *Okra cooked with onions, tomatoes, and an exotic blend of Indian spices.*

Here's a third trick for reading between the lines in menus: hunt for what I call "linguistic fillers." Consider for example positive but vague words like *delicious* and synonyms *tasty, mouth-watering, flavorful, scrumptious,* and *savory,* or words like *terrific, wonderful, delightful,* and *sublime.* These words seem to promise something special about what you're going to get, but in a subjective enough way that the restaurant sneakily avoids incurring any sort of actual obligation (you can't sue because you thought your scrod wasn't scrumptious). Another type is what my colleague Arnold Zwicky calls "appealing adjectives": words like *zesty, rich, golden brown, crispy,* or *crunchy.* These aren't completely uninformative (*golden brown* means something different from *crunchy*) but whether something is *zesty* is a matter of opinion.

Both of these categories of linguistic filler words are associated with lower prices. After controlling for the factors mentioned above (the food itself, the type of cuisine, the average price and location of the restaurant), we saw the relationship between the words on the menu and the price. For each positive vague word like *delicious, tasty,* or *terrific* you see on a dish, the average price of the dish is nine percent less. Each appealing adjective like *rich, chunky,* or *zesty* is associated with a price that is two percent lower.

Our finding is one of association rather than causation. That is, we can't say for sure whether restaurants actually base their price on the number of times they call the dish *delicious,* or whether they decided to call the dish *delicious* after looking at the price, or whether some other unknown factor (what we technically call an *exogenous* factor) is causing both the price and the wording. All we can say for certain is that lower prices and filler words seem to go together. Nonetheless, we have a hypothesis about what's going on. We suspect that empty words are linked with lower prices because they are in fact fillers; stuff you put in the description of a dish when you don't have something really valuable like *crab* or *porterhouse* to talk about instead. Steven Levitt and Stephen Dubner in *Freakonomics* show that this same principle applies to real estate advertising as well. They found that houses whose real estate ads had words like *fantastic* or *charming* tended to sell for lower prices, while houses whose ads had words like *maple* and *granite* tended to sell for higher prices. Their hypothesis was that real estate agents used vague positive words like *fantastic* to mask the lack of any specific positive qualities in the house. Indeed, in restaurants, the words that correlate with higher prices are not the empty words like *fantastic* but the words describing truly valuable products like lobster, truffle, or caviar.

Here are some examples of sentences stuffed with fillers; see how many total fillers you notice in these three dishes:

> BLT Salad: *a flavorful, colorful and delicious salad mixture of crispy bacon bits, lettuce, tomatoes, red and green onions and garlic croutons tossed with bleu cheese dressing*

> Homemade Meatloaf Sandwich: *Flavorful, juicy, & delicious. Served warm with our BBQ ketchup, caramelized onions, & melted American cheese*

> Mango Chicken: *Delicious golden fried white meat chicken nuggets sauteed in a sweet savory sauce, with freshly sliced mango chunks, carrots and bell peppers*

I counted at least 13: *delicious* (three times), *flavorful* (twice), *colorful*, *crispy*, *juicy*, *warm*, *golden*, *sweet*, *savory*, and *freshly*.

These filler words tell us something else about the restaurant. Consider the restaurants that have very long, wordy menus with lots of filler words. You might think these could be the very expensive

restaurants with the high-powered menu-writing marketing consul-
tants. Or it could be the very cheap restaurants, using filler words to
make up for not-very-fancy food.

In fact, it's neither: long, wordy menus with lots of filler words occur
in the middle-priced restaurants, chains like Ruby Tuesday, T.G.I Friday's, Cheesecake Factory, or California Pizza Kitchen or local places.

Descriptive adjectives like *fresh*, *rich*, *spicy*, *crispy*, *crunchy*, *tangy*,
juicy, *zesty*, *chunky*, *smoky*, *salty*, *cheesy*, *fluffy*, *flaky*, and *buttery* appear
significantly more often in menus from these middle-priced restaurants:

Crisp Golden Brown Belgian Waffle with Fresh Fruit

Mushroom Omelette: *Our fluffy omelette filled with fresh mushrooms
and topped with a rich mushroom sherry sauce*

Chicken Marsala: *Tender chicken breast in a rich marsala wine sauce
with fresh mushrooms*

Rustic Apple Galette: *Hand crafted tart in five inches of
butter flaky french puff pastry. We layer fresh ripe apples and
bake to a golden brown*

Why would it be middle-priced and not expensive restaurants that use
more of these adjectives?

To understand the answer to this we have to consider the function of these adjectives. The literal meaning of "delicious" is that the
food tastes good. The literal meaning of "ripe" is that the apple wasn't
picked when it was still sour and green. But why would a restaurant
serve unripe apples or cook bad-tasting food? Doesn't it go without
saying that the food will taste good and the apples be ripe?

One of the most important language philosophers of the twentieth century, H. Paul Grice, gave an answer to this problem. Grice pointed out that when we are trying to understand a speaker, we assume that they are acting rationally. If they say something is fresh, there must be some reason to say it's fresh; speakers don't just add in random words. (Grice called this the "maxim of quantity"; there is also a related "maxim of relevance" that says that speakers try to say relevant things.) So if I hear someone say that something is fresh (or ripe, or fluffy, or golden brown), I immediately consider why it would be relevant to mention ripeness. We generally mention ripeness because there is an implicit comparison with unripeness. It's something like saying, You might worry that this fruit is unripe, but don't worry, I hereby reassure you that it's ripe. That is, just the mention of ripeness brings up the possibility that there might be some people that might not think it's ripe, and I'm mentioning this to convince them.

Linguist Mark Liberman suggests that we think of this overmentioning as a symptom of "status anxiety." Expensive restaurants don't use the word *ripe* (or *fresh* or *crispy*) because we assume that food that should be ripe is ripe, and everything is fresh. Middle-priced restaurants are worried that you won't assume that because they aren't fancy enough, so they go out of their way to reassure you. Protesting too much.

We can see a similar implication of Grice's idea in the use of the word *real* on menus. You'll find the word on lots of menus, but exactly which foods the restaurants claim are "real" depends sharply on the price. Cheap restaurants promise you real whipped cream, real mashed potatoes, and real bacon:

Chocolate Chip Pancakes: *served with real whipped cream.*

Home Made Meatloaf: *Served with Real Mashed Potatoes, Vegetables, and Gravy.*

Chicken Cutlet: *Melted Swiss Cheese on a Roll with Lettuce, Tomato, Russian Dressing and Real Bacon Bits.*

In slightly more expensive ($$) restaurants, real is used mainly to describe crab and maple syrup:

California Roll: *real crab and avocado*

Blueberry Whole Grain Pancakes: *With real maple syrup*

By contrast, *real* is barely used at all for more expensive ($$$ and $$$$) restaurants. This isn't because the bacon isn't real at these restaurants, but rather because consumers already assume that the bacon and whipped cream and crab are real. For a pricy restaurant to call its crab "real" would be to suggest that its realness might be in question and has to be defended. Once again, Grice's principle is in play: if a restaurant says the butter is real, there must be a reason to say so, and a normal reason you might go to the trouble of saying that something is real is that you are worried the person you're talking to thinks it's fake and you want to reassure them. Expensive restaurants certainly don't want to imply that any of their customers might think their butter is fake.

The history of which foods are called "real" or "genuine" on menus is a mini lesson on what was considered valuable enough to create a fake substitute. The 1990s had real bacon (not Bacon Bits). The 1970s and 1980s had real whipped cream (not Cool Whip) and real sour cream (not Imo). The 1960s menus had real butter (not margarine). The 1940s and 1930s had genuine calves' liver.

Around 1900 the foods most frequently called "real" or "genuine" weren't any of these. Back then it was fake beer and fake turtles that people were worried about. Menus of the day boast of "real German beer" and "real turtle." German pale lager came to us in the great

German immigrations of the nineteenth century (along with hamburgers, frankfurters, seltzer, home-fried potatoes, potato salad, and the delicatessen). Before this, Americans only drank dark English-style ale. The pale cold-fermented lagers brewed by ethnic German entrepreneurs like Miller, Pabst, Schlitz, and Busch became popular by the turn of the nineteenth century, and restaurants boasted of being able to serve this new prestige product. Turtle soup was also a sought-after delicacy of the day, so much so that mock turtle soup, made of brains and calves' heads (and not of Mock Turtles, whatever Lewis Carroll said) was common as a cheaper substitute. In fact, Jane Ziegelman tells us in her book *97 Orchard: An Edible History of Five Immigrant Families* that New York restaurants "often nailed a real tortoise shell to the doorpost" as a sign that they served real green turtle soup.

The signs we use for prestige these days are less obvious than that tortoise shell, but they are still there in the menu. Of course these days we don't use macaronic French. Our modern fancy menus are light and terse, with no cheap filler adjectives or endless protestations about what's "real." When you're demonstrating high status, less is more, in words as in food. Fancy menus are lightly seasoned with something else instead: carefully selected obscure food words and pastoral images of green pastures and heirloom vegetables. If they offer you a menu at all.

And you should probably avoid that menu loaded with linguistic fillers like *crispy, crunchy, tangy, juicy, zesty, chunky, smoky,* or *fluffy,* adjectives written by a menu writer trying too hard to convince you. As for the word "exotic," if you see it, don't pay the surcharge that it implies. Instead, do what Calvin Trillin would do: sneak off down the street to the place that is authentic enough not to have to protest it so much.

Two

Entrée

LIVING IN SAN FRANCISCO means visitors, and visitors mean an excuse to wander down Bernal Hill and explore various delicious dinner options along Mission Street. My houseguests are always open-minded eaters, but they do sometimes find odd things to complain about. My cranky British friend Paul is irked by the interminable questions at cafes here ("Single or double? Small, medium, large? For here or to go? Milk or soy? Whole milk or nonfat?"). "Just give me a bloody coffee," says Paul, who thinks Americans have control issues. Indeed, as we just saw, the profusion of choices offered by cafes, diners, fast-food, and other inexpensive outlets is matched only by the control we abdicate when selecting the tasting menus at our expensive restaurants.

Paul is also annoyed by our parochial word usage. For example, the word *entrée* in the United States means a main course while in France and the UK *entrée* means what we would call the appetizer course. Thus a French meal might consist of an entrée, the main course (the *plat*), and dessert, while a corresponding American meal would have appetizer, entrée, and dessert. Since the word *entrée* comes originally from French and literally means "entrance," we Americans, Paul suggested to me at dinner one night, must have botched up the meaning of this word at some point.

Paul's hypothesis seems reasonable, and since he also complains about my fork and knife etiquette (it turns out I don't align my fork and knife in the proper position on the plate to signal I'm done eating), I have lately been feeling quite the uncultured colonial from the Wild West.

The late Alan Davidson told us in his magisterial *Oxford Companion to Food* that (even if Paul is right) the meaning of entrée is just not worth investigating:

> entrée, entremet: *A couple of French terms which no doubt retain interest for persons attending hotel and restaurant courses conducted under the shadow of French classical traditions, but have ceased to have any real use, partly because most people cannot remember what they mean and partly because their meanings have changed over time and vary from one part of the world to another. Forget them.*

But the redoubtable Davidson, although right about practically everything else, is off the mark here; the language of food ought to have an enormous amount to tell us about our history, our society, and our selves. So instead I'll side with the late historian Fernand Braudel who once suggested that these same French terms might be cues to understanding food's cultural history:

> *We might . . . follow fashion in food through the revealing history of certain words which are still in use but which have changed in meaning several times: entrées, entremet, ragoûts, etc.*

Entrée is a good next step in our adventure in the language of food for another reason as well: it is an organizing word, describing the structure of a meal rather than a food itself, and thus bridges the previous chapter's study of menu language with the succeeding chapters describing foods from main courses to desserts.

As for Paul's hypothesis that the modern French meaning of entrée is the original one: *au contraire!* Let's start with that modern French definition:

Mets qui se sert au début du repas, après le potage ou après les hors-d'œuvre.
[A dish served at the beginning of the meal, after the soup or after the hors d'oeuvres.]

Extracts from the menus from Aux Lyonnais in Paris and Frances in San Francisco (both Michelin 1-star restaurants) show the differing uses: the French *entrée* as the appetizer, the American *entrée* (or *entree*) as the main.

Aux Lyonnais:

ENTREES

Planche de charcuterie lyonnaise
Terrine de gibier, condiment coing/poivre
Jeunes poireaux servis tièdes, garniture mimosa
Fine crème de laitue, cuisses de grenouille dorées

PLATS

Saint-Jacques en coquille lutée, salade d'hiver
Quenelles à la lyonnaise, sauce Nantua
Vol-au-vent du dimanche en famille
Notre boudin noir à la lyonnaise, oignons au vinaigre

Frances:

APPETIZERS

Lacinato Kale Salad—Pecorino, Grilled Satsuma
Mandarin, Fennel, Medjool Date
Squid Ink Pappardelle & Shellfish Ragoût—Green Garlic,
Dungeness Crab, Gulf Prawn
Salad of Spring Greens—English Pea, Poached Farm
Egg, Crisp Shallot and Potato

ENTREES   *Five-Dot Ranch Bavette Steak—Butter Bean Ragoût,*
Foraged Mushrooms, Bloomsdale Spinach
Sonoma Duck Breast—Charred Satsuma Mandarin, Lady
Apple, Cipollini Onion
Market Fish—Green Garlic, Full Belly Potatoes, Salsify,
Roasted Fennel Purée

How did this difference in meaning develop? The word *entrée* first appears in France in 1555. In the sixteenth century, a banquet began with a course called *entrée de table* ("entering to/of the table") and ends with one called *issue de table* ("exiting the table"). Here are two menus in Middle French (explaining the archaic forms and variable spelling) from the 1555 book *Livre Fort Excellent de Cuysine Tres-Utile et Profitable* excerpted from culinary historian Jean-Louis Flandrin's excellent book *Arranging the Meal: A History of Table Service in France*:

Cest que fault pour faire ung banquet ou nopces après pasques
[What you need for a banquet or wedding after Easter]

MENU 1	MENU 2
Bon pain [Bread]	Bon pain [Bread]
Bon vin [Wine]	Bon vin [Wine]
Entrée de table [Table entrée]	Entrée de table [Table entrée]
Potages [Soups]	Aultre entrée de table pour yver
Rost [Roast]	[Another table entrée for winter]
Second Rost [2nd roast]	Potaiges [Soups]
Tiers service de rost [3rd roast]	Rost [Roast]
Issue de Tables [Table exit]	Issue de Tables [Table exit]

As these menus show, the entrée is the first course of the meal, there can be multiple entrées, and after the entrée comes the soup, one or more roasts, and then a final course. Entrées in fourteenth- through sixteenth-century France were hearty sauced meat dishes (Beef Palate with Gooseberries, Wood Pigeons with Pomegranate, Chicken fricassee in verjus, Venison sirloins, Leg of lamb hash), savory pastries (Hot small venison pies), or offal (Roasted calf's liver, Salted lamb tongues, Browned kid heads).

Over the next hundred years, the soup began to be eaten earlier in the menu, so that by about 1650 the soup was always the first course, followed by the entrée. In *Le Cuisinier François* (*The French Cook*), La Varenne's famous 1651 cookbook, an entrée was still a hot meat dish, distinguished from the roast course. The roast course was a spit roast, usually of fowl or sometimes rabbit or suckling animals, while the entrée was a more complicated made dish of meat, often with a sauce, and something requiring some effort in the kitchen. The cookbook gives such lovely seventeenth-century entrées as Ducks in Ragout, Sausages of Partridge White-Meat, a Daube of a Leg of Mutton, and Fricaseed Chicken. An entrée was not cold, nor was it composed of vegetables or eggs. (Dishes that were cold or composed of vegetable or eggs were called *entremets*). So the entrée in 1651 is a hot meat course eaten after the soup and before the roast.

By a hundred years later, in the eighteenth century, the French, English (and colonial American) banquet meal had standardized in a tradition called *à la Française* or sometimes *à l'Anglaise*. Meals were often in two courses, each course consisting of an entire tableful of food. All the offerings were laid out on the table, with the most important in the middle and the soup or fish perhaps at the head of the table, entrées scattered about, and the smallest courses (the *hors d'oeuvres*, literally "outside the main work") placed around the edges (that is, "outside" of the main stuff).

After the soup was eaten, it was taken away and replaced on the table by another dish, called the *relevé* in French or the *remove* in English. A remove might be a fish, a joint, or a dish of veal. The other dishes (the entrées and entremets) stayed on the table. Sometimes a fish course was itself removed, just like the soup. Then the joint might be carved while the entrees and hors d'oeuvres were passed around. After this first course was completed, the dishes would all be cleared away and a second course would be brought in, based around the roast, usually hare or various fowl such as turkey, partridge, or chicken, together with other dishes.

The figure opposite shows how the dishes were laid on the table in the two courses or servings à la Française from the first cookbook published in the American colonies, Eliza Smith's very popular English cookbook *The Compleat Housewife: or, Accomplished Gentlewoman's Companion*, first published in 1727 in England, and published in the American colonies in the 1742 edition.

Note the "soop," with the Breast of Veal "ragood" remove, and the entrées like Leg of Lamb, 2 Carp Stew'd, and A Pig Roasted. Recall that the classic French roast course consisted of roast fowl; that would be the 4 Partridges and 2 Quails in the second course; roast beef and pork were served in the first course as entrées or removes. Also note that at this point, the word *entrée* was not yet used in English; at least it's not mentioned in Eliza Smith, and the first usage listed in the *Oxford English Dictionary* is decades later, in William Verral's 1759 *A Complete System of Cookery*, where it is marked in italics as a newly borrowed foreign word.

The next change in the ordering of meals was another hundred years later, in the nineteenth century, to a method known as service *à la Russe*, significantly closer to modern coursed dinners. Instead of the food being all piled on the table to get cold, dishes are brought in one course at a time on plates served directly to the guests. Thus, for example, meat is carved at the sideboard or the kitchen by servants rather than by the host at the table. Since the table was no longer covered in food, it was decorated with flowers and so on. And since the guests couldn't know what food they were going to eat just by looking at the table, a small list of dishes was placed by each setting. The name for this list was borrowed (first in French and then English) from a shortening of the Latin word *minūtus*, "small, finely divided, or detailed." It was called a *menu*.

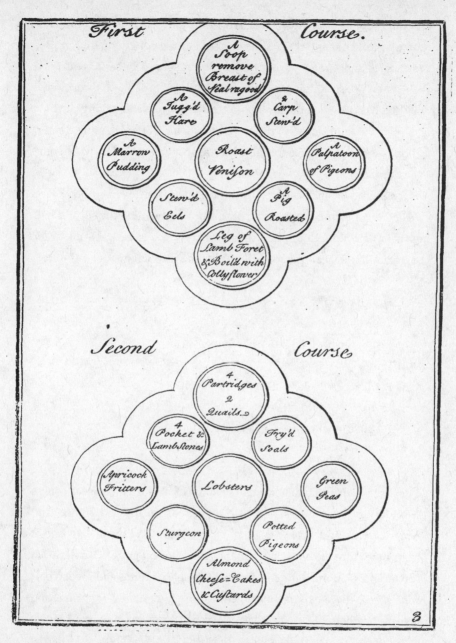

Placement of dishes in the two courses,
from Eliza Smith's 1758 The Compleat Housewife
(16th edition)

This service à la Russe took over in France in the nineteenth century; in England and the US the custom shifted roughly between 1850 and 1890, and our modern meals are now served in serial courses à la Russe. We still maintain remnants in the US of the old-fashioned method of putting all the food on the table at once and having the host carve at the table, in very traditional meals like Thanksgiving dinner. (Thanksgiving is archaic in all other aspects as well, but we'll come back to that.)

By the nineteenth century the hors d'oeuvres began to be served earlier, even before the soup. So at this point (meaning the second half of the nineteenth century and the first half of the twentieth), the order of a traditional meal was something like the following:

1. Hors d'oeuvres
2. Soup
3. Fish (possibly followed by a remove)
4. Entrée
5. Break (sherbet, rum, absinthe, or punch)
6. Roast
7. Possible other courses (salads, etc.)
8. Dessert

The word *entrée* maintained this meaning of a substantial meat course served after the soup/fish and before the roast in Britain, France, and America until well after the First World War. The menu opposite is from 1907 from the newly built Blanco's, the legendary O'Farrell Street restaurant and bordello whose fantastic marble columns and rococo balconies were the site of the unbridled drinking, gambling, whoring, and general bad behavior that characterized San Francisco's Barbary Coast days but also symbolized the city's rise from the ashes of the 1906 earthquake. Blanco's later became the Music Box, the burlesque owned by San Francisco's beloved fan dancer Sally Rand. It's now the Great American

Music Hall, one of the most beautiful concert venues in the city, but if you go around to the back alley you can still see the faded Blanco's sign painted on the brick. Notice on the menu some of the pseudo-French we talked about in the previous chapter ("Celery en Branch," the misspelling of "Parisienne," and some unexpected accents).

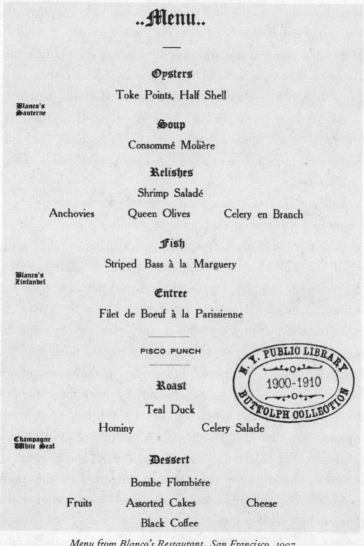

Menu from Blanco's Restaurant, San Francisco, 1907

As for the Pisco punch that separates the entrée from the roast, it was San Francisco's signature drink in the nineteenth century. The punch was made from Pisco brandy, lemon juice, and pineapple syrup, and was an "insidious concoction which in its time had caused the unseating of South American governments and women to set world's records in various and interesting fields of activity," as cocktail historian David Wondrich recounts from a later memoir. Pisco punch was popularized and maybe even invented here at the old Bank Exchange at the corner of Montgomery and Washington, which made it through the earthquake of '06 only to be replaced by the Transamerica Pyramid.

By 30 years later, the word *entrée* has expanded a bit in meaning. In US menus from the 1930s, the word is still used in its classic sense as a substantial "made" meat dish distinguished from roasts, but by now sometimes the term includes fish, and has lost the sense of a course in a particular order.

After the war, as separate roast and fish courses dropped out of common usage, the word *entrée* expanded once again to signify any main course. A 1946 menu from the "World Famous Cliff House," perched on the cliffs at Land's End overlooking the Pacific, refers to all main courses, including "Grilled Fillet of Sea Bass, Parsley Butter" as entrees. (The Cliff House is still there, but now the waves crash over the ruins of the Sutro Baths below, originally built by millionaire populist Adolph Sutro in 1896 with vast swimming pools fed by the ocean. In the romantic foggy midnights of my youth, we used to sneak around those ruins and through the long dark tunnels that run into the cliff.) By 1956 *entrée* came to be used even when there is no meat at all; that year in fact Alioto's on Fisherman's Wharf offered "Fish Dinners" consisting of Crab Cocktail, Soup or Salad, Entree, and Dessert.

American meals by the 1950s thus standardized on the modern three-course meal consisting of appetizer, entrée, and dessert, perhaps augmented by a salad or soup.

What about in France? The French use of the word *entrée* in Escoffier's

1921 *Le Guide Culinaire* was still the traditional one ("made" hot meat dishes served in the classic sequence before a roast). Escoffier classifies as entrées almost any meat or poultry dish that we would now consider a main course: steaks (entrecotes or filet de boeuf, tournedos), cassoulet, lamb or veal cutlets, ham, sausage, braised leg of lamb (gigot), stews or sautes of chicken, pigeon or turkey, braised goose, foie gras. Escoffier has over 500 pages of entrée recipes. Only roast fowl and small game animals are classified as roasts, in a small 14-paged roast section.

Thus, the change from the classic central heavy meat entrée to the modern light first course must have come after 1921 in France but before 1962, by which point the recipes Julia Child gives for entrées are light dishes, mainly quiches, soufflés, and quenelles. We see similar light dishes listed as typical entrées in the modern *Larousse Gastronomique*, the French culinary encyclopedia.

Actually, an *older* edition of the *Larousse Gastronomique*—the very first one from 1938, in fact—gives us even more insight in its definition of entrée:

> *Ce mot ne signifie pas du tout, comme bien des personnes semblent le croire, le premier plat d'un menu. L'entrée est le mets qui suit, dan l'ordonnance d'un repas, le plat qui est désigneé sous le nom de relevé, plat qui, lui-même, est servi après le poisson (ou le mets en tenant lieu) et qui, par conséquent, vient en troisième ligne sur le menu.*
>
> *[This word does not mean, as many seem to believe, the first dish in a meal. In the ordering of a meal, the entrée is the dish that follows the relevé, the dish served after the fish (or after the dish that takes the place of the fish) and, therefore, comes third in the meal.]*

What we have here is a "language maven" complaining about a change in the language. (*Aux armes!* The French masses are using the word *entrée* incorrectly!) Language mavens have probably been around pretty much since there were two speakers to complain about the vocabulary, pronunciation, or grammar of a third. They can be very useful for historical linguists, because grammar writers don't complain about a change in the language until it's already been widely adopted. So we can be pretty certain that in popular usage, *entrée* mostly meant "first course" in French by 1938.

So, to review: The word *entrée* originally (in 1555) meant the opening course of a meal, one consisting of substantial hot "made" meat dishes, usually with a sauce, and then evolved to mean the same kind of dishes but served as a third course after a soup and a fish, and before a roast fowl course. American usage kept this sense of a substantial meat course, and as distinct roast and fish courses dropped away from common usage, the meaning of *entrée* in American English was no longer opposed to fish or roast dishes, leaving the entrée as the single main course.

In French, the word changed its meaning by the 1930s to mean a light course of eggs or seafood, essentially taking on much of the meaning of earlier terms like hors d'oeuvres or entremets. The change was presumably helped along by the fact that the literal French meaning ("entering, entrance") was still transparent to French speakers, and perhaps as more speakers began to eat multicourse meals the word attached itself more readily to a first or entering course. So both French and American English retain some aspects of the original meaning of the word; French the "first course" aspect of the meaning (although that had actually died out by 1651) and American the "main meat course" aspect, which has been the main part of its meaning for 500 years.

This shift has a deeper lesson about language change. We are carefully taught to clamp down on changes in language as if new ways of speaking are unnatural, adopted by ignorant speakers out of stupidity or even malice. Yet linguistic research demonstrates that the gradual changes in a language over time often lead to significant improvements in the language's clarity or efficiency, as happened here with *entrée*. Everyday speakers in both France and America changed the meaning of *entrée* from an obscure third course in an archaic, aristocratic meal structure to a useful term for an appetizer (in France) or a main course (in America), sensibly ignoring the complaints of the 1938 editors of the *Larousse Gastronomique*.

What about the use of entrée now? One of the advantages of the narrow houses and dense neighborhoods of San Francisco is that the restaurants are all very close by, so a short walk down to Mission Street quickly answers that question. I checked all the menus of the 50 restaurants within a few blocks of us (Mexican, Thai, Chinese, Peruvian, Japanese, Indian, Salvadoran, Cambodian, Sardinian, Nepalese, Italian, Jordanian, Lebanese, barbecue, southern, plus the pairwise combinations like Chinese Peruvian roast chicken, Japanese French bakeries, and Indian pizza). The word *entrée* was used only at five restaurants. Not surprisingly these serve mainly European American rather than Asian or Latin American food.

The vast increase in the number of ethnic restaurants and the fading of French words like entrée as a marker of social prestige in the United States are part of a general trend in food, music, and art that sociologists call *cultural omnivorousness*. Previously high culture was defined solely by a limited number of "legitimate" genres: classical music or opera, or French haute cuisine or wine. The modern high-culture omnivore, however, can be a fan of 1920s blues, or 1950s Cuban mambo, or the ethnic or regional foods championed by writers like Calvin Trillin. High status is signaled now not just by knowing fancy French terms, but also by being able to name all the different kinds of Italian pasta, or appreciating the most authentic ethnic cuisine, or knowing just where to find the best kind of fish sauce. Even potato chips are advertised by appealing to this desire to be authentic.

Omnivorousness explains the decline, detailed in the previous chapter, of the use of pseudo-French as a modern marker of status on menus. And omnivorousness is perhaps one reason we are seeing the decline of the word *entrée* in menus and in books and magazines as well. The Google Ngram corpus, a very useful online resource that counts the frequency of words over time in books, magazines, and newspapers, demonstrates entrée's rise in the 1970s and 1980s and then the fall since 1996:

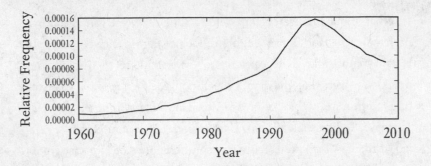

If entrée is declining in use, what is it being replaced by? Some menus use "main course," Italian restaurants often use "secondi," and French restaurants might use "plat." But the most frequent answer in new restaurants is, Nothing; appetizers and entrées are listed without a label at all, and diners have to figure it out, like the less-is-more implicitness we saw in menus. In the highest-status restaurants, whether the food is an appetizer or entrée portion, how crispy or fluffy it is, or even exactly what you are going to be served can literally go without saying.

Entrée has more to tell us than Alan Davidson guessed: it concisely encapsulates an entire history of culinary status, from the structure of fabulous Renaissance meals, to the early role of French as a signal of high status, to the more recent decline of French as the sole language of culinary prestige, replaced by omnivorousness and by more tacit signals of status.

The high status of French isn't completely gone, however; Paul and I automatically assumed the French meaning was the "correct" one even though it's actually the American borrowing that retained entrée's Renaissance sense of a hearty meat course.

In the next chapter we'll turn to a word whose change in meaning reflects an even larger social transformation, while still retaining aspects of its meaning that are thousands of years old.

Three

From Sikbāj to Fish and Chips

SINCE THE DAYS WHEN the native Ohlone people caught and ate the bounty of oysters and abalone and crab that thrived throughout the bay, San Francisco has been a good place for seafood. The first restaurants here were mainly Chinese, serving fish caught by the redwood fishing sampans that set out from the Chinese fishing villages on the beach south of Rincon Hill. Tadich Grill (founded by Croatian immigrants in 1848) has been using Croatian methods of mesquite-grilling fish since the early twentieth century, the Old Clam House has served clam chowder at the foot of Bernal Hill since 1861 when it was still waterfront property with a plank road to downtown, and Dungeness crab has been in demand for San Francisco Italian Thanksgivings and Christmas Eve cioppinos since the nineteenth century.

And then there's ceviche (or seviche or cebiche), the tangy fish or seafood marinated in lime and onion that's the official national dish of Peru, a gift to San Francisco from the Peruvians who also brought the Pisco that made Pisco punch. Peruvians have been in San Francisco since the 1850s, when what's now called Jackson Square at the southern foot of Telegraph Hill was called Little Chile and was filled with the Chileans, Peruvians, and Sonorans drawn by the gold rush. This was before the transcontinental railway was built, so ships from Valparaiso and Lima brought the earliest men to the gold fields. Chilean and Peruvian miners introduced techniques like dry digging and the "chili mill" that they had learned in the great silver mines of the Andes, the mines that produced the Spanish silver dollar or "piece of eight" that was the first world currency. Now San Francisco has so many cevicherias that I have found myself in many a pleasant debate about which is best, from cozy gems in the neighborhoods to bright whitewashed dining rooms overlooking the water.

What is ceviche? The Royal Spanish Academy's *Diccionario de la lengua española* defines *cebiche* as:

> *Plato de pescado o marisco crudo cortado en trozos pequeños y preparado*
> *en un adobo de jugo de limón o naranja agria, cebolla picada, sal y ají.*
> *[A dish of raw fish or seafood diced and prepared in a marinade of lime or*
> *sour orange juice, diced onion, salt and chile.]*

In Peru, ceviche is often made with *aji amarillo* (Peruvian yellow chile), and served with corn and potatoes or sweet potatoes.

Ceviche turns out to have a historical link to the seafood dishes of many nations, from fish and chips in Britain to tempura in Japan to escabeche in Spain. All of them, as well as some others that we'll get to, turn out to be immigrants themselves, and descend directly from the favorite dish of the Shahs of Persia more than 1500 years ago.

The story starts in the mid-sixth century in Persia. Khosrau I Anushirvan (501–579 CE) was the Shahanshah ("king of kings") of the Sassanid Persian empire, which stretched from present-day Armenia, Turkey, and Syria in the west, through Iran and Iraq to parts of Pakistan in the east. This was an extraordinary period of Persian civilization. The capital, Ctesiphon, on the banks of the Tigris in Mesopotamia (modern-day Iraq; ancient Babylonia), was perhaps the largest city in the world at the time, famous for its murals and a center of music, poetry, and art. Although the state religion was strictly Zoroastrian, Jewish scholars wrote the Talmud here, Plato and Aristotle were translated into Persian, and the rules for backgammon were first written down.

King Khosrau and Borzūya the scholar, from the 1483 German rendering Das buch der weißhait *of John of Caput's Latin translation of the* Panchatantra

This part of the Fertile Crescent was irrigated by an extensive canal system that was significantly extended by Khosrau. Persia was at the center of the global economy, exporting its own pearls and textiles, and helping bring Chinese paper and silk and Indian spices and the Indian game of chess to Europe.

Another borrowing from India in Khosrau's time was the *Panchatantra*, a collection of c. 200 BCE Sanskrit animal fables that the Persian physician Borzūya brought back and translated into Persian, and which was the source of stories in *One Thousand and One Nights* and Western nursery tales like the French fables of Jean de La Fontaine. There is a beautiful fable about Borzūya's trip itself, told in the Persian national epic "The Shahnameh," in which Borzūya asks King Khosrau for permission to travel to India to acquire an herb from a magic mountain that when sprinkled over a corpse could raise the dead. But when he arrives in India a sage reveals to him that the corpse is "ignorance," the herb is "words," and the mountain was "knowledge." Ignorance can only be cured by words in books, so Borzūya brings back the *Panchatantra*.

Ctesiphon is long gone now, but as we'll see, Khosrau's favorite food lives on. He loved a dish of sweet-and-sour stewed beef called *sikbāj*, from *sik*, Middle Persian for "vinegar." Sikbāj must have been amazingly delicious, because it was a favorite of kings and concubines for at least 300 years, and celebrated in story after story. In one story, Khosrau sent a great number of cooks into separate kitchens, saying, "Let each one of you prepare his best dish." I am sure the cynical among you will not be surprised to hear that it turned out that all the chefs made the shah's favorite, sikbāj.

The Sassanid empire fell as Islam spread, and by 750, the Islamic Abbasid caliphate was established in formerly Persian areas of Mesopotamia. The Abbasids built a new city 20 miles from Ctesiphon, Madinat al-Salam, "the city of peace," in a former market town called Baghdad. The Abbasids were heavily influenced by Sassanid culture, hiring local Persian-trained chefs who knew how to cook sikbāj. The dish became the favorite of the new rulers, like Harun al-Rashid (786–809). I love the stories of Caliph Harun in *One Thousand and One Nights*, and how he would go in disguise at night through the city of Baghdad with his vizier Jafar, listening to the complaints of the people, and I imagine some of these adventures must have happened after a big dinner of sikbāj. In fact Harun's recipe for sikbāj and others are given in the oldest surviving cookbook in Arabic, *Kitāb al-Tabīkh* (*The Book of Cookery*) compiled by Ibn Sayyār al-Warrāq, c. 950–1000 CE. Here's the recipe that al-Warrāq claims is the original sixth-century Persian version eaten by Khosrau, slightly shortened from Nawal Nasrallah's translation:

Meat Stew with Vinegar (sikbāj)

Wash 4 pounds of beef, put in a pot, cover with sweet vinegar, and bring to a boil three times until almost done.

Then pour out the vinegar, add 4 pounds of lamb, cover completely with fresh undiluted vinegar, and boil again.

Now clean and disjoint a chicken and add it to the pot, along with fresh watercress, parsley, and cilantro, a few snips of rue, and 20 citron leaves. Boil until the meat is almost cooked. Discard the greens.

Add 4 cleaned plump chicks and bring to a boil again. Add 3 ounces of ground coriander, thyme-mint, 1 ounce of whole garlic cloves (threaded onto toothpicks) and cook until everything is done.

Finally add honey or sugar syrup (use a quarter the amount of vinegar you used), 6 grams ground saffron, and 2 grams ground lovage. Stop feeding the fire and let the pot simmer until it stops bubbling. Take the pot off the fire and ladle it, God willing.

The details of sikbāj vary from recipe to recipe, but in all of them it is a rich beef stew, often with chicken or lamb too, flavored by many herbs and often by smoked woods, and always preserved with lots of vinegar. Besides its perky flavor, vinegar has been known since Babylonian times to be an excellent preservative (acetic acid is a potent antimicrobial, killing salmonella and E. coli). In fact, it seems likely that sikbāj is a variant of even older local vinegary meat stews. In the 1980s Assyriologist Jean Bottéro translated the world's oldest cookbook: a set of clay tablets, written in Akkadian in 1700 BCE, probably in Babylon, only 55 miles south of Baghdad. Recipes for meat stews on these clay slabs, the Yale Culinary Tablets, make such similar uses of vinegar, smoked woods, and herbs like rue that it seems likely that sikbāj is a variant of local stews that had been cooked in southern Mesopotamia for thousands of years.

Very quickly, sikbāj moved around the Islamic world, perhaps because it seems to have been a favorite dish of sailors, who are often more dependent on preserved foods. The story is told that the ninth-century Caliph al-Mutawakkil was once sitting with his courtiers and singers on a terrace overlooking one of the canals of Baghdad when he smelled a delicious sikbāj stew cooking on a nearby ship. The caliph ordered the pot to be brought to him, and enjoyed the sikbāj so much that he returned the pot to the sailor filled with money.

It's possible that it was these sailors that first started making sikbāj with fish instead of meat. The first mention of a fish sikbāj is in *The Book of the Wonders of India*, a set of stories collected by a Persian sea captain, Buzurg Ibn Shahriyar, fantastical tales about the Muslim and Jewish sea merchants that were trading among the (Abbasid) Muslim empire, India, and China. In one story set in 912 CE, a Jewish merchant, Isaac bin Yehuda, returns to Oman with a gift for the ruler: a beautiful black porcelain vase. "I have brought you a dish of sikbāj from China," said Isaac. The ruler is skeptical that even a preserved sikbāj could last that long, so Isaac opened the vase to show it was full of fish made out of gold, with ruby eyes, "surrounded by musk of the first quality."

This story reveals that already by the tenth century sikbāj could be made of fish. The first recipe we have for these fish sikbāj comes somewhat later, in the thirteenth-century medieval Egyptian cookbook *Kanz Al-Fawa'id Fi Tanwi' Al-Mawa'id, or The Treasury of Useful*

Advice for the Composition of a Varied Table. Sikbāj now is a fried fish dredged in flour and then sauced with vinegar and honey and spices. Here's the recipe as translated by Lilia Zouali in her excellent *Medieval Cuisine of the Islamic World*:

Fish sikbāj, Egypt, 13th century

Provide yourself with some fresh fish, vinegar, honey, atrāf tib [spice mix], pepper, onion, saffron, sesame oil, and flour.

Wash the fish and cut it into pieces then fry in the sesame oil after dredging in the flour. When [they] are ready, take them out.

Slice the onion and brown it in the sesame oil.

In the mortar, crush the pepper and atrāf tib. Dissolve the saffron in vinegar and honey and add it. When [the sauce] is ready, pour it over the fish.

The recipe continued to move westward along the ports of the Mediterranean, the name and the recipe metamorphosing as it did so. By the

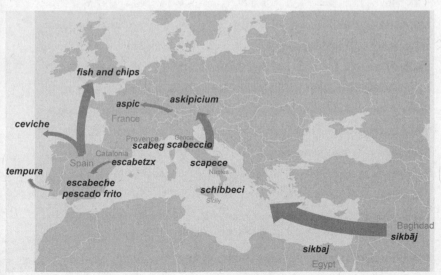

The journeys of sikbāj

early fourteenth century there were recipes for *escabetx* in Catalan, the Romance language spoken in what is now northeastern Spain and by the late fourteenth century in southwestern France for *scabeg*, written in Occitan, the medieval language spoken in Provence, the southern part of France. Later in Italy we see the word in the dialects from Sicilian (*schibbeci*), to Neapolitan (*scapece*), to Genoese (*scabeccio*).

In all these areas the word refers to a fried fish dish. For example, a Catalan cookbook from the first half of the 1300s, the *Book of Sent Soví* (Saint Sofia), has a recipe called *Si fols fer escabetx* (If you want to make escabeche) that describes fried fish made into minced fishballs and served cold with a sauce made of onions in vinegar and spices. In Muslim regions like Baghdad or Spain, by contrast, cookbooks like the *Book of Dishes (Kitab al-tabikh)* still mostly describe sikbāj as a meat stew with vinegar.

Why did the fish rather than meat sikbāj become so prevalent in these Romance languages? One clue is geographical: these scapeces and scabegs all appear in ports along the Mediterranean (in southern but not northern France, in coastal but not inland Italy), consistent with the idea that it was sailors who continued to spread sikbāj.

But the key difference between Italy and France, on the one hand, and Spain and Baghdad on the other, is that the *sikbāj* eaters of Italy and France were Christians. Medieval Christians had very strict dietary restrictions, abstaining from meat, dairy, and eggs during Lent, on Fridays and sometimes Saturdays and Wednesdays, and on numerous other fast days like Ember days. Medieval food scholar Melitta Adamson estimates that medieval fast days amounted to more than a third of the year for most Christians. Cookbooks were full of fish recipes for these extensive fast periods. Even as late as 1651, the famous French cookbook of La Varenne, *The French Cook*, is divided into three sections: meat recipes, Lent recipes, and "lean" recipes for non-Lenten fast days like Fridays.

While the fish descendent of sikbāj was traveling from port to port, another Christian borrowing of the sikbāj stew took a different form. In the fourteenth century Arabic cookbooks and medical texts were translated into Latin and, as Italian scholar Anna Martellotti shows us, the full name *al-sikbāj* began to be transcribed as *assicpicium* and *askipicium*. Medieval medical texts often focused on broths and their medicinal qualities, and Latin medical texts emphasized the broth of the cold sikbāj. When sikbāj was eaten cold, the vinegary broth results in a jelly, and *assicpicium* became *aspic* in French, still our modern word for a cold jellied broth.

By 1492, the Reconquista had extended Christian influence over Spain and Portugal as well, and cookbooks from neighboring Catalonia, like Master Robert's 1520 *Llibre del Coch*, began to be translated into Spanish, bringing words for many seafood and other gastronomic terms into Spanish, and the new Spanish word *escabeche* seems to have been one of them. Meanwhile, other descendants of sikbāj had appeared in Arabic cookbooks in Spain under different names, including another fried fish recipe very similar to the twelfth-century Egyptian sikbāj, called "dusted fish," in which fish is dipped into a spicy egg batter, fried in oil, and then eaten with vinegar and oil.

By the early 1500s, Spain and Portugal thus had a number of closely related dishes involving fried fish with vinegar, usually eaten cold, which derived from various versions of sikbāj. In escabeche the fish was first fried, with or without crumbs or batter, and then soaked in vinegar and onions. In *pescado frito*, there were no onions, and the fish was invariably battered before being fried and then eaten cold with vinegar.

Sikbāj had reached the western edge of Europe; but its travels were not over. In 1532–33, Francisco Pizarro González, the Spanish conquistador from Estremedura in Spain, led the army that conquered Peru. Pizzaro's soldiers brought many European foods to Peru, including onions and citrus fruits (limes, lemons, sour oranges), but also found many local foods like potatoes and corn. They also brought a version of escabeche, probably one using sour orange juice instead of vinegar (an early Spanish dictionary, the 1732 edition of the Real Academia Española's *Diccionario de la lengua castellana*, suggests that citrus used to be an alternative in escabeche):

> *Escabeche. A kind of sauce and marinade, made with white wine or vinegar, bay leaves, cut lemons, and other ingredients, for preserving fish and other delicacies.*

The Spanish encountered indigenous coastal groups like the Moche who lived off fish and molluscs such as snails; Gutiérrez de Santa Clara (1522–1603), one of Pizarro's soldiers, reported that "los indios desta costa . . . todo el pescado que toman en el río, o en la mar, se lo comen crudo" [the Indians on this coast . . . all the fish they take from the river or the sea, they eat raw].

Local lore in Peru suggests that the Moche flavored this raw fish with chile. Modern ceviche (fish, lime juice, onions, chile, salt; see recipe below) is thus probably a mestizo dish that incorporates chile and raw fish from the Moche's tradition, and onions and limes or sour oranges from the Spanish escabeche. Most scholars (such as Peruvian historian Juan José Vega and the Royal Spanish Academy's *Diccionario de la lengua española*) believe that the word *ceviche* thus derives from a shortening of *escabeche*, although we may never know for sure—the word doesn't appear in writing until almost 300 years later in lyrics for an 1820 song, where it is spelled *sebiche*.

Ceviche

1 pound fish (red snapper or halibut), cut into ½"–¾" cubes
½ red onion, sliced thin
⅓ cup + 1 tablespoon fresh key lime juice
¼ cup fish broth
2 teaspoons aji amarillo (Peruvian yellow chile) sauce

2 teaspoons chopped cilantro leaves

1 habanero pepper, minced

¼ teaspoon salt (to taste)

Marinate onions with lime juice in a medium bowl in refrigerator. Meanwhile, mix fish broth, aji amarillo paste, minced pepper, salt, and cilantro in a small jar and set aside. Fifteen minutes before serving, mix cut fish thoroughly with the lime juice and onions, and marinate in refrigerator for 10–15 minutes. Then add fish broth mixture into the bowl with lime juice and fish, and mix well. Serve with sliced cooked sweet potato, boiled Peruvian choclo corn kernels, or the toasted Peruvian dried corn called cancha.

Now just about the time Pizarro was bringing escabeche to Peru, another descendent of sikbāj, a version of pescado frito, was also brought to Japan, this time by the Portuguese Jesuits. The Portuguese first arrived in Japan in 1543, and established an active colony in Nagasaki, where Jesuit missionaries lived and Portuguese merchants traded Chinese products from their colony in Macao. Around 1639 a recipe for battered fried fish appears in the *Southern Barbarian Cookbook*, a collection of Portuguese and Spanish recipes written in Japanese. This cookbook included recipes for confectionary and baked goods (the Japanese word for bread [*pan*] and the names for various cakes and candies all come from Portuguese), and gives the following recipe for what is clearly a version of pescado frito:

Fish dish

It is fine to use any fish. Cut the fish into round slices. Douse in flour and fry in oil. Afterward, sprinkle with powdered clove and grated garlic. Prepare a stock as desired and simmer.

By around 1750 this dish is called *tempura* in Japanese; Japanese food scholar Eric C. Rath suggests that the name comes from *tenporari*, the name of a related dish in the 1639 *Barbarian Cookbook*, a chicken fried with six spices (black pepper, powdered cinnamon and cloves, ginger, garlic, onions) and then served in stock. This word is likely a borrowing of the Portuguese noun *tempero* (seasoning) and the related verb *temperar* (to flavor).

Just as the Spanish and Portuguese conquistadors, Jesuits, and merchants were traveling to Asia and the New World, another group left Spain and Portugal: Jews, expelled by both countries. Many of these Sephardic Jews moved to Holland and then England. In 1544, Manuel Brudo, a Portuguese crypto-Jewish doctor, wrote about the fried fish eaten by Portuguese exiles in Henry VIII's London. Once England rescinded its own ban on Jews in the seventeenth and eighteenth centuries, the community grew, and fried fish dishes became widely associated with Jews.

By 1796, a cold battered fried fish with vinegar appeared in Britain in Hannah Glasse's *The Art of Cookery, Made Plain and Easy*. Here's her recipe for battered and fried fish soaked in vinegar and served cold, called

The Jews Way of preserving Salmon, and all Sorts of Fish.

Take either salmon, cod, or any large fish, cut off the head, wash it clean, and cut it in slices as crimped cod is, dry it very well in a cloth, then flour it, and dip it in yolks of eggs, and fry it in a great deal of oil till it is of a fine brown and well done; take it out, and lay it to drain till it is very dry and cold. . . . have your pickle ready, made of the best white wine vinegar; when it is quite cold pour it on your fish, and a little oil on the top; they will keep good a twelvemonth, and are to be eat cold with oil and vinegar: they will go good to the East Indies.

This final note in Glasse's recipe reminds us why this dish originated as a favorite of sailors and why it spread so quickly up the coasts of the Mediterranean. Fish sikbāj and its descendants were made of an ingredient readily available at sea, and kept well for long periods, in this case preserved by the antimicrobial powers of the acetic acid in the vinegar, an immensely useful property in the days before refrigeration. As we'll see in the next chapter, sailors and the need for food preservation played a similar role in the story of how an Asian salted fish developed into both ketchup and sushi, and even indirectly led to the invention of the cocktail.

By the early nineteenth century, the Jews began selling this cold fried fish in the streets of London. In *Oliver Twist*, first serialized in 1838, Dickens talks of the fried-fish warehouses of London's East End: "Confined as the limits of Field Lane are, it has its barber, its coffee-shop, its beer-shop, and its fried-fish warehouse. It is a commercial colony of itself: the emporium of petty larceny."

In 1852, a *Times of London* reporter covering a story on London's Great Synagogue complained of being forced to pass through strange Jewish alleys "impregnated with the scents of fried fish." The 1846 *A Jewish Manual*, the first Jewish cookbook in English, written by Lady Judith Cohen Montefiore, gives a recipe similar to Glasse's, and distinguishes between Jewish fried fish and "English fried fish." In "English" recipes, Montefiore tells us, the fish is dredged in bread crumbs and then fried in butter (or presumably lard, although Montefiore doesn't talk about that) and served hot. "Jewish" fried fish, by contrast, is encased in an egg and flour batter and is fried in oil and served cold.

Roughly the same fried fish recipe, still eaten cold with vinegar, is considered "Jewish" as late as 1855 in Alexis Soyer's *Shilling Cookery for the People*:

75. Fried Fish, Jewish Fashion.

This is another excellent way of frying fish, which is constantly in use by the children of Israel, and I cannot recommend it too highly; so much so, that various kinds of fish which many people despise, are excellent cooked by this process. . . . It is excellent cold, and can be eaten with oil, vinegar, and cucumbers, in summer time, and is exceedingly cooling.

By the mid-nineteenth century, potatoes fried in drippings came to London, probably from the north of England or Ireland. Modern fish and chips arose at the latest by 1860, as Ashkenazi Jews began to move into London and integrate Sephardic foods and customs. One of the earliest known fish and chips shops was opened by Ashkenazi Jewish proprietor Joseph Malin, combining the new fried potatoes with Jewish fried fish, and serving everything warm rather than cold.

The last time I was in London food writer Anna Colquhoun and linguist Matt Purver took me to an old-fashioned Dalston chippie where you can have your lovely fried haddock battered in matzo-meal batter, made from the pulverized matzos that Jewish mothers like mine still use as a breading. (It wasn't until my twenties that I realized that matzo was not a main ingredient in other moms' recipes for veal parmesan.)

So it seems that it's not just melting-pot America whose favorite foods come from somewhere else. This family of dishes that are claimed by many nations as cultural treasures (ceviche in Peru, Chile, and Ecuador, fish and chips in Britain, tempura in Japan, escabeche in Spain, aspic in France) were prefigured by the ancient Ishtar worshippers of Babylon, invented by the Zoroastrian Persians, perfected by the Muslim Arabs, adapted by the Christians, fused with Moche dishes by the Peruvians, and brought to Asia by the Portuguese and to England by the Jews. And you can now find all these descendants of sikbāj, sometimes on the same block, in the ethnic restaurants that fill San Francisco and other bustling cities around the world.

I'd like to think that the lesson here is that we are all immigrants, that no culture is an island, that beauty is created at the confusing and painful boundaries between cultures and peoples and religions. I guess we can only look forward to the day when the battles we fight are about nothing more significant than where to go for ceviche.

Four

Ketchup, Cocktails, and Pirates

FAST FOOD IS AMERICA'S signature export, and one of its most pervasive: Every day another few outlets open in Europe or Asia, spreading the distinctively American diet to the world. It's ironic, then, that—just like England's fish and chips, Japanese tempura, or Spanish escabeche—America's hamburgers, French fries, and ketchup are not even originally ours. The borrowing is clear from what we call them: the large German contribution to American cuisine is obvious in words like *hamburger*, *frankfurter*, *delicatessen*, and *pretzel*, while *French fries* make their Franco-Belgian origins plain.

And, of course, *ketchup* is Chinese.

Chinese food has always been important in San Francisco. The Cantonese who settled the region were from the seafaring southern coastal region of Canton, and Chinese fishing and shrimping villages dotted San Francisco Bay in the nineteenth century. But the path that ketchup took from China to America didn't come through San Francisco at all. *Ketchup* originally meant "fish sauce" in a dialect of China's other southern coastal region, mountainous Fujian Province, which also gave us the word *tea* (from Fujianese "te"). Fujianese immigration to the United States has increased in recent years, so you can now sample Fujianese dishes in Chinatowns up and down the East Coast, paired with the homemade red rice wine that is a specialty of the province. The history of this red rice wine is intertwined with that of ketchup—but while the wine has stayed largely the same over the centuries, ketchup has undergone quite a transformation.

The story begins thousands of years ago, when people living along the coasts and rivers of Southeast Asia and what is now southern China began to preserve local fish and shrimp by salting and fermenting it into rich savory pastes. These groups didn't leave written records but we know they spoke three ancient languages that linguists call Mon-Khmer (the ancestor of modern Vietnamese and Cambodian), Tai-Kadai (the ancestor of modern Thai and Laotian), and Hmong-Mien (the ancestor of modern Hmong). All three left traces of their languages in the old names of many rivers and mountains throughout southern China, and in the words and grammar of the southern Chinese dialects.

Especially further south and inland the Mon-Khmer and Tai lived on the freshwater fish that were plentiful in their rice paddies in the rainy seasons. To make it through the dry season they devised sophisticated preservation methods, layering local fish in jars with cooked rice and salt, covered with bamboo leaves, and left to ferment. The enzymes in the fish convert the starch in the rice to lactic acid, resulting in a salty pickled fish that could be eaten by scraping off the goopy fermented rice. Chinese historians recorded this recipe by the fifth century CE, and the exact same methods are still used by the Kam, a Tai-speaking hill tribe who make this dish, called *ba som* (sour fish) in the hills of China's Guangxi province, the province where Janet's father grew up. Anthropologist Chris Hilton, who lived with the Kam, describes a thirty-year-old ba som that literally melted in his mouth, salty but mellow like "a Parma ham," with a "distinct sourness."

The Chinese people, who came from further north along the Yellow River, called these southerners the "Yi" or the "Hundred Yue," and around 200 BCE Emperor Wu of the Chinese Han dynasty began to expand the newly unified nation of China south and east toward the coast, invading the Mon-Khmer and Tai areas of what is now coastal Fujian and Guangdong. Chinese soldiers and colonists poured in, pushing the Mon-Khmer speakers south into what is now Vietnam and Cambodia, and the Tai speakers west and south into Thailand and Laos, with some tribes like the Kam remaining west in the hills of Guangxi. Evidence from early Chinese sources demonstrates that it was during this period that the Chinese adopted these fish sauces; here's one fifth-century account:

When the Han emperor Wu chased the Yi barbarians to the seashore, he smelled a potent, delicious aroma, but could not see where it came from. He sent an emissary to investigate. A fisherman revealed that the source was a ditch in which was piled layer upon layer of fish entrails. The covering of earth could not prevent the aroma from escaping. The emperor tasted a sample of the product and was pleased with the flavor.

The Mon-Khmer and Tai speakers who remained in Fujian and Guangdong (Canton) intermarried and assimilated, becoming thoroughly Chinese but continuing to make their indigenous fish and shrimp pastes. Soon this fermented seafood was adopted widely throughout the Chinese empire and other products began to be developed there, including a fermented soybean paste (the ancestor of Japanese *miso*) that eventually gave rise to soy sauce and a paste made from the leftover fermented mash from wine making, which spread to neighboring countries as preservatives and flavoring agents.

By 700 CE, for example, the Japanese began to use this Southeast Asian method of fermenting fish together with rice, calling this newly borrowed food *sushi*. This early fermented fish, now technically called *narezushi* in Japanese, is the ancestor of modern sushi. Sushi evolved to its modern fresh form in the eighteenth century as the lactic fermentation was replaced with vinegar, and again in the nineteenth century when the fish began to be eaten immediately rather than waiting for it to ferment.

Meanwhile, back in the original coastal areas of Fujian and Guangdong, fish and shrimp pastes remained a local specialty, as did another ancient fermented sauce: red-fermented rice (called *hongzao* in Mandarin), the lees or mash (used fermented rice) left over from making red rice wine. (The technique probably spread even further; sake lees, *sake kasu*, are used in Japan too as a marinade and flavoring in *kasuzuke* dishes like grilled kasuzuke butterfish.) Fujianese red rice wine and the resulting dishes like Red Wine Chicken, chicken browned in sesame oil with ginger and garlic and then braised in wine lees, became famous throughout China. You might like that dish too so I'm including the recipe here:

Fujian Red Rice Wine Chicken 红糟鸡

2 tablespoons sesame oil

1 large knob of ginger, sliced

3 smashed and peeled cloves of garlic

3 chicken thighs, each cut through the bone into 3 pieces

3 tablespoons red rice wine lees

½ cup Fujian red rice wine (or Shaoxing rice wine)

2 tablespoons soy sauce (to taste)

1 teaspoon brown sugar (or pieces of Chinese rock sugar)

Salt to taste

4 dried shitake mushrooms, reconstituted in about ½ cup boiling
    water, removed and sliced, reserving the water

Heat sesame oil and sauté ginger and garlic until fragrant. Add chicken and sear the chicken pieces until browned, then flip and brown the other side. Push chicken aside, fry the red wine lees briefly until fragrant, then add the wine, soy, mushrooms, and mushroom liquid, stirring until the chicken is well coated. Turn the heat to low and simmer 10 or more minutes or until chicken is done and sauce begins to thicken, stirring occasionally.

By the year 1200 CE, this shrimp-paste and red-rice eating region of Fujian became the bustling center of seafaring China. The port city of Quanzhou was one of the greatest and richest in the world, filled with Arab and Persian traders who prayed at the city's seven mosques. Quanzhou was the start of the Maritime Silk Road, and Marco Polo marveled at the vast number of ships in the harbor as he passed through on his way from China to Persia. By the fifteenth century Fujianese shipwrights built the great treasure fleet of Chinese Admiral Zheng He that sailed to Persia and as far as Madagascar in Africa, and Fujianese-built ships took Chinese seamen and settlers to ports throughout Southeast Asia.

In Southeast Asia, fermented fish products rather than soy products had remained the most popular seasonings, and the Vietnamese, Khmer, and Thai had developed many sophisticated fermented seafood products, like the fish sauce called *nuoc mam* in Vietnamese or *nam pla* in Thai, a pungent liquid with a beautiful red-caramel color. Fish sauces occur in Europe and the Middle East as well, probably developing independently of the Asian sauces. The ancient Babylonians had a fish sauce called *siqqu*, and classical Greece had a sauce called *garos* that probably came from their colonies along the Black Sea, a region that is still famous for salted fish products like caviar. *Garos* became the Roman fish sauce *garum*, eaten and made throughout the Roman world. The garum from Hispania was particularly prized; you can go tour the ruins of the garum factories under the streets of Barcelona.

One of the most prized modern fish sauces comes from Phu Quoc, a Vietnamese island off the coast of Cambodia in the Gulf of Thailand. Janet and I visited fish sauce factories there on our honeymoon, driving our motor scooter across the island in the rain to the old corrugated steel sheds along the river, the moist warm air pungent with the stench of fermenting fish. It's all very romantic. Anchovies from the gulf were mixed with salt in huge ancient wooden tanks 10 feet high, painted bright Asian red but otherwise looking (at least to a couple of San Franciscans) like wine tanks in a Napa winery, with thoroughly modern stopcocks bored in and hoses snaking everywhere for mixing the sauce as it ferments.

Maybe these sixteenth-century Fujianese traders and seamen saw some of the same factories, and in any case they loved the fish sauce too, naming it *ke-tchup*, "preserved-fish sauce" in Hokkien—the language of southern Fujian and Taiwan. (Hokkien, Cantonese, and Mandarin are as linguistically different from each other as, say, Italian and French. I once took cooking classes in Taiwan, where Mandarin

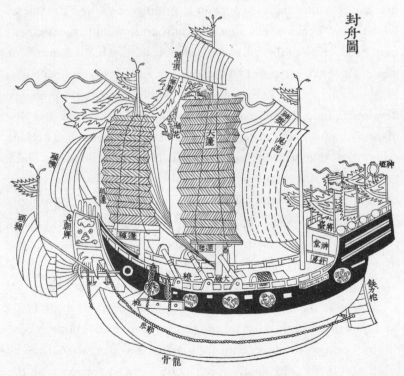

A Chinese oceangoing junk running before the wind
From Zhou Huang's Liuqiu Guo Zhi Lue (Account of the Ryukyu Islands), *written in 1757*

is the official language but Hokkien is very widely spoken; the other students had to translate into Mandarin for me when the chefs drifted into Hokkien. I did manage to learn how to make Hakka braised pork belly and keep my wok clean.)

Of course, Hokkien isn't written with the Roman alphabet, which explains why there are so many different spellings: *ke-tchup*, *catsup*, *catchup*, and *katchup* are all attempts by English, Dutch, or Portuguese speakers of the time to capture the sounds of the Chinese word. The word *ke-tchup* has died out of modern Hokkien, although I was still able to find it in old missionary dictionaries from the nineteenth century. The syllable *tchup*—pronounced *zhi* 汁 in Mandarin—still means "sauce" in Hokkien and in Cantonese. The syllable *ke* means "preserved fish" in Hokkien. *Ke* also looks like part of the Cantonese word for tomato, *faan-ke*, but that's a coincidence, since Chinese dialects have lots of words that sound like *ke* and tomatoes weren't added to the sauce until more than a century later.

Fujianese settlers took ke-tchup, soy, and their fermented red rice with them to Indonesia, Malaysia, and the Philippines. In Indonesia, they established Chinese sauce-making factories, small family businesses that fermented soy sauce and fish sauce. Soon the word *kecap* was adopted by Indonesians. It must have originally been borrowed from Hokkien in its original meaning of "fish sauce," but as other sauces became more prominent over the intervening 400 years, kecap has generalized its meaning and now in Bahasa Indonesia, the language of Indonesia, *kecap* just means "sauce" (sweet soy sauce is *kecap manis*, fish sauce is *kecap ikan*, and so on). Linguists call this kind of generalization "semantic bleaching," because part of the meaning (the salty fish part) got bleached out. (Almost the exact same kind of bleaching happened in the history of the English word *sauce*, which comes from the Latin word *salsus* originally meaning "salted"; just as in the Indonesian case, generalizing from meaning a briny sauce to meaning just any sauce at all.)

The red rice mash changed as well, turning out to be useful for more than just a flavoring for clay pot dishes. The immigrants began to turn red rice wine into *arrack*, an early ancestor of rum, distilling the fermented rice together with molasses and palm wine. The word *arrack* comes from the Arabic *'araq* (sweat), and is related to words for other distilled spirits like anise-flavored Levantine *arak* and the Croatian plum brandy *rakia*, as we'll see. Arrack is a bit fiery and rough, as befits its archaic nature; you can taste it for yourself, since Batavia arrack (van Oosten brand) is still imported.

Chinese factories were established to make arrack on Java and Sumatra, using the Chinese pot still, a traditional Chinese method that boils the wort and drips the resulting arrack as condensing steam through tubes. The customers were presumably local, other Chinese and native Javans, or at least they were until two more groups of people wandered into Batavia and Bantam: British and Dutch merchants who had come to Southeast Asia looking for spices, textiles, and porcelain. Liquor was not yet well known at this time in England; this was before the invention of gin, and although Ireland and Scotland had already been drinking *usquebagh*, spirits in England were still purely medicinal. Edmund Scott, an English trader on Java, thus described arrack as "a kind of hot drink that is used in most of those parts of the world instead of wine." British sailors in the tropics mostly drank sour wine and even sourer beer due to the fact that neither stood up well to tropical heat (even with the extra hops of India Pale Ale, a type of beer that in any case wasn't developed until a few hundred years later).

Thus when Scott learned of arrack in 1604 from the Chinese tavern-keeper next door who distilled it in a backyard shed for his customers it was a revelation. Distilled spirits don't go bad in the tropical heat, and they don't oxidize. While this made arrack an exciting discovery for the British in general, this revelation wasn't such a happy one to Scott himself. Under the cover of the noise of boiling water and clamor of tubs full of mash in the distilling shed, the Chinese tavern-keeper next door tunneled under Scott's warehouse to steal the treasure Scott had buried in jars: 3000 silver Spanish pieces of eight from the mines in Bolivia, the same silver mines from which, 250 years later, Chilean and Peruvian miners brought mining techniques to the California gold fields of 1849. But I digress.

Before long the British were buying immense quantities of arrack, despite its expense; after all, navies full of British sailors needed something to drink, and rum hadn't yet been invented. The Chinese settlements in Java were concentrated in Batavia (modern-day Jakarta), and it was here that the main industrial production occurred. Almost immediately, around 1610, arrack became the main ingredient in what cocktail historian David Wondrich calls "the original monarch of mixed drinks": punch—a combination of arrack, citrus, sugar, water, and spice. Wondrich thinks this first cocktail was likely invented by British sailors, making good use of the lemons they were supplied with as the recently discovered cure for scurvy, and punch quickly became the "common drink" of all Europeans in Asia.

While acquiring a taste for arrack and punch, British sailors acquired a taste for something else they bought from Chinese merchants in Indonesia: ke-tchup. Shipboard fare—salt pork and the dry crackers called hardtack—was pretty bland, so ke-tchup may have helped enliven their diet, but it's also possible traders just figured they could market it back home as an exotic Asian sauce. The British had a trading post in Bengkulu on Sumatra in the 1690s and one of the earliest recipes for ketchup in 1732 is for "Ketchup, in Paste. From Bencoulin in the East Indies." It's therefore likely that it is at one of such posts on either Java or Sumatra that the word *ketchup* first came into English.

By the turn of the eighteenth century, fish sauce and arrack had become as profitable for British merchants as they were for Chinese traders, as we see from the reports of a trader for the East India Company, Charles Lockyer, who traveled to Indonesia, Malaysia, Vietnam, China, and India in 1703. His *An Account of the Trade in India*, a kind of vade mecum for would-be global capitalists, explains the vast sums of money

AN
ACCOUNT
OF THE
TRADE in *INDIA*:

CONTAINING

RULES for good Government in TRADE, Price Courants, and Tables: With Defcriptions of *Fort St. George, Acheen, Malacca, Condore, Canton, Anjengo, Muskat, Gombroon, Surat, Goa, Carwar, Telichery, Panola, Calicut*, the *Cape of Good-Hope*, and *St. Helena.*

THEIR

Inhabitants, Cuftoms, Religion, Government, Animals, Fruits, *&c.*

To which is added,

An ACCOUNT of the Management of the *DUTCH* in their Affairs in *INDIA.*

By *CHARLES LOCKYER.*

LONDON,

Printed for the Author, and fold by SAMUEL CROUCH, at the Corner of *Pope's-Head-Alley* in *Cornhill.* 1711.

The cover of Charles Lockyer's 1711 memoir of his travels in Asia to be made in Asia, and how to get rich by bargaining with the Chinese and other foreigners:

Soy comes in tubs from Jappan, and the best Ketchup *from* Tonqueen *[northern Vietnam]; yet good of both sorts, are made and sold very cheap in* China. . . . *I know not a more profitable Commodity.*

Lockyer would buy tubs of ketchup and soy and draw off the sauces into bottles for the return journey. The expensive bottled ketchup quickly became a prestige product in England. The great expense of this Asian import soon led to recipes in British and then American cookbooks for cooks attempting to make their own ketchup, imitating the taste of the expensive imported original. Ketchup wasn't the only attempt to counterfeit a luxury Asian import. Worcestershire sauce was created later in the nineteenth century to imitate a sauce from Bengal, and budget replacements for arrack were also developed, using local sugar in the Caribbean. You probably know the most popular of these imitation arracks: it is called "rum."

Here's a ketchup recipe from a 1742 London cookbook in which the fish sauce has already taken on a very British flavor, with "eschallots" (shallots) and mushrooms:

To Make KATCH-UP that will keep good Twenty Years.

Take a Gallon of strong stale Beer, one Pound of Anchovies wash'd and clean'd from the Guts, half an Ounce of Mace, half an Ounce of Cloves, a quarter of an Ounce of Pepper, three large Races of Ginger, one Pound of Eschallots, and one Quart of flap Mushrooms well rubb'd and pick'd; boil all these over a slow Fire till it is half wasted, and strain it thro' a Flannel Bag; let it stand till it is quite cold, then bottle and stop it very close. . . . This is thought to exceed what is brought from *India.*

The mushrooms that played a supporting role in this early recipe soon became a main ingredient, and from 1750 to 1850 the word *ketchup* began to mean any number of thin dark sauces made of mushrooms or even walnuts, often used to flavor melted butter. Jane Austen's family seemed to prefer this new walnut ketchup, and the household book kept by Jane's friend Martha Lloyd while she lived with Jane's family in Chawton tells us they made it by pounding green walnuts with salt and then boiling the mash with vinegar, cloves, mace, ginger, nutmeg, pepper, horseradish, and shallots.

It wasn't until the nineteenth century that people first began to add tomato to ketchups, probably first in Britain. This early recipe from 1817 still has the anchovies that betray its fish sauce ancestry:

Tomata Catsup

Gather a gallon of fine, red, and full ripe tomatas; mash them with one pound of salt; let them rest for three days, press off the juice, and to each quart add a quarter of a pound of anchovies, two ounces of shallots, and an ounce of ground black pepper; boil up together for half an hour, strain through a sieve, and put to it the following spices; a quarter of an ounce of mace, the same of all-spice and ginger, half an ounce of nutmeg, a drachm of coriander seed, and half a drachm of cochineal; pound all together; let them simmer gently for twenty minutes, and strain through a bag: when cold, bottle it, adding to each bottle a wineglass of brandy. It will keep for seven years.

By the mid-1850s, tastes changed and anchovies seem to disappear from the recipes. After the Civil War, manufacturers in America responded to the greatly increased demand by increasing ketchup production, tailoring their recipes to American consumers who began to prefer their ketchup a bit sweeter and thicker than the British. By around 1910 manufacturers like Heinz found that adding even more sugar and also lots of vinegar helped produce a ketchup that preserved better, leading to our modern sweet-and-sour formula. The spelling was another common difference between Britain and America; while both spellings were used in both countries, *ketchup* was more common in Britain and *catsup* in America, until about 30 years ago, when *ketchup* took over here as well. (Heinz originally chose the spelling "ketchup" to distinguish the product from competitors' "catsup," but when Heinz began to dominate the market other manufacturers switched to Heinz's spelling.)

The Chinese origins of our national sauce aren't just a fun bit of culinary trivia—ketchup's history offers us new insights into global economic history. If you subscribe to a traditional Western model of Asian economics, China turned inward in 1450 during the Ming dynasty and became isolated and economically irrelevant, leading to stagnation and a low standard of living until the West finally dragged Asia into the world economy in the nineteenth and twentieth centuries.

But the vast production and trade of ke-tchup (not to mention arrack and less delicious goods like textiles and porcelain) well into the eighteenth century tell a different tale. The late economist Andre G. Frank and scholars like Kenneth Pomerantz and Robert C. Allen have shown that while the Chinese government did ban private sea trade, these bans were repeatedly rescinded, and in any case were simply ignored by Hokkien sailors, who continued to sail and trade illegally on a massive scale. Charles Lockyer, for example, complains throughout his memoir about intense competition from the Chinese, describing, in every country he visited, harbors crowded with Chinese ships packed with goods, trading voluminously from China along every coast and island east to Indonesia and west as far as Burma.

Fujianese pirates also played a huge role in this trade. Chinese officials repeatedly complained that the entire city of Amoy was given over to pirates. The private navy of the Fujianese warlord Zheng

Chenggong was the largest navy in Asia, conquering Taiwan from the Dutch East Indies Company in 1662 and trading enormous quantities of silk and porcelain to the west for Spanish silver.

In fact, by the time British sailors brought ketchup back to England in the late seventeenth century, China was the richest nation in the world by any measure—including standard of living, life span, and per capita income—and produced the bulk of the whole world's GNP. China's control of intra-Asia trade together with its superior manufacturing technology (in textiles, clothing, ceramics, and distillation) meant that China dominated the world economy until the Industrial Revolution.

These facts explain why the Portuguese, British, and Dutch were so eager to get to Asia: most of the world's trade took place only there. But Europe had no manufacturing base that was comparable to Asia's until 1800. All Europe had to offer in exchange for Asia's considerable luxury goods were gold and silver from the new colonial mines that had been established in Bolivia, Peru, and Mexico. The mines, discovered in the sixteenth century and worked by Andean and African slaves, produced the silver for vast floods of Spanish silver *reals* of eight. Silver was the only thing the Chinese government would accept, and Spanish silver pieces of eight became the first international currency, the dollar of its time, explaining why Edmund Scott had jars of them buried under his warehouse in Java in 1604.

It wasn't just the larcenous Chinese tavern-keeper next door who had designs on those silver reals. The Manila galleons carrying silver from Acapulco to Manila were under constant attack from pirates. These included the Fujianese pirate Zheng Chenggong mentioned above (the warlord also known as Koxinga) whose vast pirate armada let him conquer Taiwan from the Dutch and almost invade the Philippines. English and Dutch pirates were after them as well, including Sir Francis Drake, who captured tons of silver from the Spanish treasure ships and coastal cities of Peru and Chile before landing in 1579 just north of San Francisco at Drake's Bay and claiming "New Albion" for England. In the other direction, the great Spanish treasure fleet carrying silver reals as well as silk and porcelain from Veracruz to Spain was targeted by the *original* pirates of the Caribbean, represented in my childhood by Stevenson's Long John Silver whose parrot Cap'n Flint would screech out "Pieces of Eight! Pieces of Eight! Pieces of Eight!" until he was out of breath.

The silver real was de facto currency for the British colonies as well, circulated widely even in the United States well into the nineteenth century. (In the 1960s when I was reading *Treasure Island*, a quarter was still called "two bits," a usage that dates back to small silver coins that were worth one-eighth of a Spanish real.)

Europeans sent vast numbers of these silver reals of eight back to Asia to buy high-quality Asian-manufactured silk, cotton, porcelain, arrack, soy, and prestigious ketchup. As Charles Mann argues in his book *1493*, it was thus the Chinese desire for silver, and Europe's desire for Asian exports, that drove Europe's intense phase of exploration and colonization in the New World. The encounter between Western appetites and Eastern products created our modern "world-spanning interconnected civilizations," to borrow Mann's phrase.

The story of ketchup—from the fermented fish sauces of China and Southeast Asia to the sushi of Japan to our modern sweet tomato chutney—is, after all, a story of globalization and of centuries of economic domination by a world superpower. But the superpower isn't America, and the century isn't ours. Think of those little plastic ketchup packets under the seat of your car as a reminder of China's domination of the global world economy for most of the last millennium.

Five

A Toast to Toast

SAN FRANCISCO HAS always been a pretty good town for drinking to someone's health. I already introduced the Pisco punch, made from Pisco brandy, lemon juice, and pineapple syrup that people toasted with after the gold rush. These days on sunny afternoons I'm fond of clinking glasses with a *michelada*, a Mexican summer beer cocktail with fresh lime juice, hot sauce, and—if you're lucky—a dusting of the chili lime powder called "salsa en polvo" (salsa powder):

Michelada

1¼ ounces fresh squeezed key lime juice
½ teaspoon hot sauce
½ teaspoon Worcestershire sauce
½ teaspoon chamoy (fruity chili sauce)
½ teaspoon Maggi
1 Negra Modelo (or a Pacifico if it's very hot outside)
ice cubes to fill a tall glass
Mexican chili lime powder (like Tajín) (optional; for the glass rim)

Rub a lime around the rim of a tall chilled glass and then dip the rim in chili lime powder. In a small jar or shaker, mix the rest of the ingredients, add to the glass with ice, and top with beer.

Unusual cocktails mixed with fresh herbs and fruits and a mix of alcohols are quite the rage all across the country recently. The Chamomile High Club at Maven in the Lower Haight mixes hop-forward India Pale Ale with bourbon and flavors of lemon, chamomile, and apricot. (Hops are a preservative, and the extra hops of India Pale Ale originally helped it stand up to the long journey to India in the stifling hot cargo holds.) Or you can have all the flavors from one bottle with Fernet Branca, the Italian bitters that every bar serves here, flavored with chamomile, elderflower, galangal, aloe, myrrh, and other herbs.

At weddings, champagne is more traditional. But at our friend Marta's wedding—she's originally from Croatia—Janet and I happily toasted the bride and groom with *rakia* instead. Rakia is the generic name for the fruit-based brandies of southeast Europe: Albania, Bulgaria, Croatia, Romania, Serbia, Slovenia. While rakia may be made from apricots, cherries, or grapes, the most common type of rakia is plum, called *šljivovica* or *slivovitz*, made by fermenting plum fruit into a kind of plum cider and then distilling off the liquor. You toast with rakia by saying, "živjeli!" (To life!); phrases meaning "health" or "life" are employed for toasting in many European languages: French *santé*, Irish *slainte*, Polish *na zdrowie*, Spanish *salud*, Hungarian *egészségedre*.

Toasting to the bride and groom, the parents, the grandparents, and so on can add up to a lot of drinking. Even more so for the bride and groom, if they walk around and toast at each table, a Chinese tradition that is now more widely prevalent in San Francisco. At a big wedding with 30 tables of guests, the groom wouldn't get halfway around the room before becoming what my Uncle Herbie would call *shikker*, Yiddish for "drunk," with the result of, well, not much of a wedding night. When Janet and I got married, my brother-in-law John, a man who is serious about his whisky, took me aside and suggested I might want to quietly fill my glass with tea or cider instead of whisky for all the toasts, a piece of family wisdom that got me through the evening.

I assume we weren't the first couple to adopt this strategy. Which raises the question: Why do we toast people's health with alcohol? What does a drink have to do with honoring someone or wishing them health? And why is it called a *toast*?

As we'll see, the histories of the words *toast*, *cider*, and even that Yiddish word *shikker* are all related, the name *rakia* has a relevant story too, and furthermore, delicious herb-infused drinks of mixed liquors were invented, not in the last century, but at the very dawn of human civilization.

The original meaning of the word *toast* was bread that had been grilled by the fire, from the popular Latin *tostāre* (to grill). I'm a fan of toast; my invariant breakfast of a toasted bagel and a cup of coffee is a source of amusement for Janet, whose Cantonese sensibilities lead her to believe that all meals can be improved by a little bacon. And thick slabs of artisanal toast with pumpkin butter or homemade jam are the latest breakfast trend at San Francisco cafes like the Mill. The association of toast solely with breakfast, however, is purely modern.

Until the seventeenth century, for example, wine and ale were often drunk with a piece of toast in it. This tradition is quite old; the Elizabethans did it too, as we can see from Shakespeare's *Merry Wives of Windsor*: "FALSTAFF. Go fetch me a quart of sack; put a toast in 't." While it seems quite strange to us now, the toast was used to add flavor and substance to the drink, and was often spiced with herbs like *borage*, a sweet-tasting herb that is no longer in common use, and with sugar.

In the seventeenth century, just as this tradition of flavoring wine with toast was actually beginning to die out, the custom developed at English dinners to have the whole table drink to someone's health. And then someone else's. (And then again. All that drinking doesn't seem very healthy to me, but as my British friends point out, I come from a nation founded by Puritans. Indeed, the Puritans of the time thought it was a bad idea too, and railed against the "drinking and pledging of healthes" as "sinfull, and utterly unlawfull unto Christians.") Frequently these toasts were made to the health of a lady, and the favored lady became known as the *toast* of the company.

A report from the time suggests that the term was used because she flavored the party just as the spiced toast and herbs flavored the wine. Popular ladies "grew into a toast" or became the "toast of the town," as we see in this (snide?) comment from a gossip magazine of 1709:

> *A Beauty, whose Health is drank from Heddington to Hinksey, . . . has no more the Title of Lady, but reigns an undisputed Toast.*

A Carol for a Wassail Bowl, *by the Victorian illustrator Myles Birket Foster*

One of the things the Elizabethans drank with toast was called wassail. Wassail was a hot spiced ale, especially one that was brought in on the Twelfth Night of Christmas and offered to the company from a wassail bowl. In the early 1600s, Christmas carols describe the tradition of women carrying the wassail bowl from door to door while singing songs and soliciting donations.

In another wassail tradition, in the apple-growing West of England, people would "wassail the trees," placing a piece of toast soaked in cider in the trees and singing around the trees as a good luck ritual. For this reason some wassail recipes have cider or apples in them in addition to the hot ale. Here's one:

Wassail

4 baking apples, cored
⅓ cup brown sugar
½ cup apple juice

1½ cups Madeira
1 bottle ale (12 ounces)
1 bottle hard apple cider (22 ounces)
1 cup apple juice
10 whole cloves
10 whole allspice berries
1 cinnamon stick
2 strips orange peel, 2"
1 teaspoon ground ginger
1 teaspoon ground nutmeg

Preheat oven to 350 degrees. Put cored apples in a glass baking dish and fill each with brown sugar. Pour apple juice (½ cup) into baking dish and bake apples until tender, about an hour.

Meanwhile put cloves, allspice, cinnamon, and orange peel into cheesecloth bag or mesh strainer.

Put ale, cider, apple juice (1 cup), and Madeira into a heavy pot or slow cooker and add spice bag, ground ginger, and nutmeg. Gently simmer (do not boil) while apples are baking.

Add apples and liquid from baking dish into pot. Ladle into cups and serve.

The word *wassail* was first used to describe the drink in 1494, in the days of Henry VII. But the drink itself comes from the earlier sweetened ales of medieval Britain. Wine or spiced wine and cider were all conventional back then but ale was perhaps the most prevalent, sometimes in the form of bragget, an ale sweetened with honey or mead. Ale in medieval England was a dark brew made of malted barley and other grains but, unlike modern beer or ale, made without hops. As I mentioned above, hops are a preservative, so without them (their usage was only adopted from the Netherlands in the fifteenth/sixteenth century) ale went bad very quickly and so was drunk fresh, usually within a few days of brewing. Ales were a safe drink because they were made of boiled water, and many ales had a low alcohol content, with the result that everyone drank quite a lot of them in the Middle Ages and ale was thus an important source of calories and nutrients for the general population.

The idea of putting toast in the ale is even older. In the Middle Ages slices of toast soaked in wine, water, or broth, called *sops*, were often used as a way to add heat, flavor, and calories to hot liquids like broth or wine. The most common meal of the Middle Ages, the thick one-pot stews called *pottages*, were generally served over slices of hot toast or bread.

In *The Canterbury Tales*, Chaucer's Franklin, a hearty old epicure whose house "snowed of meat and drink," loved to have a sop in his morning wine ("wel loved he by the morwe a sop in wyn"). The earliest written recipes mentioning toasted bread or toast in English all describe slices of bread toasted and then served "all hot" soaked in wine and spices, like these recipes for "sowpes in galyngale" from the 1390 *Forme of Cury*, the first English cookbook, written by the master cooks of King Richard II, or "soups dorye" from a fifteenth-century cookbook:

Sowpes in galyngale. Take powdour of galyngale, wyne, sugur and salt; and boile it yfere. Take breded ytosted, and lay the sewe onward, and serue it forth

[*Sops in galangal.* Take galangal powder, wine, sugar, and salt, and boil together. Take toasted bread, pour the sauce over it, and serve it forth]

Soupes dorye . . . take Paynemayn an kytte it an toste it an wete it in wyne

[*Golden sops* . . . Take payndemayn (white bread) and cut it and toast it and wet it in wine]

In fact the word *sop*, perhaps via its sixth-century late Latin relative *suppa*, gave rise by the tenth century to the Old French word *soper* (to have supper) and *soupe*, from which come our words *supper* and *soup*. Soup thus first meant the soaked toast, and then generalized to mean the broth eaten with it, and supper meant the light evening meal of sops or soup, as opposed to a heavier midday "dinner." In the United States, the word was retained in various regional dialects with various slightly different meanings. As a young child in New York, *supper* was my word for the evening meal, and I remember moving to California at the age of four, being laughed at by other kids for using this old-fashioned word, and informing my parents that we had to call the evening meal *dinner*.

The word *wassail* comes from the English of a thousand years ago, when you toasted someone's health with wine or ale by saying *waes hael* (be healthy); the word *hael* is the ancestor of our modern words *hale* and *healthy*. English thus had a word just like Croatian *ževjeli*, French *santé*, or German *prost*.

The correct response to *waes hael* was *drink hael* (drink healthy). We know this because in 1180, the English monk and social critic Nigellus Wireker wrote that English students studying abroad in Paris at the fancy new "university" were spending too much of their time in "waes hael" and "drink hael" and not enough in their studies. I guess the fundamentals of university life have not changed in the last 900 years.

In some places complex ritualized toasts like the waes hael/drink hael (call-and-response) are deeply embedded in the culture. In the country of Georgia, for example, feasts are characterized by endless series of toasts with wine. There can be 20 or more toasts in an evening. Toasters around the room rise to toast the guest of honor, the Land of Georgia, families, the toastmaster (called the *tamada*), and so on.

In fact, to take a brief digression on the ancient origins of wine, converging evidence from biology, archaeology, and linguistics suggests that it is in this same Caucasian region of modern Georgia or Armenia that the wild grape was first domesticated and wine was made. The earliest known domesticated grape seeds have been found in this region, dating from 6000 BCE. The region has the greatest diversity in wild grape genes, and DNA evidence suggests that the wine grape *vinis vinifera vinifera* was first domesticated from the wild grape *vinis vinferia sylvestris* here. The earliest chemical remains of wine come from jars found slightly farther east in a Neolithic village called Hajji Firuz Tepe in Iran's Zagros Mountains, dating from 5000 BCE. And some linguists believe that **γwino* (the * means this is a hypothesized proto word), the ancient word for wine in Kartvelian, the language family that includes Georgian, is the origin of the word for wine in neighboring language families like Indo-European (English *wine* and *vine*, Latin *vinum*, Albanian *vere*, Greek *oinos*, Armenian *gini*, Hittite *wiyana*) and Semitic (**wajn*, Arabic *wayn*, Hebrew *yayin*, Akkadian *inu*). University of Pennsylvania researcher Patrick McGovern calls this idea the "Noah hypothesis," after the biblical Noah, who planted a vineyard on Mount Ararat (now in eastern Turkey at the Armenian border): "And the ark rested in the seventh month, on the seventeenth day of the month, upon the mountains of Ararat . . . and Noah . . . planted a vineyard."

These Semitic and Indo-European cultures that may have borrowed the word for wine also show early evidence for a concept related to toasting, the idea of *libation*. A libation, an offering of mead (a fermented honey beverage) or wine or oil poured to the gods before drinking, was central to Greek religion, appearing as early as Homer. At later Greek symposia, a libation from the first *krater* of wine was poured to Zeus before drinking from it, from the second to the heroes, and so on.

These libations date back even earlier, to the ancestors of Greek culture, the Indo-Europeans, who poured libations for the gods to avert bad fate. We know this from linguistic evidence; languages across the Indo-European language family have many words for libation, often linked with words relating to health, security, or guarantees. Thus Greek *spendo* and Hittite *spand* indicates a wine libation that is poured while asking the gods to guarantee someone's security or safe return, while the related Latin *spondeo* means "to guarantee," from which we get our word *spouse*, from the Roman marriage ceremony in which one promises to guarantee the security of one's spouse. The root **g'heu* (*pour*) is the ancestor of Latin *fundere* (to pour, from which come English words like *fund*, *refund*, *found*, *fuse*, *suffuse*), and of Sanskrit *hav-*, used for the liquid offerings in Vedic ritual, and of Iranian *zav-*, meaning to make an offering, and Iranian *zaotar*, meaning priest.

Drink offerings seem to be just as old in the Middle East. A 2400 to 2600 BCE carving at the British Museum shows a priest from the Sumerian city of Ur pouring a libation. Similar images of libations come from the third millennium BCE from the Akkadians, a Semitic people who took over Mesopotamia after the Sumerians.

The libations in Mesopotamia, both Sumerian and Akkadian, were generally with beer rather than wine. Grapes weren't easy to grow this far south, and beer, called *shikaru* in Akkadian, was the common drink. Shikaru was made from barley as beer still is today, but it was also often brewed together with honey or palm wine that could result in a higher alcohol content (more sugar to ferment means more resulting alcohol). The earliest extant written recipe in the world is an 1800 BCE recipe for beer brewed with herbs and honey and wine in an ode to the Sumerian beer goddess Ninkasi:

A HYMN TO NINKASI

Ninkasi, it is you . . . mixing . . . the beerbread with sweet aromatics.

It is you who bake the beerbread in the big oven, and put in order the piles of hulled grain.

It is you who water the earth-covered malt

It is you who soak the malt in a jar;

It is you who spread the cooked mash on large reed mats

It is you who hold with both hands the great sweetwort, brewing it with honey and wine.

You [add?] . . . the sweetwort to the vessel.

You place the fermenting vat, which makes a pleasant sound, . . . on top of a large collector vat.

It is you who pour out the filtered beer of the collector vat; it is like the onrush of the Tigris and the Euphrates

Libations are also recorded from a later Semitic people, the Hebrews, in the earliest parts of the Hebrew Bible, such as the drink offering Jacob makes in Genesis: "And Jacob set up a Pillar in the place where he had spoken with him, a Pillar of Stone; and he poured out a drink offering on it, and poured oil on it" (Genesis 35:14). This offering was usually of wine (Hebrew *yayin*) or oil, but could also be a drink called *sheker*, a word borrowed from the Akkadian word *shikaru*. Hebrew sheker similarly meant beer, or a modified beer with extra alcohol due to fermented honey or palm wine: "in the holy *place* shalt thou cause the strong wine [sheker] to be poured unto the LORD *for* a drink offering" (Numbers 28:7).

We don't know why the custom of libations with wine or beer developed. Wine may have been associated with health due to the antipathogenic properties of the alcohol or the infused herbs. Wine from 3150 BCE jars produced in the southern Levant (modern Palestine or Israel) seems to have been infused with antioxidant herbs like savory, coriander, wormwood, or thyme. Some of these are the components of the spice mixture known as *za'atar*, still prevalent throughout the Levant. Wine, beer, oil, and flour (another common early libation) were also industrial foods, highly valued because of the effort necessary to process them, and convenient to spill out a bit as a sacrifice.

Alternatively, toasting may have begun as a way of strengthening ties of friendship between people; early Chinese writings prescribe toasts as part of elaborate social rituals. Other anthropologists have suggested that toasting and libation may have originally had to do with the evil eye, a superstition widespread in Indo-European and Semitic cultures that boasting about your good fortune can cause the gods to harm you. Because the evil eye was a dessicating force (withering fruit trees, or drying up cows' milk), liquid was a kind of cure or placation for the Greek gods who might resent hubris in mortals. The curative power of liquids also explains the old folk custom of spitting three times to scare off the evil eye (opera singers still say *toi toi toi* before going on stage, a verbal representation of this spitting).

Toasting may also be related to health or appetite that Indo-European, Semitic, and many other cultures wish for before eating as well, like French *bon appetit*, Levantine Arabic *sahtein* (two healths), Yiddish *ess gezunterheit* (eat in health), or Greek *kali orexi* (good appetite).

In any case, the Hebrew word *sheker* had a continued life as the meaning "fortified beer" generalized to refer to any kind of strong drink. Saint Jerome in his fourth-century Latin Bible translation, the Vulgate,

An alembic of the Middle Ages. The liquid to be distilled is placed in the cucurbit A and heated over a gentle fire. Alcohol has a lower boiling point than water, and rises as vapor into the still-head B, which is then externally cooled (for example, by cloth soaked in cold water), causing the condensed alcohol (or other distillate) to drip down the tube C into the collecting reservoir E.

borrowed it into Latin as *sicera*, which he defined as beer, mead, palm wine, or fruit cider. In the early Middle Ages *sheker* was borrowed into Yiddish *shikker* to mean "drunk," while in France the word *sicera*, now pronounced *sidre*, became the name of the fermented apple juice that became popular in France, especially in Normandy and Brittany. After 1066 the Normans brought the drink and the new English word *cider* to Britain.

It was just at this time that the technology of distillation was perfected by Persian and Arab alchemists, extending the work of earlier Egyptian Greek and Byzantine alchemists. The *alembic* (from Arabic *al-anbiq*, from Greek *ambyx*; also the ancestor of the word *lambic* referring to the spontaneously fermented Belgian beer) is a flask whose lid has a tube coming off it; when a liquid is boiled in the flask, the vapor rises into the tube and drips out as it cools and condenses.

By the early Renaissance alcohol distillation began to spread west to Europe and east to Central Asia. In Western Europe, apple ciders and grape wines were distilled into eau-de-vies and brandies. Peruvians and Chileans produced their brandy Pisco by distilling wine. In southeast Europe, plum cider was distilled into the *rakia* that we toasted with at Marta's wedding.

All this history, of course, is there in the words. The word *rakia* comes from ʿ*araq*, meaning "sweat" in Arabic, a vivid metaphor for the condensing alcohol dripping from the spout of the still. Other descendants of the word ʿ*araq* are used all over the world for the local distilled spirits. We already met *arrack*, the red rice liquor of Indonesia, in the previous chapter, and there are many others: the anise-flavored Levantine *arak* of Lebanon, Israel, Syria, and Jordan or *raki* of Turkey, Persian *aragh*, the gesho-leaf flavored *araki* of Ethiopia, the coconut liquor of Sri Lanka also called *arrack*, or Mongolian *arkhi*, distilled from fermented mare's milk. What these areas have in common is their history of Muslim populations, contact, or influence, from Ottoman-controlled southeast Europe in the west through the Persian influence on the Mongols to Muslim Indonesia in the east. (Although intoxicants are banned in Islam, drinking of specific kinds of alcoholic beverages in various amounts was sometimes allowed and in any case seems to have persisted in different regions.) These words (and other Arabic words like *alcohol*) are thus a reminder of the important role of Arab and Muslim scientists in developing and propagating distillation and distilled spirits.

As for cider and shikker, they both still carry the phonetic traces of *shikaru*, the Akkadian honeyed beer and the world's oldest written recipe, and this ancient method of getting higher alcohol content by fortifying beer with honey or fruit. In fact, the very earliest manmade alcoholic beverage we know of is a similar beer/cider mixture of fermented honey, rice, and grape or hawthorn fruit whose traces have been found on pottery from 7000 to 6600 BCE in China's Henan province.

In other words, the chamomile, thyme, and fruits of our hip modern cocktails and summer micheladas are not a new innovation at all, but the modern reflex of an ancient tradition that began with the world's very first mixed drinks 9000 years ago, and continued through history with the Levantine thyme-infused wines and Mesopotamian honeyed beers of 2000 BCE, the wassails of Henry VII, the toast-and-borage-spiced wine of eighteenth-century England, and our modern mulled ciders. And the strong hops flavors in modern IPAs bring to mind the barrels of India Pale Ale in the sweltering cargo holds of the East Indiamen crossing the equator to what were then called Bombay, Madras, and Calcutta.

Libations are still around too. Modern hiphop culture has a libationary tradition of "pouring one out"—tipping out malt liquor on the ground before drinking, to honor a friend or relative who has passed away—described in songs like Tupac Shakur's "Pour Out a Little Liquor." (It's especially appropriate that malt liquor, a fortified beer made by adding sugar before fermenting, is itself another descendent of shikaru.)

Modern cocktail names have gotten more interesting, though. The bar Trick Dog in the Mission names drinks after Pantone colors or old 45 rpm singles, Alembic by the park serves a Sichuan pepper-infused Nine Volt, and the Lower Haight's Maven has drinks with names like Widow's Kiss and Nauti' Mermaid, whose straightforward appeal to women and sex recalls those eighteenth-century tipplers whose drinking to the health of the "Lady we mention in our Liquors" first gave rise to the word *toast*, although now it's as likely to be the women doing the toasting.

In any case, now that our Punch break is over, let's talk turkey.

Six

Who Are You Calling a Turkey?

I LOVE THANKSGIVING, when the rains finally begin to come to San Francisco and it feels almost like we have seasons. The streets are bustling with people buying ingredients for their mother's fabulous stuffing or tamale or dessert recipes, and, most important, my choirs start to have their winter concerts. Last Thanksgiving I missed seeing various friends' choir concerts, making me feel almost as much a musical Scrooge as Edgar Allan Poe, who famously said:

> *I never can hear a crowd of people singing and gesticulating altogether at an Italian opera without fancying myself at Athens, listening to that particular tragedy by Sophocles in which he introduces a full chorus of turkeys who set about bewailing the death of Meleager.*

Poe is referring to *Meleager*, the lost tragedy of Sophocles, which, as you've probably assumed, didn't actually have a chorus of turkeys. This is certainly not to disparage their vocal stylings, but turkeys simply didn't make it to Europe until 1511—a good 2000 years after Sophocles wrote his tragedies in Athens. So how did they show up at the Greek amphitheater two millennia early? And why does this bird always seem to be named after countries? Besides Turkey the list includes India, the source of the name in dozens of languages including French *dinde*, from a contraction of the original d'Inde, "of India," Turkish *hindi*, and Polish *indik*. And there's Peru (the source of the word *peru* in both Hindi and Portuguese) and even Ethiopia (in Levantine Arabic the turkey is *dik habash*, "Ethiopian bird").

As we'll see, the answer involves Aztec chefs, a confusion between two birds caused by Portuguese government secrecy and, indirectly, the origins of the modern stock exchange. And as with ketchup, it turns out that turkey and other favorite foods traveled around the world to get here, although in this case it's a round-trip voyage that started with the Native Americans of this hemisphere.

The journey begins thousands of years ago in south-central Mexico. Many different species of wild turkeys still range from the eastern and southern United States down to Mexico, but our domestic turkey comes from only one of these, *Meleagris gallopavo gallopavo*, the species that Native Americans domesticated in Michoacán or Puebla sometime between 800 BCE and 100 CE.

We don't know who the turkey domesticators were, but they passed the turkey on to the Aztecs when the Aztecs moved down into the Valley of Mexico from the north. The turkey became important enough to play a role in Aztec mythology, where the jeweled turkey is a manifestation of Tezcatlipoca, the trickster god.

By the fifteenth century, there were vast numbers of domestic turkeys throughout the Aztec world. Cortés described the streets set aside for poultry markets in Tenochtitlán (Mexico City), and 8000 turkeys were sold every five days, all year round, in Tepeyac, just one of several suburban markets of the city.

The words for turkey in Nahuatl, the Aztec language, are *totolin* for turkey hen and *huexolotl* for male turkey. *Huexolotl* gave rise to the modern Mexican Spanish word for turkey, *guajolote*. (English words from Nahuatl include *avocado*, *tomato*, *chocolate*, and *chile*.)

Aztecs and the neighboring peoples made turkey with several different chile sauces. The Nahuatl word for sauce or stew is *molli*, the

*Turkey in stews and tamales at the A{tec feast in honor
of a newborn child, from the sixteenth-century illustrations
in the Florentine codex*

ancestor of the modern Mexican Spanish word *mole*, and many different moles were made, thick like ketchup or thin like soup, from various
kinds of chiles, venison, rabbit, duck, iguana, armadillo, frogs, tomatillos or tomatoes, vegetables like amaranth leaves, and herbs like hoja
santa or avocado leaves.

But one of the most common ingredients in *mole* was turkey. Bernardino de Sahagún's sixteenth-century *General History of the Things
of New Spain* tells us that Aztec rulers were served turkey moles made
with chile, tomatoes, and ground squash seeds (*totolin pat{calmolli*), as
well as turkey in yellow chile, turkey in green chile, and turkey tamales. In a 1650 description of a Oaxacan turkey mole called *totolmole*
(from *totolin* [turkey hen], plus *mole*) turkey was stewed in a broth flavored with dried ground chilhuaucle (a black smoky chile still used for
Oaxacan mole), pumpkin seeds, and hoja santa or avocado leaves.

The arrival of the Spanish in the New World led to the famous

Columbian exchange of foods between the Old and New worlds. Foods like rice, pork (and hence lard), cheese, onion, garlic, pepper, cinnamon, and sugar all crossed the Atlantic to Mexico, as did Spanish stews like chicken *guisos* with sauteed onion and garlic and Moorish spices like cinnamon, cumin, cloves, anise, and sesame. Soon recipes for guisos and moles in early Mexican manuscripts began to merge, mixing chile with European spices and the resulting moles and chilmoles and pipians became a foundation of modern Mexican cuisine.

By the eighteenth or early nineteenth century, recipes appear for dishes like the most famous turkey dish of all, *mole poblano de guajolote* (Turkey with Puebla Mole), for which every chef in Puebla has a recipe. Its most famous ingredient, chocolate, was mainly treated as a drink by the Nahuatl, and doesn't appear in moles until an 1817 cookbook, whose recipe for mole de guajolote (flavored with chile, garlic, onions, vinegar, sugar, cumin, cloves, pepper, and cinnamon) is followed immediately by a recipe for *mole de monjas* (Nuns' Mole) that adds chocolate and toasted almonds. Modern recipes are even more spectacular, including cloves, anise, cinnamon, coriander, sesame, chile, garlic, raisins, almonds, tomatoes or tomatillos, and pumpkin seeds as well as chocolate.

The profusion of ingredients and magical deliciousness of mole poblano de guajolote has led to many myths about the origin of the recipe, delightful folktales about winds blowing spices into mixing bowls, or boxes of chocolate accidentally falling into the pot, or a nun having to create a dish in a hurry for an important visitor from Spain, all quite dramatic but with no basis in truth. Almost all recipes develop not by spontaneous creation but by evolution, as each inventive chef adds a key ingredient or modifies a process here or there. Probably the only grain of truth in these stories is the role of nuns in convents, who in Mexico as in Europe probably played an important role in preserving and passing on recipes.

In any case, modern turkey moles, from the simply delicious turkey mole tamale steamed in banana leaves at La Oaxaqueña down on Mission Street to the phenomenally complex mole poblano de guajolote, are a modern edible symbol of mestizo history, blending ingredients from Christian and Moorish Spain with the turkey, chocolate, and chile of the New World to create an ancient fusion food at the boundaries of the two cultures. Here's a shortened list of ingredients from Rick Bayless's recipe:

Ingredients from Rick Bayless's Recipe
for Mole Poblano de Guajolote

a 10- to 12-pound turkey, cut into pieces

The chiles:
16 medium dried chiles mulatos
5 medium dried chiles anchos
6 dried chiles pasillas
1 canned chile chipotle, seeded

Nuts and seeds:
¼ cup sesame seeds
½ teaspoon coriander seeds
½ cup lard or vegetable oil
heaping ⅓ cup unskinned almonds

Flavorings & thickeners:
⅓ cup raisins
½ medium onion, sliced
2 cloves garlic, peeled
1 corn tortilla, stale or dried out
2 slices firm white bread, stale or dried out
1 ripe, large tomato, roasted, cored, and peeled

Spices:
⅔ 3.3-ounce tablet Mexican chocolate, roughly chopped
10 black peppercorns
4 cloves
½ teaspoon aniseed
1 inch cinnamon stick

Salt, about 2 teaspoons
Sugar, about ¼ cup
¼ cup lard or vegetable oil
2½ quarts poultry broth

The recipe is long, and involves toasting the seeds; frying the chiles and then soaking them in boiling water; frying almonds, raisins, onion, and garlic; frying the tortilla and bread; pureeing the mixture; pureeing the chiles; frying the turkey; frying the sauce; and finally baking the turkey with the sauce.

While mole poblano de guajolote resulted from the east-west direction of the Columbian exchange, the turkey itself (along with corn, squash, pumpkin, beans, potato, sweet potato, tomatoes, chile pepper, all domesticated in the New World thousands of years earlier) went to Europe simultaneously in the opposite direction.

The turkey's trip to Europe came very quickly after Columbus ate what were probably turkeys on the coast of Honduras in 1502. The Spanish explorers called them *gallopavo* (chicken-peacock), and sent them to Spain by 1512. The spread of turkeys through Europe was astonishingly rapid; by the mid-1500s turkeys were already in England, France, Germany, and Scandinavia.

The first few turkeys were brought over by the Spanish, but it was the Portuguese rather than the Spanish who did the most to introduce the turkey to Europe. And it was the Portuguese government policy of secrecy that more than anything caused the misnaming of turkeys that persists to this day.

It all began because of spices. The world emporium for spices at this time was the city of Calicut in Kerala, India, where black pepper from the hills of south India and spices from the Spice Islands were sold to Muslim traders who shipped them to the Levant (the eastern Mediterranean) via Yemen or Hormuz. Then the Ottomans and Venetians took over, controlling the reshipment of spices, and other goods like exotic animals from Africa, to the rest of Europe.

In an attempt to break the Ottoman and Venetian monopolies on this trade, Portuguese mariners, starting with Vasco da Gama in 1497, sailed around Africa to reach Calicut directly by sea. On the way, they established colonies in the Cape Verde Islands and down the coast of West Africa, a region they called Guinea, slave-raiding and trading for ivory, gold, and local birds like the guinea fowl. Reaching Calicut in 1502, they quickly began to import spices as well.

At the same time, the Portuguese acquired turkeys from the Spanish. The Spanish origin is clear in the Portuguese name for turkeys, *galinha do Peru* (Peruvian chicken). The *Virreinato del Perú* (the Viceroyalty of Peru) was the name for the entire Spanish empire in South America, modern-day Peru, Chile, Colombia, Panama, Ecuador, Bolivia, Paraguay, Uruguay, and Argentina. The Portuguese most likely got turkey from the mid-Atlantic trade islands (the Canary or Cape Verde islands) where ships stopped to provision between the Americas, Africa, and Europe.

Portuguese ships sailed back to Lisbon with products from all three colonial territories: spices and textiles from Calicut; ivory, gold, feathers, and exotic birds from West Africa; and turkey and corn from the Americas. Customs were paid in Lisbon, and then goods were shipped out again to Antwerp, the trading capital of northern Europe at the time. Sixteenth-century Antwerp was a bustling commercial metropolis experiencing its golden age and full of traders: the Portuguese with their colonial finds, the Germans with their copper and silver products, the Dutch with their herring, and the English, the largest contingent, with their textiles.

In Antwerp, the Portuguese maintained a trading station and warehouse called a *feitoria* in which goods were stored (this is also the original meaning of our English word *factory*). The trader would bring goods to various open-air markets in squares throughout the city where wholesalers from the major trading nations of Europe would come and bargain for the Portuguese pepper, ivory, grain, and birds,

The Antwerp Bourse, from a nineteenth-century postcard using Antwerp's French name, Anvers

German silver, English textiles, Dutch herring and so on, presumably amid cacophonies of squawking turkeys and piles of goods and food.

By the middle of the century exchange trading moved to the newly built Antwerp Bourse, the world's first building built specifically for financial and commodities trading, and from which both French and English get the word *Bourse*, meaning trading exchange. The exchange enabled common pricings to be established, and because goods could be sold by sample or even sight unseen, everyone avoided a lot of messy bird droppings.

Meanwhile, France and England had been importing a satiny black African bird that looked extraordinarily similar to a small female turkey. Known today as a guinea fowl, the French and English first called this bird *galine de Turquie* (Turkish chicken) or *Turkey cock*, after the originally Turkish Mamluk sultans who first sold the bird to the Europeans in the 1400s. It was also called *poule d'Inde* (hen of India) because it was imported from Ethiopia (in the fifteenth century, "India" could mean Ethiopia as well as India).

By 1550 the Portuguese began to reimport this African "turkey cock" guinea fowl from West Africa (where there are long oral traditions of breeding guinea fowl among the Mandinka and the Hausa) at the exact same time as they were shipping turkeys from the New World. Both quickly became sought-after commodities.

At the same time, the Portuguese government imposed strict secrecy on all of its maritime explorations, with the goal of protecting its advantage in international trade. Publication of its discoveries was forbidden and maps and charts were strictly censored. Portuguese globes and nautical charts were not allowed to show the coast of West Africa, navigators were subject to an oath of silence, and the death penalty was prescribed for pilots who sold nautical charts to foreigners. It was thus impossible to know that one bird came from the Americas and the other from Africa. Because Portuguese goods were routed through Lisbon to pay customs, the two birds may have arrived at Antwerp on the same Portuguese ships, and might even have been traded sight unseen to the English or Germans in the new bourse. The two similar-looking birds were frequently confused, in Antwerp and throughout Europe.

The result is that the English "turkey cock" or "cocks of Inde," and the French "poules d'Inde" were used sometimes for turkeys, sometimes for guinea fowl, for the next hundred years. The two birds were confused in Dutch too, and even Shakespeare sometimes got it wrong, using "turkey" in Henry IV, part I (act II, scene 1) when he meant guinea hen.

The English confusion between the two birds was only resolved when both were commercially farmed in England. In any case, our modern word arrived just in time for "turkey" to be actually eaten in the Renaissance, thus explaining the ubiquity of giant turkey legs in today's "Renaissance Faires."

Other languages were left with a similarly confused atlas of names; French *dinde* from "d'Inde," Dutch *kalkoen*, many names (like Polish

French naturalist Pierre Belon's drawing of turkeys ("Cocs d'Inde"),
from his 1555 book L'Histoire de la Nature des Oyseaux (The
Natural History of Birds)

indik) dating from later reference to the Americas as the West Indies, and Levantine Arabic *dik habash* alone still pointing to Ethiopia, the source of the guinea fowl. German used to have a dozen names for turkey (*Truthahn, Puter, Indianisch, Janisch, Bubelhahn, Welscher Guli*, etc.).

Another memorial to the early confusion remains in the genus name for turkey that Linnaeus, the Swedish zoologist who is the father of modern taxonomy, mistakenly took from the Greek name for guinea fowl: *meleagris*, explaining Sophocles' chorus of "turkeys." Ovid tells us that the name *meleagris* for guinea fowl came from the Greek hero *Meleager*, who was foretold at birth to live only as long as a log burning in his mother's fire. Although his mother saved the log, Meleager later met a tragic end anyhow and his black-clad sisters cried so many tears over his tomb that Artemis turned them into guinea fowl, *Meleagrides*, changing their tears into white spots all over their bodies.

The turkey became particularly popular in England. It was eaten widely by the 1560s and was a standard roasting bird for Christmas and other feasts by 1573, when a poem celebrated: "Christmas husbandlie fare . . . pies of the best, . . . and turkey well drest."

It was just at this time that the turkey made the journey back to the United States. The English colonists brought domestic turkeys with them to Jamestown in 1607 and the Massachusetts Bay Colony in 1629, and in both places compared the "wilde Turkies" to "our English Turky."

You probably know that the Pilgrims of Plymouth Colony didn't really have a "First Thanksgiving" turkey feast (although they certainly ate a lot of wild turkey). While there were many days of thanksgiving declared at different points in the American colonies, a day of thanksgiving for the passionately religious Separatists would have been a religious holiday to be spent in church, not a dinner party with the neighbors. Instead, the joint feast to which "Massasoit with some ninety men" brought five deer is described in a 1621 Pilgrim letter as celebrating "our harvest being gotten in," and owes more to the autumn harvest festivals long celebrated in England.

So if the English and the Wampanoag did eat turkey together at that feast (and we may never know for sure), it was not a newly invented American ceremony, but a fine old English tradition of Christmas and festival roast turkey celebrations.

Thanksgiving itself took hold partly from the efforts of Sarah Josepha Hale, a prominent nineteenth-century magazine editor, antislavery novelist, and supporter of female education (and the author of the nursery rhyme "Mary Had a Little Lamb") whose activism for a national day of thanksgiving to unify the country eventually convinced Abraham Lincoln in 1863. Within 20 years Thanksgiving was linked in schools and newspapers with the Pilgrims and the schoolchildren of our great immigrant wave of 1880 to 1910 (including my Grandma Anna) brought home a new holiday, a metaphor of gratitude for safe arrival in a new land.

Or at least they brought home the desserts. Like the mestizo mole, the sweet dishes that grew to symbolize Thanksgiving combine New World ingredients (cranberries, sweet potatoes, pumpkins, pecans) with the medieval spices, sweet and sour flavors, and custards that date back to the Arabic influence on Andalusia and Italy. By 1658 an English pumpkin pie recipe with eggs and butter was flavored with sugar, cinnamon, nutmeg, and cloves, sliced apples, and also savory spices like pepper, thyme, and rosemary. Our modern American pumpkin pie appears in the first cookbook written by an American, Amelia Simmons's 1796 *American Cookery*:

Pompkin.

One quart stewed and strained, 3 pints cream, 9 beaten eggs, sugar, mace, nutmeg and ginger, laid into paste . . . and baked in dishes three quarters of an hour.

Recipes for pecan pie are more recent. The earliest I have seen, called Texas Pecan Pie, appeared in *The Ladies Home Journal* in 1898 (pecan is the Texas state pie):

Texas Pecan Pie

One cup of sugar, one cup of sweet milk, half a cup of pecan kernels chopped fine, three eggs and tablespoonful of flour. When cooked, spread the well-beaten whites of two eggs on top, brown, sprinkle a few of the chopped kernels over.

The milk, eggs, and sugar in these early recipes (corn syrup only came later) remind us that the original pecan pie, like pumpkin pie, was really a custard, a descendant of early European recipes for custard pies. Recipes for an open-topped pie crust filled with egg yolks, cream, and spices appear in fifteenth-century cookbooks from both England and Portugal. You can still find them as *pastel de nata* in Portuguese bakeries, and the Portuguese brought them to Macao, where they became hugely popular by their Cantonese name *daan tat* or "egg tarts." Egg tarts are now a mainstay of *dim sum* and many Chinese bakeries sell both a Portuguese and a Chinese version. You can even get them at KFC in Macao now. Here in San Francisco, it's the Golden Gate Bakery on Grant Avenue whose egg tarts make an excellent dessert addition for a Chinese American Thanksgiving.

Unlike most other Thanksgiving food names, the word *pecan* is Native American. English borrowed it from Illinois, a language of the Algonquin family. The original word was *pakani*, although we now pronounce our borrowing in many ways. My best friend from kindergarten, James, got married on a warm summer evening along the Brazos River of eastern Texas in what I was distinctly informed were "pickAHN" groves. But the word is PEE-can in New England and the Eastern Seaboard, pee-CAN in Wisconsin and Michigan, and something closer to peeKAHN in the west and many other parts of the country.

Why this difference? The region of the pronunciation pickAHN corresponds remarkably to the native range of the pecan tree. This is because the pickAHN pronunciation is closest to the original in the Illinois language (/paka:ni/). In other words, people in the area where the Illinois gave the word to English still use a traditional pronunciation, while dialects farther away have a modified pronunciation influenced by the spelling.

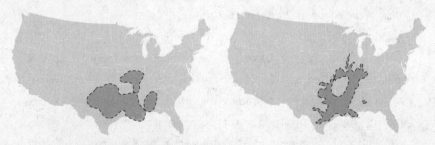

Two pecan maps. Left: *Rough outline of dialect regions where pickAHN is the dominant pronunciation (based on the research of Bert Vaux and Joshua Katz).* Right: *Rough outline of natural habitat of the pecan tree (data from US Forest Service maps).*

Although it's not widely known, the guinea fowl came to America too, as part of the slave trade. Slave ships to the Americas included West African flocks as provisions, and slaves raised guinea fowl on small plots of land. The late African American chef and food writer Edna Lewis, the granddaughter of freed slaves, talks about guinea fowl as one of the important foods she grew up with in Freetown, Virginia, passed on "from generation to generation by African-Americans." Her cookbook *The Taste of Country Cooking* describes traditional ways of stewing guinea fowl in clay pots that—based on archaeological evidence of pots from early slave settlements—probably date back to African Mandinka recipes for stewing guinea fowl in earthenware pots hundreds of years ago in West Africa.

So the real message of turkey is not that Portuguese trade secrecy caused sixteenth-century Europeans to confuse two birds, although it did, or that the turkey was traded in Europe's first commodities exchange building, although it probably was, or even any of the fantastic myths about a collection of spices being blown by the wind into a seventeenth-century stockpot in Puebla, Meleager's sisters being turned into guinea fowl, or Pilgrims inviting Massassoit for a Thanksgiving turkey dinner.

The real meaning of our Thanksgiving foods is that the Africans and the English managed, despite the horrors of slavery and the terrible hardship of exile, to bring the food of their homelands to help create the cuisine of our new country, just as the Native Americans and the Spanish, despite struggles and massacres and suffering, managed to merge elements of their cuisines to create the mestizo mole poblano de guajolote that helps preserve the food culture of their ancestors.

That's another beautiful myth about America, and maybe this is finally one we can believe: that we've created something truly extraordinary in our stone-soup mestizo America by throwing into the pot, each of us, ingredients from the beautiful traditions our grandmothers and grandfathers passed down to us.

Seven

Sex, Drugs, and Sushi Rolls

YOU CAN ALWAYS GET a good argument going in San Francisco by asking people for their favorite taqueria. I lean toward the *carnitas* at La Taqueria on Mission, but our friend Calvin can be pretty eloquent on the subject of the *al pastor* at Taqueria Vallarta on Twenty-Fourth. San Franciscans are similarly contentious about the best dim sum, and have been politely disagreeing about tamales since the 1880s, when the city was famous for the vendors plying the streets every evening with pails of hot chicken tamales. (Some things, of course, are simply not a matter of opinion, like the best place for roast duck—it's Cheung Hing out in the Sunset, but don't tell anybody else, the line is already too long.)

It's not just San Francisco. You can't go on the Internet these days without stumbling over someone's lengthy review of a restaurant, wine, beer, book, movie, or brand of dental floss. We are a nation of opinion-holders. Perhaps we always have been: in De Tocqueville's prophetic study of the American character, the 1835 *Democracy in America*, he noted that in the United States "public opinion is divided into a thousand minute shades of difference upon questions of very little moment."

Consider online restaurant reviews, those summaries of the wisdom of the crowd that have become a familiar way to discover new places to eat. Take a look at this sample from a positive restaurant review (a rating of 5 out of 5) on Yelp (modified slightly for anonymity):

I LOVE this place!!!!! Fresh, straightforward, very high quality, very traditional little neighborhood sushi place. . . . takes such great care in making each dish . . . You can tell the chef really takes pride in his work. . . . everything I've tried so far is DELICIOUS!!!!

And here are bits of one negative review (a rating of 1 out of 5):

The bartender was either new or just absolutely horrible . . . we waited 10 min before we even got her attention to order . . . and then we had to wait 45—FORTY FIVE!—minutes for our entrees . . . Dessert was another 45 min. wait, followed by us having to stalk the waitress to get the check . . . he didn't make eye contact or even break his stride to wait for a response . . . the chocolate soufflé was disappointing . . . I will not return.

As eaters we use reviews to help decide where to eat (maybe give that second restaurant a miss), whether to buy a new book or see a movie. But as linguists we use these reviews for something altogether different: to help understand human nature. Reviews show humans at their most opinionated and honest, and the metaphors, emotions, and sentiment displayed in reviews are an important cue to human psychology.

In a series of studies, my colleagues and I have employed the techniques of computational linguistics to examine these reviews. With Victor Chahuneau, Noah Smith, and Bryan Routledge from Carnegie Mellon University, my colleagues on the menu study of Chapter 1, I've investigated a million online restaurant reviews on Yelp, from seven cities (San Francisco, New York, Chicago, Boston, LA, Philadelphia, Washington), covering people's impressions between about 2005 and 2011, the same cities and restaurants from our study of menus. With computer scientists Julian McAuley and Jure Leskovec, I looked at 5 million reviews written by thousands of reviewers on websites like BeerAdvocate for beers they drank from 2003 to 2011.

As we'll see, the way people talk about skunky beer, disappointing service, or amazing meals is a covert clue to universals of human language (like the human propensity for optimism and positive emotions and the difficulty of finding words to characterize smells), the metaphors we use in daily life (why drugs are a metaphor for some foods but sex is a metaphor for others), and the aspects of daily life that people find especially traumatizing.

Let's start with a simple question. What words are most associated with good reviews, or with bad reviews? To find out, we count how much more often a word occurs in good reviews than bad reviews (or conversely, more often in bad reviews than good reviews).

Not surprisingly, good reviews (whether for restaurants or beer) are most associated with what are called *positive emotional words* or *positive sentiment words*. Here are some:

love delicious best amazing great favorite perfect excellent awesome wonderful fantastic incredible

Bad reviews use *negative emotional words* or *negative sentiment* words:

horrible bad worst terrible awful disgusting bland gross mediocre tasteless sucks nasty dirty inedible yuck stale

Words like *horrible* or *terrible* used to mean "inducing horror" or "inducing terror," and *awesome* or *wonderful* meant "inducing awe" or "full of wonder." But humans naturally exaggerate, and so over time people used these words in cases where there wasn't actual terror or true wonder.

The result is what we call *semantic bleaching*: the "awe" has been bleached out of the meaning of *awesome*. Semantic bleaching is pervasive with these emotional or affective words, even applying to verbs like "love." Linguist and lexicographer Erin McKean notes that it was only recently, in the late 1800s, that young women began to generalize the word *love* from its romantic core sense to talk about their relationship to inanimate objects like food. As late as 1915 an older woman in L. M. Montgomery's *Anne of the Island* complains about how exaggerated it was that young women applied the word to food:

> *The girls nowadays indulge in such exaggerated statements that one never can tell what they* do *mean. It wasn't so in my young days.* Then *a girl did not say she* loved *turnips, in just the same tone as she might have said she loved her mother or her Saviour.*

Semantic bleaching is also responsible for meaning changes in words like *sauce* or *salsa* from their original meaning of "salted," but I am getting ahead of myself. For now there's much more to learn from reviews.

Let's start with the negative reviews. Consider the very specific and creative words used to express dislike (*sodalike, metallic, wet dog water, force-carbonated, razor thin*) in this strongly phrased negative beer review from BeerAdvocate:

> *Clear light amber with a sodalike head of white that immediately fizzles to nothing. Very sodalike appearance. Aroma is sweet candy apricot with slight metallic wheat notes. Flavor is wet dog water infused with artificial apricot. Bad, bad, bad. Mouthfeel is razor thin, watery, and highly force-carbonated. Drinkability? Ask my kitchen sink!*

My colleagues and I automatically extracted the positive and negative words. While reviewers generally called beers they disliked "watery" or "bland," they tended to describe the way they were "bad" by using different negative words for different senses, distinguishing whether the beer smelled or tasted bad (*corny, skunky, metallic, stale, chemical*), looked bad (*piss, yellow, disgusting, colorless, skanky*), or felt bad in the mouth (*thin, flat, fizzy, overcarbonated*).

By contrast, when people liked a beer, they used the same few vague positive words we saw at the beginning of the chapter—*amazing, perfect, wonderful, fantastic, awesome, incredible, great*—regardless of whether they were rating taste, smell, feel, or look.

The existence of more types of words, with more differentiated meanings, for describing negative opinions than positive ones occurs across many languages and for many kinds of words, and is called *negative differentiation*. Humans seem to feel that negative feelings or situations are very different from each other, requiring distinct words. Happy feelings or good situations, by contrast, seem more similar to each other, and a smaller set of words will do.

Negative differentiation comes up in all sorts of domains. For example, across languages there seem to be more adjectives to describe pain than pleasure. We use more varied vocabulary to describe people we dislike than people we like. People even describe attractive faces as more similar to each other while unattractive faces differ more from each other. This generalization that there are more different ways to be negative than to be positive was most famously stated by Tolstoy at the beginning of Anna Karenina: "Happy families are all alike; every unhappy family is unhappy in its own way."

Words for smell seem particularly disposed to the negative trend. English, for example, has no commonly used positive word meaning "smells good" that corresponds to *delicious* for taste or *beautiful* for sight. Languages generally seem to have a smaller vocabulary for smell than for other senses, relying on words for tastes (like *sweet* or *salty*) or names of objects (like *gamy, musky, skunky, or metallic*).

Some languages do have somewhat richer olfactory vocabularies, like Janet's native language, Cantonese. Unlike English, Cantonese has a common word that means "smells good," *heung* 香, often translated as "fragrant." *Fragrant* in English is rare and poetic, but the everyday Cantonese *heung* (and its Mandarin cognate *xiang*) is just how you say you like the smell of what's cooking. It's such a frequent word that you've all seen it: *heung* is the first part of the name *Heung Gong* (Hong Kong; "smells-good harbor").

Cantonese is particularly rich in words for negative smells. Here are some:

suk1	the bacterial smell of spoiled rice or tofu
ngaat3	the ammoniacal smell of urine, ammonia
yik1	the smell of rancid or oxidized oil or peanuts
hong2	the stale, rancid smell of old grain (uncooked rice, flour, cookies)
seng1	fishy, bloody smell
sou1	musky, muttony, gamy, body odor smell
lou3	the smell of overheated tires or burnt hair

Note the numbers following each word. Cantonese has six tones, characteristic rising or falling pitches, and the meaning of a word varies depending on the tone used. The richness of this language is not limited to ways to say *stinky*.

Many of the words listed above exist in other Chinese dialects as well, and some are very ancient. An essay on cuisine in a third-century BCE Chinese encyclopedia (which Chinese cuisine scholar Fuchsia Dunlop calls "perhaps the world's oldest extant gastronomic treatise") records the ancient advice of the sixteenth-century BCE cook Yi Yin on how to eliminate fishy (*seng1* 腥) and gamy (*sou1* 臊) smells.

Sadly, use of this ancient and rich negative smell vocabulary seems to be dying out of Cantonese. Studies show that younger Hong Kong speakers know fewer of these words than their elders, as sanitization and plastic wrap eliminate opportunities to experience what linguist

Hilario de Sousa delicately calls "the variety of olfactory sensations experienced by their ancestors."

The minimal smell vocabularies of many languages may be recent and due to urbanization (languages retaining the vocabulary are often spoken outside the cities), ancient and genetic (many genes coding for the detection of specific odors are turned off in humans, perhaps dating back to the development of tricolor vision in primates), or related to human variation in smell perception. For example, genetic variations lead to differences in detecting the grassy smell of sauvignon blanc, partially caused by the flavor compound cis-3-hexen-1-ol. The ability to detect the sulfurous smell of asparagus in urine has similar genetic links; according to one recent experiment, about 8 percent of people don't produce it, and about 6 percent can't smell it. (My biologist wife, upon reading that paper, immediately conducted an impromptu experiment on yours truly by cooking up a big batch of asparagus.) The vast variation over the many different abilities of smell might have made it harder for a language to develop a stable shared olfactory vocabulary.

The greater differentiation of negative smells is but one aspect of *negativity bias*, the idea that humans are biased to be especially aware of negative situations. Bad reviews like the one at the start of the chapter display another. To understand, we need to look beyond the negative emotional words like *horrible*, *terrible*, *awful*, and *nasty* and focus instead on the story being told. Yes, story.

Linguist Douglas Biber has shown that we use past tense, communication verbs (said, told), and event words (then, after) much more frequently when telling stories, and the negative reviews are filled with these features. Let's also look at the common nouns most strongly associated with them:

manager customer minutes money waitress waiter bill attitude management business apology mistake table charge order hostess tip

Not a one of these words refers to food! Instead, bad reviews are stories about bad things done by other people. The waiter or waitress made some mistake, messed up the order or the bill, or had a bad attitude, the manager didn't help, the hostess caused a long wait, and so on.

In addition, bad reviews overwhelmingly use the pronouns we or us ("We waited," "our entrées," "us having to"). While other reviews use those pronouns too, "we" and "us" are vastly overrepresented in negative ones. What is the common denominator of these three features: negative emotional words like *terrible* and *horrible*, narrative stories about other people, and a vast increase in *we* and *us*, all strongly linked to 1-star reviews?

The answer comes from the pioneering work of Texas psychology professor James Pennebaker, who for decades has studied how words like function words are veiled cues to people's personalities, attitudes, and feelings. Pennebaker has particularly studied the aftereffects of trauma. His "social stage model of coping" suggests that immediately after a traumatic event, people feel a need to tell stories about the event, stories expressing their negative emotion, and suggests that traumatized people seek comfort in groups by emphasizing their belonging, using the words *we* or *us* with high frequency.

Pennebaker and his colleagues identified these tendencies in bloggers talking about their feelings after September 11, 2001, in fans writing about the death of Princess Diana, and in student newspaper articles after campus tragedies. In each case, what people write is just like terrible reviews of restaurants: narratives, stories about the negative things that happened to them, bulwarked against these negative emotions by the solidarity of *us* and *we*. In other words, bad reviews display all the linguistic symptoms of minor trauma.

We always confirm our automated methods by carefully reading selected samples of the reviews. And the tendency toward negative bias is clear, from the negative differentiation in describing skunky beers to the trauma narratives of bad restaurants.

Why do we find negative things more intense and more differentiated than positive things? One possibility is that negative things in the world really are more different from each other than positive things. Perhaps there really is more difference between being evil, brutal, sad, sick, or skunky than there is between being good, gentle, happy, well, or nice. Another possibility is that negative things aren't actually more different or more potent than positive things, but it's evolutionarily useful for us to treat them as if they were so. Humans need to worry about and be exceptionally good at distinguishing among negative events. The intuition of this theory is that there are a lot of ways for things to go wrong in life, and even though they may be very rare (like tiger attacks and earthquakes and bee stings), they require very different responses. Having different words to talk about how to avoid them helped our ancestors outlive the tiger and the earthquake.

Of course, reviews aren't all negative. What are the metaphors and other linguistic structures that reviewers use in positive reviews of food or wine?

Let's start by talking about sex.

Adrienne Lehrer, a linguistics professor at the University of Arizona, studied how wine reviews changed over time from 1975 to 2000. She noticed that in the 1980s wine reviewers began to increase their use of the body as a metaphor, starting to use words like *fleshy, muscular, sinewy, big-boned,* or *broad-shouldered*. At the same time, influential wine writers like Robert Parker began to emphasize the sensual pleasure of wine, repeating words like "sexy" and "sensual," describing wines as "supple and seductive," "offering voluptuously textured, hedonistic drinking," or even "liquid Viagra." Literature professor Sean Shesgreen says that all this erotic talk about wine as "pretty and caressing," "ravishing," "pillowy," and "overendowed" affirms that "in the kaleidoscope of Americans' fixations, gastronomy has eclipsed sex."

This metaphor of sex seems especially associated with expensive foods as well. We examined this in the million restaurant reviews by extracting every mention of sex (or related words like *sexy, seductive, orgasms,* or *lust*) in the reviews. We then used regression, a statistical technique that allowed us to ask how these mentions of sex were associated with people's ratings of a restaurant, after controlling for factors like the type of cuisine and the city.

Reviewers who liked a restaurant were indeed more likely to use sexual metaphors. But we also discovered an economic interaction; mentions of sex like these are especially frequent for expensive restaurants:

> *the apple tarty ice cream pastry caramely thing was just* **orgasmic**
> *sumptuous flavors, jaw-droppingly good,* **sexy** *food*
> *succulent pork belly paired with* **seductively** *seared foie gras*

The association is quite strong: the more mentions of sex in a restaurant review, the higher the price of the restaurant.

People use a very different metaphor when they like the food at cheap restaurants. In reviewing inexpensive restaurants, they use the language of addiction or drugs instead of sex to talk about their fries or garlic noodles:

> *garlic noodles . . . are now my* **drug of choice**
> *these cupcakes are like* **crack**
> *be warned the wings are* **addicting**
> *. . . every time* **I need a fix.** *That fried chicken is so damn good!*
> *I swear the fries have* **crack** *or some sort of* **addicting drugs** *in them*

The examples above show what we "crave" or are "addicted to": chicken wings and fried chicken, cupcakes, garlic noodles, French fries, and burgers. It's the snack foods and bar foods, guilty pleasures because of their fat, sugar, and deep-fried goodness that invite the comparison to drugs. Researchers still aren't sure of the biochemical link between junk-food cravings and drug addiction, but in any case the cravings for fat and also sugar are quite strong. A study that varied the fat and sugar in chocolate milkshakes suggests that sugar may light up the reward center of the brain even more effectively than fat. Writer Adam Gopnik describes nights during his experiment in giving up dessert when he would wake up and—like a golem controlled by external command—sleepily wander toward the freezer and the ice cream.

In any case, the linguistic ubiquity of this metaphor of drugs demonstrates how deep this addictive understanding of junk food and desserts is embedded in our culture. By placing the blame on the food, we're distancing ourselves from our own "sin" of eating fried or sugary snacks: "It's not my fault: the cupcake made me do it." Our research also found that women are more likely than men to use drug metaphors in reviews, suggesting that they are especially pressured to conform to healthy or low-calorie eating.

What are people eating when they talk about sex in reviews? We can study this by looking at food words that occur more frequently near sexual words. Two kinds of foods are associated with sex. One is sushi, because of the modern trend of giving sexy names to sushi like these:

sex on the beach roll	sexy mama roll
foreplay roll	sexy lady roll
sweet temptation roll	hot sexy shrimp roll
orgasmic spicy tuna roll	sexy lizzy roll

The other food most frequently associated with sex is dessert:

molten chocolate cake . . . honestly an **orgasm** *on a plate*

I still **lust** *for the silky panna cotta and* **tantalizing** *sorbet*

marshmallows . . . so . . . sticky and sweet, they're nearly **pornographic**

warm chestnut mochi chocolate cake . . . **seductively** *gooey on the inside*

The examples above also exhibit another class of words associated with both dessert and sex: texture words like *sticky, silky, gooey*. Here are the sensory words most commonly used to describe desserts in the million reviews:

rich moist warm sweet dense hot creamy flaky light fluffy sticky dry gooey smooth crisp oozing satin soft velvety thick melty silky oozing thin crunchy spongy

All of these are from the sensory domain of "feel," of textures and temperatures. When we talk about desserts, we talk about their feel in the mouth, not their appearance, smell, taste, or sound. Americans usually describe desserts as soft or dripping wet, a tendency that linguist Susan Strauss, in her comparison of TV advertising in the US, Japan, and Korea, found to be a general property of food advertising in American English. US commercials emphasize tender, gooey, rich, creamy food, and associate softness and dripping sweetness with sensual hedonism and pleasure.

This association between soft, sticky things and pleasure isn't a necessary connection. For example, Strauss found that Korean food commercials emphasize hard, texturally stimulating food, using words like *wulthung pwulthung hata* (solid and bumpy), *ccalis hata* (stinging, stimulating), *thok ssota* (stinging), and *elelhata* (spicy to the extent that one's nerves are numbed).

The link between dessert and sex is visible in many aspects of our culture, from the sensual advertising of chocolate to women (like Ghirardelli's slogan, "Moments of Timeless Pleasure") to modern music, where my students Debra Pacio and Linda Yu found that recent songs like Kelis's "Milkshake" or Li'l Wayne's "Lollipop" use dessert and especially candy as a metaphor for sex. There is a gender effect with dessert too. Our study shows that women are more likely than men to mention desserts in their reviews.

Dessert is also so prized that people find it very difficult to say anything bad about it. Notice the overwhelmingly positive sentiment of the 20 most frequent sentiment words associated with dessert:

delicious amazing yummy decadent divine yum good OK wow fabulous scrumptious delectable wonderful delish refreshing awesome perfect incredible fantastic heavenly

In fact, the more Yelp reviewers mention dessert, the more they like the restaurant. Reviewers who don't mention a dessert give the restaurants an average review score of 3.6 (out of 5). But reviewers who mention a dessert in their review give a higher average review score, 3.9 out of 5. And when people do talk about dessert, the more times they mention dessert in the review, the higher the rating they give to the restaurant.

This positivity exhibited by reviews, filled with metaphors of sex and dessert, turns out to be astonishingly strong. Despite the negativity bias that makes us especially sensitive to negative situations, people are actually much more positive than they are negative.

One sign of our positive nature is word frequency. Positive words, though weak in variety, occur much more often in reviews than negative words. Restaurant reviewers use words like *great*, *delicious*, and *amazing* 3 to 10 times more often than words like *bland*, *bad*, or *terrible*.

Review scores themselves are also skewed toward the positive. Reviewing scores on most sites go from 1 to 5, so the median score should be 3. Instead the median score, whether for restaurants or beers, is about 4 out of 5. My colleague down the hall Chris Potts has shown that this skew is true wherever people review things on the web—books, movies, cameras, you name it.

This tendency toward the positive is not a recent trend caused by the Internet, but has been shaping our language for millennia. Linguists are deeply interested in linguistic phenomena that hold across all languages, key to our goal of discovering true human universals. A bias toward positivity in vocabulary is one of the strongest universals we have found. This idea that people are positive is called the *Pollyanna effect*, after the heroine of Eleanor Porter's 1909 book for children, Pollyanna, an orphan who always looked on the bright side. In common usage "Pollyanna-ish" describes a naïve or foolish optimism, but the Pollyanna effect is a more neutral observation of humans' remarkable tendency toward optimism.

The Pollyanna effect is not just specific to reviews. If you ask Google how frequent a word is (or check the frequency in a carefully constructed academic database of texts), positive words are (on average) more frequent than negative words. English *good* is more frequent than *bad*, *happy* than *sad*; Chinese *kaixin* 开心 (happy) is more frequent than *nanguo* 难过 (sad); Spanish *feliz* is more frequent than *triste*.

More subtly, positive words have a special linguistic status called *unmarked*. *Markedness* has to do with oppositions: in pairs of words like happy/unhappy, good/bad, capable/incapable, or honest/dishonest, the first of each pair is unmarked or neutral and the second is marked. There are many linguistic cues to which member of a pair is unmarked. The unmarked form is shorter (marked *unhappy* and *dishonest* have an extra *un-* and *dis-* than unmarked *happy* and *honest*). Unmarked words tend to come first in "X and Y" phrases like "good and evil" or "right and wrong." Unmarked words are neutral in questions. Asking "Is your accountant honest?" is the neutral way to find out about the honesty of your accountant. If I instead ask, "Is your accountant dishonest?" that suggests that I already have some reason to believe you have a cheating accountant. Sure enough, across languages, the unmarked form is much more likely to be positive (*happy, honest*) rather than negative (*unhappy, dishonest*); it's very rare across languages for a negative word like *sad* to be the basic form and *unsad* to be the way to say "happy." Thus we have English words *unhappy*, *incapable*, *uncomfortable*, but not *unsad*, *un-itchy*, *unklutzy*.

The Pollyanna effect has been confirmed in dozens of languages and cultures, and comes up in all sorts of nonlinguistic ways as well. When psychologists ask people to think of items or remember them from a list, they name more positive things than negative things. When people forward news stories, they are more likely to forward the positive stories than the negative ones.

In other words, although humans have a lot of ways of talking about negative events, and are especially traumatized when other people are rude or mean to them, although people differ in all sorts of ways, perceive different tastes and smells, and range hugely in their personalities, these differences only serve to highlight a fundamental similarity as humans: we are a positive, optimistic race. We tend to notice and talk about the good things in life. Like dessert. And sex.

And all of this, joy and trauma, is visible in those reviews on the web, offering a little insight into the human psyche along with advice on where to go for dinner.

Just don't forget to order dessert.

Eight

Potato Chips and the Nature of the Self

SAN FRANCISCANS ARE a festive people, although we can be a little confused about exactly what we're celebrating. There's the Chinese New Year Parade, which is not held on Chinese New Year, and Carnival, a fabulous parade we have in May instead of in February. Then there's Burning Man, which used to be on Baker Beach but we don't even hold in the state anymore, and the Bay to Breakers race, which for most participants is more of a (barely) mobile drunken costume party than a race.

My favorite, however, is the Hardly Strictly Bluegrass festival, which, in keeping with the fluidity of categories here, does not mainly consist of bluegrass. It's a free autumn music festival created by late local legend (and fluid category himself) Warren Hellman, the scion of an old California Jewish immigrant family, a lifelong Republican and billionaire private equity manager who supported labor unions and played labor protest songs in a bluegrass band, and was beloved in the city for giving away a lot of his fortune making music free to everyone. Hardly Strictly gets 600,000 attendees (in a city of 800,000 people!) who come to see Emmy Lou Harris and Doc Watson and Steve Earle and Janet's favorite, Elvis Costello. You can't beat listening to Elvis Costello on a sunny Saturday in Golden Gate Park, but the icing on the cake, as it were, is the kettle corn that they make in huge fired vats, stirring with a big paddle. Kettle corn, or really any kind of sugary popcorn confection, from Cracker Jack to Fiddle Faddle to a confection of my childhood called Screaming Yellow Zonkers! all have the crucial salt–sugar balance that is definitive of a perfect snack.

Everyone has a favorite junk food, whether it's French fries (with ketchup, naturally), the chili cheese dogs that Janet favors when we're visiting her brother Ricky in LA, those "snack bars" that my runner friends pretend aren't junk food, or the Cheetos snacks adored by my nephews and labeled—by food scientist Steven Witherly in Michael Moss's book *Salt Sugar Fat*—"one of the most marvelously constructed foods on the planet."

Junk food is a popular topic in my Stanford seminar on the Language of Food, a fact that will not surprise you if you have ever been a teenager. Moss's book and others are fascinating studies of the unscrupulous ways that snack manufacturers design their products to create bliss points and food addictions. But for this class, instead of the nefarious production of nutritional waste, we focus on the equally morally fraught attempt to convince you to buy it. What are the subtle linguistic techniques used by snack advertisers?

Josh Freedman, now a young political researcher in Washington DC, was an even younger freshman in my class in 2008 when he and I became interested in studying the language of food advertising. But what food to study? We needed one that was easily available and potentially eaten by everyone, but it had to have many similar brands and be accompanied by sufficient advertising language, which ruled out kettle corn or chili cheese dogs or even bananas.

The obvious solution came to Josh in the supermarket one day: potato chips, the great American snack whose bags are obligingly covered with lots of lovely advertising words. Josh is a brilliant budding social scientist, but he was also a college student, which meant he was too broke to actually purchase the potato chips. So he sat down in the aisle of the supermarket and used his phone to take pictures of the front and back of each bag. Later we relied on the vast financial resources of Stanford University to actually buy 12 carefully selected bags of potato chips. Six of them were more expensive (Boulder Canyon, "Dirty," Kettle Brand, Popchips, Terra, Michael Season's, averaging 68 cents per ounce) and six were less expensive (Hawaiian, Herr's, Lay's, Tim's, Utz, and Wise, averaging 40 cents per ounce).

We then typed in all the advertising text from the back of the chips, coded it up in various ways, and examined how the words differed between the two classes of chips.

To gain some insight into what we found, take a few seconds to look at this (anonymized) excerpt from the back of one of the expensive potato chip bags we examined:

"Anonymous Brand"
potato chips are
· All natural
· Cholesterol free
· Kettle cooked in a peanut oil blend
· Kosher certified

And contain:
· No MSG
· No artificial colors
· No artificial flavors
· No preservatives
· No wheat glutens
· No hydrogenated oil
· No trans fats
· No artificial sweeteners

At *"Anonymous Brand"* we don't wash out the natural potato flavor, which makes our chips crunchier and tastier.

After seeing this example you can probably guess the one universal characteristic of potato chip advertising: potato chips turn out to be a health food, at least in the special world inhabited by advertising copywriters. All the bags were covered with language emphasizing how healthy and good for your body the chips are, using phrases like "healthier," "o grams trans fat," "low fat," "no cholesterol," "lowest sodium level."

Now you and I both know that potato chips are not actually healthy. And so do the restaurant reviewers studied in the previous chapter who lightheartedly used words like "crave" and "jonesing" and "fix" to characterize similar deep-fried snacks as addictive drugs. The linguistic evidence demonstrates that potato chip advertisers are similarly aware of the unhealthiness of their products, and they know we know it. In Chapter 1 we used the ideas of the philosopher H. P. Grice to argue that when a menu protests too much about the freshness or crispiness of its food, it means the menu writer suspects the customer needs to be convinced. Similarly with chips: the ridiculous emphasis on health is an admission that the manufacturers are well aware that you may be skeptical of the nutritional value of their products.

Even beyond this overall flood of health talk, we found a huge difference between the words used to describe expensive chips and inexpensive chips. Health-related claims occur on expensive chips six times as often as on inexpensive chips, as often as six times per bag!

This difference in health language is not, as far as we can tell, due to actual differences in the chips. For example, none of the 12 kinds of chips contains trans fats, but the text on inexpensive chips doesn't emphasize this—it's mentioned on only two out of the six inexpensive chip bags. By contrast, text on every one of the six expensive chip bags emphasizes the lack of trans fats. In other words, advertisers try to sell chips to richer, presumably more health-conscious consumers by pretending, or at least actively encouraging the belief, that the chips are good for them, or at least just healthy enough to overcome the guilt.

That's not the only marketing trick for targeting the rich. Another tool is to use more complex words and complex sentences. The simplest way of measuring these is counting the number of letters in the average word. We also counted the number of words in the average sentence. The widespread Flesch-Kincaid measure of language complexity simply averages these two counts to assign a very rough "grade level" to a text. Sure enough, we found that advertising text on inexpensive chips uses simpler sentences and simpler words, on average at the eighth-grade level. Notice the simple grammar and vocabulary in this sample from an inexpensive chip:

> *What gives our chips their exceptional great taste? It's no secret. It's the way they're made!*

The advertising on expensive chips is written at the tenth- to eleventh-grade level; notice the more complex words ("stage of preparation" versus "way they're made") and structure in this sample:

> *We use totally natural ingredients, hand-rake every batch, and test chips at every stage of preparation to ensure quality and taste.*

So advertisers aren't just trying to get you to believe that potato chips are good for your health. Advertisers, like writers of menus, figure that the more money you have, the more you'll be pleased to have an advertiser talk to you in complicated language. Maybe those expensive student loans were worth it after all.

Also similar to menus for expensive restaurants, text describing expensive chips is riddled with natural authenticity, calling chips "natural," obsessed with the lack of anything artificial or fake, and emphasizing the handcrafted wholesomeness of the manufacturing process. Researchers call this *craft authenticity*, and you've seen it in phrases like "sea salt," "nothing fake or phony," "absolutely nothing artificial," "only the finest potatoes," or "hand-rake every batch."

We found one final characteristic of advertisements on expensive chips. The ads are chock-full of the language of differentiation and comparison. Expensive chips use words like *more* or *less*, suffixes like *—er,* or superlative words (most, least, best, finest). Phrases like "in a class of their own" or "deliciously different" or statements that these chips have "a crunchy bite you won't find in any other chip" or "less fat than other leading brands" assert that the expensive chip possesses some quality or ingredient (goodness or fat) to a greater or lesser extent than other chips.

Expensive chips also have a lot more negative markers, like the word *no* or phrases like "never fried" or the word *don't* in "we don't wash out the natural potato flavor." Negation emphasizes bad qualities that a chip does not have, subtly suggesting that other brands have this bad quality. The message is that other chips are unhealthy, unnatural, or addictive (recall the drug metaphors of the previous chapter). Here is some copy we took directly from the back of one of the chip bags:

> nothing fake or phony.
> *no fake colors, no fake flavors,*
> *no fluorescent orange fingertips,*
> *no wiping your greasy chip hand*
> *on your jeans. no, really.*

To get a more fine-grained analysis, we also ran a regression, the same statistical tool we used to analyze the menus and reviews in earlier chapters, to test exactly how much these negative words were correlated with the price. We found that a bag of potato chips costs four cents more per ounce for every additional negative word on the bag. This does not mean that advertisers literally raise the price when they add negation; we didn't attempt to find a causal link between the two. Our results are merely an association, suggesting that these go together. But it does mean that if you see six negative words on the back of the package you're going to be paying about a quarter more per ounce.

Why should words related to what a product isn't, or words related to differentiating a product from others, be linked to its expense? The answer comes from French sociologist Pierre Bourdieu, whose famous book *Distinction* surveyed French society in the 1960s, examining the daily habits and tastes of the upper class and the working class. Bourdieu showed that our position in society heavily influences our tastes, with the working class expressing "popular" tastes for the "Blue Danube Waltz" while the high-status class preferred the "Well-Tempered Clavier" or Brueghel. In food, the lower class expressed preferences for traditional hearty meals, heavy in starch and fat and generous in portion size. The high-status classes instead tended to value more exotic foods like curry and other ethnic foods newly arrived in France at the time, or health foods like brown rice.

Bourdieu argues that there is nothing inherently better about curry versus cassoulet; that hip or fashionable tastes are just a way for the upper class to display their high status, to *distinguish* themselves from other classes. Taste, says Bourdieu, is "first and foremost . . . negation . . . of the tastes of others." A high-status group maintains its status by legitimizing some tastes but not others, independent of inherent artistic merit, and by passing on these tastes as cultural preferences.

Bourdieu's model explains the massive amounts of comparison (less fat, finest potatoes) and negation (not, never) in expensive chip advertising as a way of explicitly emphasizing these distinctions. Upper-class taste in food advertising is defined by contrast with tastes of other classes; what it is to be upper class is to be *not* working class.

But advertising copywriters don't just target the rich. The text on inexpensive chips targets a specific audience too. Josh and I found

David Ogilvy in Manhattan in 1954
© Bettmann/CORBIS

that less expensive chips emphasized family recipes or a grounding in American history and geography. These advertisers harkened back to a *traditional authenticity* by using phrases like "the chips that built our company," "85-year-old recipe," "time-honored tradition," "classic American snacks," or "[from] the great Pacific Northwest." Advertisers presume that customers of less expensive chips are more concerned with family and tradition than distinction, uniqueness, and health.

This idea of using different linguistic devices to target different audiences comes from the father of advertising, ad executive giant David Ogilvy, the 1948 founder of Ogilvy and Mather and inspiration for *Mad Men*. Ogilvy was a famous eccentric, coming to work in a billowing black cape or creating a scene at restaurants by ordering a plate of ketchup as his entire meal. As a twenty-five-year-old salesman in 1936, Ogilvy wrote a sales manual for the famous European stove, the Aga, that *Fortune* magazine called "probably the best sales manual ever written." This excerpt from it explains his idea of customizing language:

> There are certain universal rules. Dress quietly and shave well. Do not wear a bowler hat. . . . Perhaps the most important thing of all is to avoid standardisation in your sales talk. If you find yourself one fine day saying the same things to a bishop and a trapezist, you are done for.

Ogilvy had a lot of experiences with different (and tough) audiences; as a young chef in Paris he cooked for the president of France and met Escoffier but also remembered "the night our chef potagier threw forty-seven raw eggs across the kitchen at my head, scoring nine direct hits." And he even specifically discusses when (and when not) to use two-dollar words. In his 1963 book *Confessions of an Advertising Man* he says, "Don't use highfalutin language" when you're talking to a non-highfalutin audience.

At the minimum, Ogilvy's advice is to distinguish at least two audiences. The non-highfalutin audience is focused on family and tradition. The wealthier, middle or upper class audience is focused on education and health and striving to be unique and special, like Ogilvy himself, with his cape and his ketchup. Fitzgerald may or may not have been right that "the rich are different from you and me" but potato chip advertisers certainly think the rich *want* to be different from you and me, echoing food historian Erica J. Peters's dictum that what people eat "reflects not just who they are, but who they want to be."

Politicians use metaphors linked to the desire for traditional authenticity and interdependence when appealing to country or working-class audiences, emphasizing traditional American foods, locales, and values. And they use linguistic devices associated with country too, with phrases like "strugglin' " and "rollin' up our sleeves" that make use of the more country or working-class *-in'* suffix. The use of the *-ing* form associated with educated or upper-class speech, or the use of fancier words in general, and a focus on the language of health and nature, are an equally frequent political tactic for appealing to more upscale voters concerned about the local food supply, natural and nonartificial ingredients, and the health of our diet.

Whatever they might claim, politicians can't really eat healthy, because they have to prove their authenticity by eating cheese steaks in Philadelphia or wings in Buffalo or donuts or hot dogs pretty much everywhere. Here in San Francisco that means the politicians eat

Chinese food at the Chinese New Year Parade, tamales at the Day of the Dead parade, and in a classic San Francisco mash up, dim sum before the Gay Pride parade.

But this ability to use different selves with different audiences is not just an ability of politicians, and these two ways of being are not just associated with differences in income. In their book *Clash!* cultural psychologists Hazel Rose Markus and Alana Conner show that these two audiences are related to two aspects of our personality, two ways of viewing the world that we make use of at different times and in different amounts. What they call the *interdependent self* is our focus on our family, our traditions, and our relationships with people. The *independent self* is our focus on our need to be unique and independent. Each of us has an interdependent self and an independent self, sometimes focusing more on our need to be authentic, unique, and natural, and sometimes more on being rooted in relationships with our family, our culture, and our traditions.

In other words, like Warren Hellman, we are all fluid categories, combinations of these two models of our nation and our selves—models written on the back of every bag of potato chips.

Nine

Salad, Salsa, and the Flour of Chivalry

FLOUR AND SALT ARE an ancient combination, constituting, together with water, the minimal ingredients in bread from the most ancient times. San Franciscans have long baked using just these three ingredients, relying on our local fog-dwelling wild yeast and bacteria like *lactobacillus sanfranciscensis* instead of baker's yeast. This "natural leavening" or *levain* tradition (and the famous "sourdough"), continues with modern local bakers like Steven Sullivan at Acme or Chad Robertson at Tartine. San Francisco artist Sarah Klein has even turned it into a performance piece; she sets up a mini kitchen in lobbies of high-rise office buildings downtown, starts mixing flour, water, salt, and starter, and random passersby join in the kneading and rising and slicing and eating of the hot sourdough.

In many cultures, salt is then added again. Bread and salt (*khubẓ wa-milh*) is an Arabic phrase that means the bond created by sharing food; the Russian word for hospitality is similarly *khleb-sol* (bread-salt), and bread and salt (and candles) is what my mom gave me, following Jewish tradition, when I moved to a new house.

But the link between flour and salt goes beyond their shared constituency in bread. These two ancient white powders are some of the earliest examples of processed, refined foods, dating back to the ancient human transition from hunter-gatherer societies to settled agriculture. This transition required finding new sources of salt, since when humanity subsisted by hunting and gathering, we got enough salt from meat. This need led to an extensive industry of salt mining and seawater evaporation across the world, not to mention thousands of years of salt taxes. The transition to agriculture also meant the need to mill wheat into flour, a technology visible in Neolithic quern stones; the British Museum has a grinding stone from Syria that dates to 9500–9000 BCE.

These days we spend a lot of time on efforts to rein in our unhealthy love of refined, salty foods. Potato chip advertisers, aware of the unhealthiness of the products, overcompensate by talking about how they are "healthier" and "low fat" with the "lowest sodium." And online reviewers are equally aware, referring to "addicting wings" and "cupcakes like crack." In this chapter we'll examine the linguistic history of these ancient industrial foods to demonstrate that our craving for these salty, refined foods is old and unchanging—although they now come in more convenient snack-sized packages. We'll start by looking at the linguistic history of flour, from the period when Anglo-Saxon was enriched with a vast French vocabulary brought by the Norman invasion.

Bread itself was so central to the medieval English diet that the word for the Anglo-Saxon ruler in his great mead hall was *hlaf-weard* (loaf-keeper), from his role in controlling the mills that ground grain into flour and distributing bread to his dependents. This word is perhaps more familiar in the modern form into which it evolved: *lord*. Our word *lady* similarly comes originally from the Anglo-Saxon *hlaf-dige* (loaf-kneader).

After the 1066 invasion of the Normans, this association of food with the lordly class was maintained. The French spoken by this new ruling class began to be used instead of Anglo-Saxon for words that persist to modern-day English: pork, veal, mutton, beef, venison, bacon (from Old French *porc, veal, mouton, boeuf,* and so on). But while only the Norman lords could afford to regularly eat meat, it was

Anglo-Saxon-speaking serfs who raised the cows and pigs that the meat came from. Thus we use French *pork* for meat from the pig but still use old Anglo-Saxon words like *pig* (and *hog* and *sow*) for the animal itself. We still use Anglo-Saxon *cow*, *calf*, and *ox*, but refer to their meat with French *beef* and *veal*.

As part of this French invasion, sometime in the thirteenth century, a word spelled variously *flure*, *floure*, *flower*, *flour*, or *flowre* first appeared in English, borrowed from the French word *fleur*, meaning "the blossom of a plant," and by extension, "the best, most desirable, or choicest part of something." This second meaning occurs in the modern French word *fleur de sel*, which means the finest of the sea salts—delicate crystals harvested from the surface of evaporation pools.

The new English *flur* adopted both of the French meanings, pushing aside the old Anglo-Saxon word *blossom*, and coming to describe the best and choicest of all sorts of fancy high-class stuff. Thus we see phrases in Chaucer like "flower of chivalry" or "flower of knighthood" to describe the knights of the noble class.

Also in the thirteenth century, the phrase "flower of wheat" or "flower of meal" began to be used to describe the very finest, choicest part of wheat meal, made only of the white or endosperm of the wheat. A kernel of wheat has three parts: the endosperm, containing carbohydrates and protein; the fat and vitamin-rich "germ"; and the fibrous outer bran. Most bread in medieval times was made from the entire grain, sometimes with a portion of the bran removed. "Flower of wheat," by contrast (or *flure of huete* as it might have been spelled at the time) meant the very fine white flour created by repeatedly sifting the wheat through a fine-meshed cloth. Each pass removed more of the bran or germ, leaving a finer and whiter flour. This process of sieving through cloth was called bolting and these bolting cloths were specially woven from canvas, wool, linen, and, much later, fine silk.

The first breads made from these fine white flours were called *payndemayn* or *paindemain*, most likely derived from the Latin *panis*

A medieval woman selling bread

dominicus (lordly bread). The fine new payndemayn became a metaphor for whiteness as in Chaucer's description of the handsome Sir Thopas in *The Canterbury Tales*: "White was his face as payndemayn, his lips red as a rose."

Payndemayn is what is called for in the recipe I gave for "sops" and also in most early recipes for French toast.

French toast was a common recipe in English cookbooks, first appearing around 1420 as *payn per-dew*, from the French *pain perdu* (lost bread), presumably after the staleness of the bread. (The name "French toast" doesn't appear until the seventeenth century, and wasn't common here in the United States until the nineteenth century.) Here's one of the earliest French toast recipes, from a fifteenth-century manuscript. See if you can read the Middle English; most of the words, albeit differently spelled, are still part of modern English (like *frey hem a lytyll yn claryfyd buture* for "fry them a little in clarified butter" and *eyren drawyn thorow a streynour* for "eggs passed through a strainer"):

Payn purdyeu

Take payndemayn or fresch bredd; pare awey the crustys. Cut hit in schyverys [slices]; fry hem a lytyll yn claryfyd buture. Have yolkes of eyren [eggs] drawyn thorow a streynour & ley the brede theryn that hit be al helyd [covered] with bature. Then fry in the same buture, & serve hit forth, & strew on hote sygure.

By the fourteenth century the English word *flower* (or *flour*) could mean any of these three things: a blossom, a finely ground wheat meal, or something which was the finest or best of something—both spellings were used to describe all of these until the modern spellings standardized around 1800. Shakespeare puns on these latter two meanings in *Coriolanus*, using "the flower of all" to mean the best of everything and "the bran" to mean whatever is left over: "All from me do back receive the flower of all, and leave me but the bran."

In this Elizabethan era of Shakespeare, the rich ate a white bread successor of payndemayn called *manchet*, a fine white bread that could also be made with milk and eggs. Besides manchet and manchet rolls, finely bolted white flour was mainly eaten in cakes, cookies, and pastries. Even for the wealthy, however, white bread was reserved for special occasions.

Over the next few hundred years, white bread slowly became more and more favored. Partly this had to do with technology, as new silk bolting cloths imported from China in the eighteenth century made it possible and cheaper to make more finely bolted white flour. But mainly this had to do with the changing nature of tastes and the increasing desire for refined foods. By the mid-seventeenth century the Brown-Bakers guild specializing in dark loaves of rye, barley, or buckwheat merged with the White-Bakers guild and white bread and white flour came to dominate; social journalist Henry Mayhew reports that by 1800 brown bread was looked down upon even by the poor.

These days we can use the word *flour* to mean any finely ground grain, whether it is whole wheat flour or even corn, spelt, rice, or barley flour. But the word still maintains something of its original usage; if you asked a neighbor to lend you a cup of flour, you probably wouldn't be surprised if what you got handed was a cupful of fine, sifted, ground, white endosperm of wheat.

English does have other quite different words for flour. An English

*One of the Yale Culinary Tablets, in Akkadian
from the Old Babylonian Period, ca. 1750 BC.
Yale Babylonian Collection.*

word for flour with particularly ancient roots is our *semolina*, the coarsely ground grains of the endosperm of hard durum wheat. Semolina comes from Latin *simila* (fine flour) and Greek *semidalis*, both of which come from the Akkadian word *samidu* (high-quality meal). Akkadian was the language of ancient Assyria and Babylon, and samidu occurs in recipes in the world's oldest known cookbook, the Yale Culinary Tablets. These were written in cuneiform around 1750 BCE and also include recipes for what is probably the ancestor of the vinegar stew sikbāj.

Samidu's Latin descendant *simila* also gave rise to the English simnel cake, and to the Middle High German word *Semmel*, originally a roll made of fine wheat flour, a sense it still maintains in the Yiddish word *ʒeml*. In modern German the word *Semmel* refers to the Austrian or Bavarian white Kaiser rolls or hard rolls, also favored in the United States in Wisconsin and other areas with German or Austrian roots. Next time you eat a bratwurst on a Sheboygan hard "semmel" roll remember that the name goes all the way back to the Assyrians.

Flour is also referenced in the name *sole meunière*, the classic French dish of fish fillets dredged in flour and pan-fried crisp in butter. A *meunière* is a miller's wife, so a dish called "meunière" or "à la meunière" means one that is likely to be served in a miller's house, hence containing flour.

What about that other white powder, salt? When we think of adding flavor to our food, we think of spices and herbs, peppers and ketchups and salad dressings and soy sauce, but the original food additive was salt. Salt's importance in cuisine is visible in the vast number of foods in English with salt in their name. *Salad* and *sauce* (from French), *slaw* (from Dutch), *salsa* (from Spanish), *salami* and *salume* (from Italian) all come originally from the Latin word *sal* and originally meant exactly the same thing: "salted."

The word *salad*, originally from Medieval Latin *salata*, came to English from Old French, borrowed from Provençal *salada*. The very first written recipe for salad in English is in the first English cookbook, the 1390 *Forme of Cury*. Despite the Middle English vocabulary it's a pretty modern recipe, chock-full of greens and herbs (I've translated the ones that might be harder to figure out), dressed with oil, vinegar, garlic, and, naturally, salt:

Salat (c. 1390)

Take persel, sawge [sage], grene garlic, chibolles [scallions], letys, leek, spinoches, borage, myntes, porrettes [more leeks], fenel, and toun cressis [town cress, i.e., garden cress], rew, rosemarye, purslarye; laue and waische hem clene. Pike hem. Pluk hem small with thyn honde, and myng [mix] hem wel with rawe oile; lay on vyneger and salt, and serue it forth.

The Provençal salada that became English salad itself developed out of the Late Latin *salata*, in the context *herba salata* (salted vegetables). This medieval term was not used by the Romans of the classical period, although classical Romans definitely ate vegetables with a brine sauce. In fact Cato gives a recipe for a salted cabbage salad in his *De Agricultura*, from around 160 BCE: "If you eat it [cabbage] chopped, washed, dried, and seasoned with salt and vinegar, nothing will be more wholesome."

Much later, cabbages with salt and sometimes vinegar, often preserved longer, became prevalent in northern Europe, and later came to America. This is the origin of our *sauerkraut*, from the German "sour vegetable." An even older American immigrant is the word *cole slaw*, from Dutch *kool* (cabbage) and *sla* (salad, from a Dutch shortening of the Dutch word *salade*). The Dutch had a huge influence on the development of New York (originally New Amsterdam), with a culinary legacy in American English that also includes the words *cookie*, *cruller*, *pancake*, *waffle*, and *brandy*. The first mention of what is probably cole slaw was in 1749, when Pehr Kalm, a visiting Swedish Finnish botanist, describes an "unusual salad" served to him in Albany by his Dutch landlady Mrs. Visher, made from thin strips of sliced cabbage mixed with vinegar, oil, salt, and pepper. Kalm says this dish "has a very pleasing flavor and tastes better than one can imagine." This original *koolsla* gave way later to our modern mayonnaise-based dressing.

The word *sauce* in French and *salsa* in Spanish, Provençal, and Italian again come from popular Latin *salsus/salsa*, referring to the salty seasonings that made food delicious. Chaucer talks in 1360 of "poynaunt sauce," by which he meant a sauce that was pungent or sharp, the old meaning of *poignant*. And various recipes for sauce, by now with or without salt, start appearing in cookbooks from the thirteenth century. (There are lots of sauces in the older cookbook known as *Apicius*, a fourth-century Latin collection of recipes written by various authors, but the word used for sauce there is *ius*, the ancestor of our word *juice*.)

Many of my favorite sauces are called "green sauce," like Mexican *salsa verde* of tomatillos, onions, garlic, serranos, and cilantro, or Italian *salsa verde*, of parsley, olive oil, garlic, lemon or vinegar, and salt or anchovies. For Italian salsa verde Janet and I tend to add in whatever green herbs are growing in our gardens; here are the ingredients we tend to use:

Salsa Verde

1 cup Italian parsley leaves
¼ cup chives or wild garlic stems
leaves from 6 sprigs thyme
leaves from 2 sprigs tarragon
leaves from 2 sprigs rosemary
2 cloves garlic
¼–½ cup extra virgin olive oil
1 tablespoon lemon juice
2 anchovies
¼ teaspoon salt or to taste

Chop herbs with anchovies and garlic by hand, and then mix in oil, lemon juice, and salt.

I called it "Italian" salsa verde but from the twelfth to the fourteenth century green parsley sauces were made all across Europe. In Arabic salsa was called *sals*, and scholar Charles Perry tells us it was one of the few recipes that moved east from European Christians to the Muslim world rather than west from Muslims to Christians. A thirteenth-century cookbook from Damascus, the *Kitab al-Wusla*, told how to make "green sals" by pounding parsley leaves in a mortar with garlic, pepper, and vinegar. French *saulce vert* was made of parsley, bread crumbs, vinegar, and ginger in the fourteenth-century French cookbook *Le Viandier*, or made of parsley, rosemary, and sorrel or marjoram in *Le Menagier de Paris*.

There are other modern descendants of this sauce. In the twentieth century, Escoffier's French *sauce verte* called for pounding blanched parsley, tarragon, chervil, spinach, and watercress and using the "thick juice" to flavor mayonnaise. This mayonnaise sauce verte was modified in 1923 at San Francisco's Palace Hotel by adding sour cream and anchovies to create the recipe for Green Goddess Dressing, still served in the Garden Court at brunch.

The Palace Hotel has been around for almost 150 years; Sarah Bernhardt brought her pet baby tiger there, Enrico Caruso stayed there on the night of the '06 earthquake, and the Maxfield Parrish painting of the Pied Piper in the bar is a San Francisco landmark. My high school prom was there, too, back when Donna Summer and Peaches and Herb were at the top of the charts. In the prom picture I just dug out to show Janet, I certainly rocked the bowtie, but unlike the original recipe for Green Goddess Dressing, below, our perfectly feathered hair did not stand the test of time.

Green Goddess Dressing

1 cup traditional mayonnaise

½ cup sour cream

¼ cup snipped fresh chives or minced scallions

¼ cup minced fresh parsley

1 tablespoon fresh lemon juice

1 tablespoon white wine vinegar

3 anchovy fillets, rinsed, patted dry, and minced

salt and freshly ground pepper to taste

Stir all the ingredients together in a small bowl until well blended. Taste and adjust the seasonings. Use immediately, or cover and refrigerate.

The earliest known recipe for one of the green sauces, however, seems to be an English recipe written mainly in Latin with some

Norman French and English in a volume written over 800 years ago in 1190 by English scholar and scientist Alexander Neckam. The recipe was called *verde sause* and it called for parsley, sage, garlic, and pepper, and ends "non omittatur salis beneficium," which translates roughly to "Don't forget the salt."

Why should a simple seasoning be so pervasive in our language? The answer is that the main use of salt throughout human history was to preserve foods. Cabbage salted into sauerkraut could last through the winter. Salted sausages, salami, ham, salt pork, and salted fish (like the salt cod called *bacallao* in Spanish) were able to last long enough to allow merchants and soldiers to travel across Europe and cross the Atlantic and the Pacific.

In the ancient European world, salted pork products were a specialty of the Celts. The geographer Strabo said that hams from the Celtic regions of France and Spain were famous in Rome, and Westphalian hams from formerly Celtic regions of what is now Germany were as beloved in Rome then as they are in modern times.

The salt is still there in the names for these pork products, most obviously in "salt pork," but it's there in Italian *salami* and *salumi* too, both formed from the root *sal* (salt) plus the noun-forming suffixes –*ame* and –*ume*. And it's there in the word *sausage*, which we got from French, from late Latin *salsīcia*, originally from the phrase *salsa isicia* (salted *isicia*). *Isicia* was a kind of forcemeat, croquette or fresh sausage; there are recipes for isicia in *Apicius*. *Salsa isicia* was thus the dried salted preserved version of this sausage.

Salt is even there in corned beef, the salted beef famously associated with the Irish, modern descendants of the ancient Celts. Corned beef has nothing to do with maize. The word *corn* in Old English originally meant a "particle" or "grain" of something (in fact it is the etymological cousin of the words *grain* and *kernel*), and here refers to the grains of salt used to preserve the beef.

Salting fish to preserve it is probably even more ancient than salting meat, like the ancient fish sauces of Asia or the fish sauce called garos in Greek and garum in Latin eaten hundreds of years BCE. Salt cod was a huge staple of the Middle Ages, and played a central role in the economies of Europe and in the slave trade, where its use as a cheap food source resulted in the prevalence of salt cod in the modern cuisines of Jamaica, the Dominican Republic, and other Caribbean nations (and its availability in grocery stores in the Latin American neighborhoods of most American cities like San Francisco).

Until about 1800 then, preservation meant salting (or smoking, or soaking in vinegar, or candying in sugar), and food preservation was essential for a population to get enough to eat. Starting around 1790, two major scientific and technical advances led to superior methods of food preservation. The first was around 1790 when Nicolas Appert, a French confectioner who was used to boiling down syrups, thought to apply the boiling method to other foods in glass jars. He perfected the method by 1810, when he won an award from the French government and wrote a book explaining how to preserve soups and stews (pots-au-feu), a filet of beef, chicken and partridges, vegetables, fruit, and milk in glass jars. The second advance was refrigeration, invented in stages through the nineteenth century, widespread in commercial breweries by the 1880s, in meatpacking by 1915, and by the mid-twentieth century available to every American household.

The result of both inventions was that salt was much less important in food as a preservative. Since vegetables and meats, raw or cooked, can be canned or frozen, salt is now only needed for taste. But we've grown accustomed to salty foods. The Jewish foods I grew up on (lox, whitefish, herring, pastrami, corned beef) are all salted, preserved foods that we continue to eat even though fresh salmon, beef, and other fish are all perfectly available (and cheaper). As Bee Wilson says in her delightful *Consider the Fork*, "Bacon serves no real purpose in a refrigerated age, except that of pleasure, which can never be discounted."

The history of flour tells us a similar story. Coarse medieval bolting left plenty of bran even in the most refined white flour, so even the rich got plenty of fiber from white flour. Only with the replacement of stone grist mills with metal roller mills that completely removed bran and germ has modern white flour become totally refined and optimally unhealthy.

The linguistic histories of *flour* and *salt* thus remind us of our ancient love for refined and salted foods. Yet English also offers us a hint about a different kind of seasoning. The word *season* or *seasoning* didn't originally mean anything about adding salt or even spices or herbs to our food to add flavor. The word meant just what it sounds like: *season* comes from French *saison*, in the original meaning "to ripen fruit according to the seasons." So although I adore refined white flour and salt (after all, it's hard to beat a freshly baked sourdough baguette or the salty umami savor of fish sauce) these linguistic histories are a little reminder to enjoy the ripe fruits and seasonal vegetables and to go easier on those white powders.

Ten

Macaroon, Macaron, Macaroni

SPRING IS BEAUTIFUL in San Francisco. The wild garlic and fennel cover Bernal Hill, Dianda's Italian American Pastry down on Mission Street augments their usual delicious *amaretti* and *ricciarelli* with their special St. Honore cake for Easter, it's Persian New Year (*Nowrūz*) and the Chinese Qingming Festival, and my family prepares for Passover, which means coconut macaroons.

For the last few years the city has also been full of another, trendier, macaroon: the Parisian macaron, a delicate pastel confection made of two almond cookies sandwiched with ganache. Parisian macarons are in every fancy pâtisserie and San Francisco, never a place to miss out on a trend, even has macaron delivery. The fad for these pricey chic French almond macarons has upstaged their humble relative, the chewy coconut macaroon.

Why this sudden fad for the expensive macaron, and how is it related to the humble coconut macaroons of my childhood? And why do both these words sound so much like macaroni? The answer involves not only a story of a favorite food created at the nexus of great civilizations, like sikbāj, ketchup, or turkey, but also a link to the important role of social status that we discussed in the chapters on menus, entrée, and potato chips.

The story begins in the year 827, when Arab and Berber troops from Ifriqiya (modern Tunisia) landed in Byzantine Greek–speaking Sicily, establishing a Muslim emirate that introduced many technologies (like paper) and foods (lemons, oranges, rice, pistachios, sugar cane) to Europe. By then Sicily had been famous for its food for a thousand years; Plato commented on the superb Sicilian cuisine in his *Republic* (404d). The Arabs added to this culinary background, bringing a selection from the rich repertoire of nut-based sweets of the medieval Muslim world: the chewy nougats that became Italian *torrone*, Spanish *turrón*, American Snickers candy bars; the powdered starchy *falūdhaj* that is the ancestor of Turkish Delight; and the most famous of all, *lauzīnaj*.

Lauzīnaj was a confection of almonds ground together with sugar, mixed with rosewater, and wrapped in a delicate pastry. The chefs of the Abbasid Dynasty in Baghdad had borrowed lauzīnaj from the Sassanid kings of Persia, who ate sweets like this for *Nowrūz*. *Nowrūz*, literally "new day," was the first day of the new year in the pre–Islamic Persian calendar, celebrated on the vernal equinox. The sixth-century Sassanid king Khosrau, who loved sikbāj, also delighted in lauzīnaj, which he called the "best and finest" pastry.

Lauzīnaj was so celebrated that every medieval Arabic cookbook had a recipe, from the tenth-century cookbook of al-Warrāq to this (abridged) recipe from the thirteenth-century Baghdad cookbook *Kitāb al-Tabīkh* (*The Book of Dishes*), in Charles Perry's translation:

Lauzīnaj

Take a pound of sugar and grind it fine. Take a third of a pound of finely ground peeled almonds, mix them with the sugar, and knead it with rose-water. Then take bread made thin . . . —the thinner, the better— . . . and put the kneaded almonds and sugar on it. Then roll up . . . and cut it into small pieces.

Some recipes for lauzīnaj left off the pastry shell, others were flavored with musk or were drenched in syrup flavored with rosewater, or were sprinkled with finely pounded pistachios.

*Roger II, from a mosaic in the Church of the
Martorana in Palermo*

By 1072 the Normans had conquered Sicily (and England), and for a brief period the rule of Roger I and Roger II of Sicily was an experiment in mutual tolerance, at least compared to the rest of Europe: Greek, Arabic, and Latin were all official languages, government officials were drawn from all three cultures, and Muslims and Jews were governed by their own law. In Sicily, and in Toledo, Spain, another contact point between Muslim and Christian culture, pastries like lauzīnaj entered the European culinary repertoire and developed into desserts like the almond paste tarts called *marʒapane* and *caliscioni*.

Marʒapane (marzipan in English) comes from the Arabic word *mauthaban*, which originally meant the jars the tarts came in, and then by extension the pastry shell. The 1465 cookbook of Maestro Martino tells us that marzipan was originally filled with a mixture of almond paste, sugar, rosewater, and sometimes egg whites. The modern word *marʒipan* means the almond paste confection itself (like the beautiful colored fruit shapes that my next-door neighbor, Mrs. Scheel, made when I was a kid). Here's Martino's recipe for the marzipan filling:

Marzipan

Peel the almonds well and crush. . . . When you crush them, wet them with a bit of rose water so that they do not purge their oil. . . . take an equal weight of sugar as of almonds . . . and add also an ounce or two of good rose water; and incorporate all these things together well. . . .

Then take some wafers . . . made with sugar and wet them with rose water; dissolve them in the bottom of a pan and add this mixture or filling on top . . . cook in the oven . . . being very careful to apply moderate heat.

Caliscioni was a very similar dessert, pastries made of almond paste wrapped in or sitting on a sugar dough. Again it's the shell that gives the pastry its name; caliscioni comes from the word for stocking or legging. (*Calceus* was the Latin word for shoe; think of French *chaussure* or *chausson* or the name Chaucer, originally "makers of leggings or footwear.") Many desserts acquired their names from their former pastry "crusts"; our word *custard* was formerly *crustade*, from French *croustade*, akin to Italian *crostata*, from *crostare*, "to encrust." Here's Martino's recipe:

How to Make Caliscioni

Take a similar filling or mixture like that described above for marzipan, and prepare the dough, which you make with sugar and rose water; and lay out the dough as for ravioli; add this filling and make the caliscioni large, medium-sized, or small, as you wish.

As is clear from these recipes, marzipan and caliscioni, even a few hundred years later, were still very close to the original recipes for lauzīnaj.

The main change was that marzipan and caliscioni were baked (at low heat) while lauzīnaj was often not cooked. The details of the pastry had also changed in the transition, but the Europeans were basically still making confections of almonds, sugar, and rosewater wrapped in pastry. Sugar was still quite expensive, and so such desserts were still luxury products originally available mainly to the wealthy. Francesco Datini, a fourteenth-century merchant, wrote that marzipan torte was more expensive than a brace of peacocks.

The mention of ravioli in the caliscioni recipe brings up the second important development that was happening in Sicily at the same time: pasta. Grain-based gruels had long been common in the region, such as the Byzantine Greek gruel called *makaria* (μακαρία) eaten as a funeral food (from the Greek *makarios* [μακάριος], "blessed"). But dough products closer to true pasta were also an old custom in many parts of the Mediterranean. As far back as the first century BCE, the Greeks ate a dish made from sheets of fried dough called *laganum*, which by the fifth century had become *lagana*, layers of boiled dough alternating with stuffing (says Isidore of Seville)—the ancestor of modern lasagne. But it was in the eastern Mediterranean that true dried pasta existed, most commonly eaten in soup or as a sweet dish. We know that the word *itria* was used for both dried and fresh noodles in Aramaic in Palestine in the fifth century (the word appears in the fifth-century Jerusalem Talmud), and in the tenth century *itriyah* was an Arabic word for dried noodles that were bought from a grocer.

It was thus in Sicily that modern dried durum wheat pasta developed out of these Mediterranean dried noodles. Durum wheat is harder and higher in protein than common wheat, producing firm, elastic dough whose long life makes it easy to store and hence trade great barrels of it by ship. Sicily had been the breadbasket of the Roman Empire because of its durum wheat production, and this hard local wheat was so successfully combined with the Arab noodle traditions that by 1154, Muhammad al-Idrisi, the Moroccan-born geographer of Roger II of

Sicily, writes that Sicily was the center of dried pasta production for the whole Mediterranean, sending it by shiploads to Muslim and Christian countries. Different regions used different words for pasta, among them *tria* (from Arabic *itriyah*), *lasagne*, and *vermicelli* ("little worms"). (The idea that Marco Polo introduced pasta to Italy from China is a myth that grew accidentally out of a humorous piece from 1929 in a Minnesota trade publication called the *Macaroni Journal*; by the time Polo returned from China in 1296, pasta had been a major export commodity for almost 150 years.)

By 1200 noodles had branched north from Sicily, carried by both Jews and Christians, and in fact our first evidence for the word *vermicelli* is from France, where the eleventh-century French scholar Rashi (or possibly a commentary from one of the medieval Tosafist rabbis that followed him) uses the Yiddish word *vermiseles*, derived via old French *vermeseil* from Italian *vermicelli*, to describe dough that was either boiled or fried. *Vermiseles* soon evolved to *vremẓel* and to the modern Yiddish word *chremsel*, the name of a sweet doughy pancake now most commonly made of matzo-meal and eaten at Passover.

The pasta and the almond pastry traditions merged in Sicily, resulting in foods with characteristics of both. As we saw above, early pastas were often sweet, and could be fried or baked as well as boiled. There is a kind of duality to many recipes from this period, which exist in both a savory cheese version and a sweet almond milk or almond-paste version that was suitable for the vast number of fast days (Lent, Fridays, and so on) that populated the medieval Christian calendar, when neither meat nor dairy could be eaten.

The almond pastry caliscioni, for example, had both almond and cheese versions. In fact, both versions still exist today. The almond descendant is called *calisson d'Aix* in Aix-en-Provence, where it is now a candy made of marzipan and dried fruit, iced with egg white and sugar. Calissons have been in Provence for a while; the seer Nostradamus (in his day job as an apothecary) published an early recipe for *callisson* in

1555, in between prophecies. As for the cheese descendant of caliscioni, you've likely eaten it; now called *calzone*, it is a kind of pizza stuffed with cheese and baked or fried.

Out of this culinary morass arises, circa 1279, the word *maccarruni*, the Sicilian ancestor of our modern words *macaroni*, *macaroon*, and *macaron*. We don't know whether *maccarruni* came from Arabic, derives from another Italian dialect word (several dialect words have a root like *maccare* meaning something like "crush"), or even comes from the Greek *makaria*.

But like other dough products of the period, it's probable that the word *maccarruni* referred, perhaps in different locations, to two distinct but similar sweet doughy foods: one resembling gnocchi (flour paste with rosewater, sometimes egg whites and sugar, served with cheese), the other very much like a slightly fluffier marzipan (almond paste with rosewater, egg whites, and sugar).

The earliest recorded examples of maccarruni (or its descendant in Standard Italian, *maccherone*) refer to a sweet pasta. Boccaccio in his *Decameron* (around 1350) talks about maccherone as a kind of hand-cut dumpling or gnocchi eaten with butter and cheese. (Incidentally, this idea of lumpy gnocchi alternating with clumps of butter and cheese as metaphors for a hodgepodge of Italian and Latin was the origin of the phrase "macaronic verse.") The fifteenth-century cookbook of Martino tells us that Sicilian maccherone was made of white flour, egg whites, and rosewater, and was eaten with sweet spices and sugar, butter, and grated cheese.

Now back to almond sweets, which by the 1500s had spread beyond Sicily and Andalusia to the rest of modern-day Italy and from there to France and then England. In 1552, in a list of fantastical desserts in Rabelais' *Gargantua and Pantagruel*, we find hard written evidence that the word *macaron* meant a dessert. Shortly thereafter the name appears in English as *macaroon* (most sixteenth- and seventeenth-century French words ending in *–on* are spelled with *–oon* when borrowed into English, like *balloon*, *cartoon*, *platoon*).

What did this sweet taste like? *Martha Washington's Booke of Cookery*, a handwritten cookbook that the first First Lady's family had brought to the New World, contains the first known recipe. It was probably written in the early 1600s (notice the archaic spelling):

To Make Mackroons

Take a pound & halfe of almonds, blanch & beat them very small in a stone morter with rosewater. put to them a pound of sugar, & ye whites of 4 eggs, & beat y^m together. & put in 2 grayns of muske ground with a spoonfull or 2 of rose water. beat y^m together till y^r oven is as hot as for manchet, then put them on wafers & set them in on A plat. after a while, take them out. [y^n when] y^r oven is cool, set [y^m in] againe & dry y^m

This recipe tells us that in the first half of the seventeenth century, the macaroon still had the rosewater and musk of its medieval Arab antecedent, lauzīnaj. We also see that macaroons were set on a wafer after baking, a historical remnant of the pastry shell of the earlier recipes.

Even as this recipe was being written, however, modern French cuisine began to evolve out of its medieval antecedents, as cooks replaced imported medieval spices like musk with local herbs. The chef whose work is often considered the turning point in this transition was François Pierre de La Varenne, and the first completely modern recipe for macaroons comes from the 1652 edition of his cookbook, *The French Cook*, in which he eliminates orange water and rosewater from the earlier instantiations. He also eliminated the pastry shell; the only remnant of the former wafer is a piece of paper that the macaron sits on:

Macaron *("La maniere de faire du macaron")*

Get a pound of shelled almonds, set them to soak in some cool water and wash them until the water is clear; drain them. Grind them in a mortar moistening them with three egg whites instead of orange blossom water, and adding in four ounces of powdered sugar. Make your paste which on paper you cut in the shape of a macaroon, then cook it, but be careful not to give it too hot a fire. When cooked, take it out of the oven and put it away in a warm, dry place.

In France distinct variations for La Varenne–style macarons developed by the seventeenth century in places such as Amiens, Melun, Joyeuse, Nancy, and Niorts. In St.-Jean-de-Luz, a French Basque town just across the border from San Sebastian, Spain, we visited Maison Adam, the pâtisserie that claims to have supplied their golden-brown round "véritables macarons" to Anne of Austria when she came for the 1660 wedding of her son Louis XIV to the Infanta Maria Theresa of Spain. By the eighteenth century macarons were also commonly made in convents throughout France, both as a means of sustenance and, by selling them to the public, of financial support. After the French revolution, nuns who were ordered to leave their convents established macaron bakeries to support

themselves in cities like Nancy, where the Maison des Soeurs Macarons is still in business, and Saint-Emilion, where food writer Cindy Meyers writes that the Fabrique de Macarons Blanchez bakery sells macarons according to the "Authentic Macaron Recipe of the Old Nuns of Saint-Emilion."

Despite these minor regional variations, though, the cookie from 1650 until about 1900 was what the *Larousse Gastronomique* calls "a

Macaron de Nancy.
A macaron in the style of Nancy

small, round biscuit [cookie], crunchy outside and soft inside, made with ground almonds, sugar and egg whites."

In Italy the word *maccherone* meant only pasta by this time, so the cookies had other names like *marzapanetti* (little marzipans) in Siena or *amaretti* (little bitters) in Lombardy because they were made with bitter almond. Name mixups persisted in English until as late as 1834, with *macaroon* sometimes used to describe the pasta and *macaroni* the cookie.

Two innovations led to the modern macaroon/macaron divide. First, in America, a fad developed in the mid-1800s for an exotic food: coconuts (or rather cocoanuts, as the word was spelled in the nineteenth century and early twentieth century because of an early confusion with cocoa). Recipes for "Cocoa-nut Cake" appear as early as 1840, but use of coconut increased greatly after the Civil War along with increased trade with the Caribbean and greater production of coconut oil. Emily Dickinson was a fan; she mailed her recipe for Cocoanut Cake to a friend, and her poem "The Things That Can Never Come Back, Are Several" was first drafted on the back of another recipe for the cake. Dickinson's own recipe is written with her idiosyncratic punctuation:

Cocoanut Cake

1 cup Cocoanut ..
2 cups Flour -
1 cup Sugar -
½ cup Butter ..
½ cup Milk -
2 Eggs -
½ teaspoonful Soda
1 teaspoonful Cream Tartar
This makes one half the Rule —

Emily Dickinson (1830–1886)

By the late 1800s manufacturers had set up factories to produce shredded coconut and everyone was making faddish new desserts: coconut cream pie, coconut custard, and ambrosia (originally made from oranges, powdered sugar, and shredded coconut). Recipes for another of these coconut concoctions, coconut macaroons, also appear first quite early, around 1830, but don't take off until later in the century when they become common in Jewish cookbooks. Because the cookies do not contain flour, they became a standard during Passover celebrations, so much so that matzo manufacturers like Streit's and Manischewitz began selling both almond and coconut macaroons for Passover in the 1930s.

Here's the recipe from the first Jewish cookbook in America, Esther Levy's 1871 *Jewish Cookery Book*, in which the almond paste heretofore traditional in macaroons is replaced by grated coconut:

Coconut Macaroons

To one grated cocoanut add its weight in sugar, and the white of one egg, beaten to a snow; stir it well, and cook a little; then wet your hands and mould it into small oval cakes; grease a paper and lay them on; bake in a gentle oven.

By the 1890s, coconut macaroons appeared in many American cookbooks and became the best-selling version in America. The graph below shows the slow increase in the number of times "coconut macaroons" (any spelling) appears in the Google Ngram corpus from 1840 to 2000, with the bumps in the 1890s and 1930s and the recent rise starting in the 1960s.

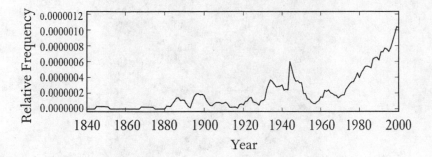

Just as coconut macaroons begin to take off midcentury in American cookbooks, a new innovation happens in France. A Parisian baker, Pierre Desfontaines (perhaps influenced by the earlier unfilled double-macaron of baker Claude Gerbet) creates a sandwich cookie by putting almond paste or ganache between two macarons. The new cookie was called *le macaron parisien* or *le macaron Gerbet* and was quickly popularized by the pastry shop and tea salon Ladurée. Today both the macaron parisien and many different versions of the traditional single macaron are prevalent throughout France.

In the United States, macaron refers only to the new ganache sandwich cookie, leaving macaroon to describe the coconut cookie, while of course macaroni for us now means only the elbow pasta.

Macaroni *used* to have a secondary meaning. In eighteenth-century England, rich young hipsters sported outlandish hairstyles (very tall powdered wigs with tiny caps on top) and affected clothing. (My prom hairdo was bad, but this was worse.) These young aristocrats were called "Macaronis" because on their travels in Italy they acquired a taste for pasta, a then-exotic foreign food fad. This may sound familiar from the song

The Macaroni. A real Character at the late
Masquerade, *a 1773 engraving by political
cartoonist Philip Dawe*

"Yankee Doodle"; the chorus mocks a disheveled "Yankee" soldier whose attempt to look sharp was to "stick a feather in his hat and call it macaroni."

The Macaronis weren't the first members of the wealthy elite to start a fad by eating exotic foreign foods. In fact, the regal or merely rich play a role in borrowing each of the foods we've talked about in this chapter. The Arab caliphs of Baghdad borrowed lauzīnaj from the Persians, wealthy Norman and Sicilian princes borrowed marzipan and dried pasta from the Arabs, rich British dandies borrowed macaroni from Italy, wealthy Americans borrowed coconuts (and other originally expensive foods like bananas) from the Caribbean, and now we've copied expensive macarons from Paris.

As for the Sassanid kings of Persia, it seems that they borrowed their lauzīnag, too. Lauzīnag means "containing almonds," but using the Semitic word for almond, *lauz*, not the Persian word, a linguistic clue that the Persians probably got the almond pastry from their Aramaic-speaking neighbors.

These borrowings, like those of sikbāj and ketchup (and sherbet, as we will see in the next chapter), illustrate the ideas of sociologists Georg Simmel and Thorstein Veblen, who at the turn of the nineteenth century noticed that fancy things (food, fashion, goods, or trends of any sort) tend to be introduced first by the wealthy elite. Like the French used in the expensive menus of Chapter 1 or Chapter 2's entrée, these newly imported luxuries function as markers of high status, exotic delicacies that only the rich can afford. Once these goods appear, Simmel and Veblen point out, the middle class naturally wants them too, and so as these foods or goods become cheaper they are consumed by more and more people and become part of the popular culture. As Rachel Laudan shows in *Cuisine and Empire*, "High cuisines were the engine of culinary change," but high-status goods eventually trickle down to the masses. Thus macaronic French becomes a sign of less expensive restaurants, and coconuts and cocoa, macaroni, nougat, and almond candy (and ketchup, originally an expensive Asian import used by English aristocrats) eventually became part of our everyday lives. Macaroni and cheese, a dish once associated with the aristocracy, became the widely popular American side dish that I grew up with, a staple for Sunday dinners in the South for both African Americans and whites, and a delight of small children everywhere. Even the expensive Parisian macaron is now available at discount prices at the wholesale warehouse Costco.

Macaroon, macaron, and macaroni remind us that the rare imported luxury of yesterday is the local popular culture of today—borrowed, maybe fluffed up a bit with egg whites or coconut to make it our own, a treat for each of us as we celebrate the coming of spring.

Eleven

Sherbet, Fireworks, and Mint Juleps

THE SAN FRANCISCO MIDSUMMER fog was late in coming last year, which means Janet and I got a fantastic view of the Fourth of July fireworks from the top of Bernal Hill (both the municipal shows and the not-quite-so-legal ones that San Franciscans set off from rooftops throughout the city). Hot days are rare in our "cool gray city of love," so random strangers were smiling at each other on Mission Street, the sidewalks were jammed with long lines in front of the ice creameries, and groups of people were picnicking in Dolores Park with icy cans of soda or cups of agua fresca or lemonade.

You may not be aware of the close relationships among these summer phenomena. Ice cream was invented by modifying a chemical process originally discovered for fireworks, and applying it to the fruit syrups that became lemonade, agua fresca, and sodas. And as we'll discuss in the next chapter, the way ice cream flavors are named turns out to have a surprising relationship with the evolutionary origin of the human smile.

Ice cream has always been popular in San Francisco; Swensons, Double Rainbow, and It's It were all founded here, and Rocky Road ice cream was invented across the bay in Oakland during the Great Depression. The latest inventions draw on the recent fads for molecular gastronomy and unusual flavor profiles. At Smitten in Hayes Valley they'll make your ice cream fresh when you order it, freezing the slurry with liquid nitrogen. At Humphry Slocombe you can get foie gras, pink grapefruit tarragon, or strawberry black olive flavors. Bi-Rite

Creamery will happily sell you honey lavender, balsamic strawberry, and that modern classic, salted caramel. Mitchell's specializes in Filipino and other tropical flavors like halo halo, lucuma, purple yam, and avocado. And Mr. and Mrs. Miscellaneous seems to keep running out of their latest hip flavor, orange blossom:

One day in the daily flavors at Mr. and Mrs. Miscellaneous, the San Francisco ice creamery

Well, actually, orange blossom is not a newfangled flavor. Orange blossom is, in fact, the original ice cream flavor, appearing in the earliest recipes by the mid-1600s, the period when ice cream was invented. Ice cream was served in the Restoration court of Charles II as early as 1671, and food scholar Elizabeth David gives us what may be the English royal recipe, handwritten in Grace Countess Granville's Receipt Book by the 1680s:

The Ice Creame

Take a fine pan Like a pudding pan ½ a ¼ of a yard deep, and the bredth of a Trencher; take your Creame & sweeton it wth Sugar and 3 spoonfulls of Orrange flower water, & fill yor pan ¾ full . . .

By about 1696, a later edition of the cookbook attributed to La Varenne suggests using fresh orange flowers:

Neige de Fleur D'orange

You must take sweet cream, and put thererto two handfuls of powdered sugar, and take petals of Orange Flowers and mince them small, and put them in your Cream, and if you have no fresh Orange Flowers you must take candied, with a drop of good Orange Flower water, and put all into a pot . . .

And by 1700 other ice cream flavors were developed as well, including pumpkin, chocolate, and lemon, and a plethora of early sorbets: sour cherry, cardamom, coriander-lemon, and strawberry.

Where did these flavors come from? And who first invented the freezing technology, the bath of salt and ice that these recipes share with modern homemade ice cream machines? The use of orange flower should give you a clue: the historical roots of ice cream and sorbet, like many of our modern foods, lie in the Muslim world.

The story begins with the fruit and flower syrups, pastes, and powders of the Arab and Persian world. In Cairo, for example, medieval cookbooks give recipes for cooking quince down into pastes with honey or sugar, flavored with vinegar and spices. Quince, a fruit that looks like a golden-yellow pear, has been renowned since classical Greece for its medicinal powers, which may account for its great acclaim. Quince paste spread from Cairo as far west as Muslim Andalusia, where it appears in a thirteenth-century cookbook manuscript. Its descendants are still popular today: in South America and Spain, where one is called *membrillo* (Spanish for "quince") and in England and the United States, where we call another descendant "marmalade" (from Portuguese *marmelo*, "quince"). *Marmalade* meant "quince paste" in English until the start of the seventeenth century, and somewhat longer in the United States. Early British recipes had the musk and rosewater of their Moorish Andalusian antecedents, but by the time the recipe made it into Amelia Simmons's 1796 *American Cookery*, the first American cookbook, the ingredients were just quince, sugar, and water:

To make Marmalade.

To two pounds of quinces, put three quarters of a pound of sugar and a pint of springwater; then put them over the fire, and boil them till they are tender; then take them up and bruize them; then put them into the liquor, let it boil three quarters of an hour, and then put it into your pots or saucers.

To digress briefly, by about the same time in Britain, the Seville orange replaced the quince as the standard marmalade ingredient and orange marmalade became a breakfast staple, starting in Scotland. Here's a Scottish recipe that food historian C. Anne Wilson gives from the 1760s:

To Make Orange Marmalade

Take the largest best Seville oranges, take the same weight of single refined sugar; grate your oranges, then cut them in two, and squeeze out the juice; throw away the pulp; cut down the skins as thin as possible, about half an inch long; put a pint of water to a pound of sugar; make it into a syrup . . . put in your rinds and gratings, and boil it till it is clear and tender; then put in your juice, and boil it till it is of a proper thickness . . .

More often than pastes, however, these medieval Arab sweet fruit concoctions were left in syrup form, where they were swallowed medicinally or combined with water to form refreshing beverages. The Arabic word for these syrups was *sharāb*, from a root meaning "drink." Here's a syrup recipe from the medieval apothecary manual of a Jewish druggist in Cairo in 1260:

Rhubarb syrup

Opens liver obstruction and strengthens the liver. Take twenty dirhams of rhubarb, sprinkle over it three ratls of water for a day and a night and simmer over a low fire and thicken with three ratls of hard loaf sugar. Let it reach the consistency of syrups, remove and use.

When these Arab medical manuals were translated into Latin this word *sharab* became the medieval Latin word *siropus*, the ancestor of our English word *syrup*.

In medieval Persia, similar syrups were extracted from flowers like rose petals or orange blossoms, or fruits like sour cherry or pomegranate. These syrups were called *sharbat*, from another form of the same Arabic word, and sharbat was also the name of the refreshing drinks made by combining the syrups with water, cooled with snow and ice brought down from the mountains. When the Ottomans came, they enthusiastically adopted these sharbat, pronouncing them sherbet in Turkish.

The idea of bringing snow and ice from the mountains and storing them in icehouses to cool drinks in the summer is an ancient worldwide custom. The earliest recorded icehouses were pits lined with tamarisk branches 4000 years ago in Mesopotamia, but icehouses were common in ancient China and Rome and they are even mentioned in the Bible. Sharbats are still quite popular in Persia and Turkey and indeed throughout the eastern Mediterranean. Claudia Roden talks nostalgically of the sharbat of her childhood in Egypt, sharbat flavored with lemon, rose, violet, tamarind, mulberry, raisin, or liquorice. Here's a modern Persian recipe from Najmieh Batmanglij:

Lime Syrup *(Sharbat-e ablimu)*

6 cups sugar

2 cups water

1½ cups fresh lime juice

Garnish:

Springs of fresh mint

Lime slices

In a pot, bring the sugar and water to a boil. Pour in the lime juice and simmer over medium heat, stirring occasionally, for 15 minutes. Cool, pour into a clean, dry bottle, and cork tightly.

In a pitcher, mix 1 part syrup, 3 parts water, and 2 ice cubes per person. Stir with a spoon and serve well chilled. Garnish with sprigs of fresh mint and slices of lime.

By the sixteenth century French and Italian travelers had brought back words of these Turkish and Iranian sherbets. In one of the earliest mentions of the word in Europe, the French naturalist Pierre Belon in 1553 described sherbets in Istanbul made of figs, plums, apricots, and raisins. Thirsty passersby would buy a glass of syrup from wandering sellers or stands, mixed with water and chilled with snow or ice to ward off the summer heat. Sherbets were most often sour. Lemons and sour cherries were some of the most popular flavors—and even vinegar was used.

In Turkey and Egypt, sherbet was often made from powders or tablets as well, as we see in this report from Jean Chardin, a seventeenth-century French traveler to Persia and the Ottoman Empire:

In Turky they keep them in Powder like Sugar: That of Alexandria, which is the most esteem'd throughout this large Empire, and which they transport from thence every where, is almost all in Powder. They keep it

*in Pots and Boxes; and when they would use it, they put a Spoonful of it
into a large glass of Water.*

While *şerbet* in modern Turkey is mostly made from syrup now, old-
style sherbet tablets, colored red and flavored with cloves, are still used
to make a hot spiced sherbet called *lohusa şerbet* served to new mothers
after the birth.

By 1662 sherbets were available across Europe. The London coffee-
house Morat's in Exchange Alley advertised "sherbets made in Turkie
of Lemons, Roses, and Violets perfumed." And by 1676 in France,
sherbets were the business of the guild of limonadiers, in charge of lemonades, iced waters, ices of fruits and flowers, sherbets, and coffee. The
Arabs had earlier brought lemons and sweetened lemon juice to Sicily
and Spain. Although at first lemons were available only to the wealthy,
by the seventeenth century lemons were more widely available in London and Paris. Nicolas Audiger, a limonadier of Paris, published *La
Maison Reglée* in 1692 with the first French recipe for lemonade:

Pour faire de bonne Limonade

Sur une pinte d'eau mettez trois jus de Citron, sept ou huit zestes,
& si les Citrons sont gros & bien à jus il n'en faut que deux, avec un
quarteron de Sucre, ou tout au plus cinq onces; lorsque le Sucre est
fondu & le tout bien incorporé, vous le passerez a la chausse, le ferez
rafraichir & le donnerez a boire.

To make good lemonade

Add the juice of three lemons to a pint of water, along with seven or
eight zests, and if the lemons are fat and full of juice you'll only need
two, with a quarter pound of sugar, or at most five ounces. When the

sugar has dissolved and is completely incorporated, strain it, chill it, and offer it to drink.

So where did the idea and the technology come from for freezing these sherbets and lemonades to become the fruit ices that we now call sorbets or sherbets? Yes, people had been putting ice and snow into drinks to cool them for over 4000 years, but freezing sweetened fruit juice or cream requires a much lower temperature than just ice can achieve. (Pure water freezes at $0°$ C, but every gram of sugar added to a liter of water drops the freezing point by about $2°$ C.) Obviously liquid nitrogen, the darling freezing technology of modernist hipster cuisine, was not available in the sixteenth century.

The insight came from fireworks. In the ninth century, during the Tang dynasty, the Chinese first realized that saltpeter (potassium nitrate) could be mixed with sulfur and coal to create the explosive mixture we now call gunpowder. Gunpowder was quickly adopted by the Muslim world, where potassium nitrate was called "Chinese snow" in Arabic.

It was in the Arab world rather than in China that the process of purifying and refining potassium nitrate was perfected, and it was in Damascus that it was discovered, probably by the physician Ibn Abī Uṣaybiʿa, in his 1242 *History of Medicine* (*Uyūn al-ānbā*)—although he credits a lost work from an earlier Muslim physician, Ibn Bakhtawayh, from 1029—that saltpeter had refrigerating properties: when potassium nitrate (saltpeter) is added to water, it chills the water. Dissolving salts like potassium nitrate (KNO_3) in water breaks the bonds between the potassium and nitrate ions, but it takes energy to break these bonds, and so heat is drawn from the surrounding water. This endothermic reaction, the basis of the modern cold pack, can drop the temperature of the water enough to freeze pure water, although not low enough to freeze fruit ices or ice cream.

By the early sixteenth century this discovery was widely used in Muslim India to chill water for drinking. At this time most of what is

*An intimate character study of the
Mughal Emperor Akbar, 1542–1605,
drawn late in his life*

today northern and central India, Pakistan, and Bangladesh, as well as parts of Afghanistan, was ruled by the Mughal emperor Akbar the Great. The Mughals were originally Turkic speakers from central Asia, and the royal line that conquered Delhi traced their descent from Genghis Khan (*Mughal* was the Persian word for "Mongol"), but had adopted the Persian language and culture. By the time of Akbar, the Persian-speaking court at Agra was a center for the arts, architecture, and literature. The Ramayana and the Mahabharata were translated from Sanskrit to Persian during this period, and Akbar's keen interest in painting and architecture led to the development of styles of art that mixed Persian, Hindu, and European forms. Like many places where scientific and culinary innovation and mixing flourished (Moorish Spain, early Norman Sicily), Akbar's reign was a beacon of relative religious tolerance, in which the tax on non-Muslims was eliminated and other religions were allowed self-government. Agra was steamy hot (as was his later court in Lahore), and drinks were cooled by spinning a long-necked flask in saltpeter-water. Here's a 1596 description from the records of his empire, the *Ain-I-Akbari*:

> *Saltpetre, which in gunpowder produces the explosive heat, is used by his Majesty as a means for cooling water, and is thus a source of joy for great and small . . . One sér of water is then put into a goglet of pewter, or silver, or any other such metal, and the mouth closed. Then two and a half sérs of saltpetre are thrown into a vessel, together with five sérs of water, and in this mixture the goglet is stirred about for a quarter of an hour, when the water in the goglet will become cold.*

Very quickly this idea of using saltpeter to cool water was adopted in Italy. Blas Villafranca, a Spanish physician working in Rome published the idea in 1550, saying that this saltpeter bath had become the

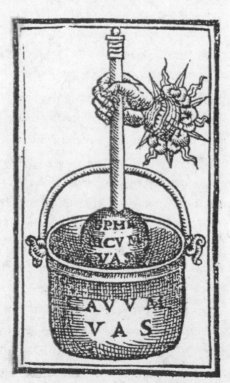

A goglet and bucket for cooling, from Blas Villafranca's Methodus Refrigerandi ex Vocato Sale Nitro Vinum Aquamque (*"Method for Cooling Wine and Water with Saltpeter"*), *after similar Mughal goglets*

common method of cooling wine in Rome. The figure on the previous page shows the method, with a bulbous flask clearly adapted from the Indian flasks. This shape makes it easy to turn the bottle in the cold bath, speeding up the cooling.

In 1589 the next step in ice cream technology was taken by the Neapolitan Giambattista Della Porta. In the second edition of his *Magia Naturalis* he experimented with adding saltpeter to snow rather than to water. The result successfully froze watered wine:

Wine may freeze in Glasses
Because of the chief thing desired at feasts, is that Wine cold as ice may be drunk, especially in summer. I will teach you how Wine shall presently, not only grow cold, but freeze, that you cannot drink it but by sucking, and drawing in of your breath. Put Wine into a Vial, and put a little water to it, that it may turn to ice the sooner. Then cast snow into a wooden vessel, and strew into it Saltpeter, powdered, or the cleansing of Saltpeter, called vulgarly Salazzo. Turn the Vial in the snow, and it will congeal by degrees.

Della Porta's combination was a happy accident; it was not saltpeter's endothermic reaction with water that caused cooling when mixed with ice, but a completely different chemical property. Adding a solute (a dissolved substance; practically anything will do) lowers the freezing point of water, by interfering with the crystal structure of the ice. Adding salt or potassium chloride slowly draws water out from its crystal mixture, and since the freezing point is lowered, turns into a salty slush. The phase shift from solid to liquid takes energy (another endothermic reaction), resulting in an even colder freezing brine that reaches -20° C, easily cold enough to freeze ice cream or fruit ices.

Sometime between 1615 and 1650, the Neapolitans combined the liquid Ottoman sherbets with the newly invented saltpeter-and-ice freezing method, resulting in a new food: frozen sherbets or frozen sorbets. The idea of freezing other liquids like milks and custards soon followed.

We don't have any of these early Italian recipes, the way we have early English and French recipes, but evidence for the Italian innovation comes from French ice cream makers like Nicolas Audiger who reported having to travel to Italy to learn how to make ices. Soon afterward the Italians also figured out that common salt worked better than saltpeter for freezing (salt is a smaller molecule than saltpeter; the smaller the molecule, the more ions from each gram of solute interfere with freezing); by 1665 the English chemist Robert Boyle said that "a Mixture of Snow and Salt" was the method "much employ'd" in Italy to chill drinks and fruit, "though little known, and less us'd here in *England*."

By the 1700s European languages had settled on names for the new invention, with the French word *sorbet* and Italian *sorbetto*, the linguistic descendants of the Turkish word *sherbet*, now defined as frozen fruit ices rather than syrups. Ice cream was given completely new names, made from words meaning "frozen" (Italian *gelato*), or "ice" (German *Eis*, French *glace*, and our own *ice cream*).

Sherbet, sorbet, syrup, and ice cream aren't the only modern descendants of these ancient sharabs and sharbats. The English word *shrub* used to be the name of a lime-sugar syrup, and also a drink made by sailors by combining the syrup with rum or arrack. In fact spirits historian David Wondrich suspects the presence of shrub on board British ships as a scurvy preventative may have influenced the invention of punch, the world's first cocktail. Shrub became widespread in eighteenth- and nineteenth-century United States, where raspberries were much more common than lemons. Raspberry shrub was made by boiling down raspberries, vinegar, and sugar into a syrup, which was bottled and then drunk with cold water in the summer.

Raspberry Shrub (1834)

Raspberry Shrub mixed with water is a pure, delicious drink for summer; and in a country where raspberries are abundant, it is good economy to make it answer instead of Port and Catalonia wine. Put raspberries in a pan, and scarcely cover them with strong vinegar. Add a pint of sugar to a pint of juice . . . scald it, skim it, and bottle it when cold.

As for the word *sherbet*, in the United States it refers to a low-dairy version of ice cream; the FDA requires that sherbet have very low (1 to 2 percent) milkfat and recipes for homemade sherbet generally use milk instead of cream (still distinguished from sorbets, which have no dairy at all).

But sherbet still retains something of its old meaning in Britain, where powders were preferred to syrups as early as the 1840s, when street vendors in London sold what was called "lemonade" or "Persian sherbet," but which were just lemon-flavored powders mixed with water. These powders used sodium carbonate to add a delightful fizz. Here's a recipe a street vendor gave journalist Henry Mayhew at the time:

Lemonade

1 lb. of carbonate of soda
1 lb. of tartaric acid
1 lb. of loaf-sugar
essence of lemon

The vendors kept the mixed powders in a jar, and for a ha'penny would mix a spoonful into a glass of water drawn from a stone jar, to produce what Mayhew called an "effervescing draught."

Modern sherbet powder is now sold in Britain as a candy powder to be eaten, very much like the Pixy Stix or Pop Rocks that kids eat here. With candies like Pop Rocks the effervescence comes from pressured carbon dioxide. The sourness, of Pop Rocks, Kool-Aid, Tang, or the powdered lemonade of my own childhood, however, still comes from tartaric, citric, or malic acid.

Tartaric acid and citric acid are yet other examples of borrowing from the Muslim world. Tartaric acid was first distilled from wine-making residue, and citric acid from citrus, by the Persian and Arab chemists of the eighth to tenth centuries. Citric and phosphoric acids are the source of the perkiness in modern Coke and Pepsi and 7UP as well, sodas that were originally nineteenth-century drugstore patent syrups full of medicinal ingredients not so different from the thirteenth-century Cairo apothecary syrups that began our story. (Some of these ingredients have their own linguistic history; "cola" comes from the kola nut, a caffeine-rich nut traded by the Mandé and other people of West Africa since the fourteenth century, and brought to the New World with slavery.)

Oh and you might even have heard of the word we used to use in English for those apothecary sugar syrups. The word was *julep*, from the Persian word *gulab* (rosewater). It's been a word for medicinal syrup since 1400, although by now we just use it in one drink, that delightful summer refresher at the Kentucky Derby, the mint julep.

In other words, every one of the icy refreshments of our summer: ice cream, gelato, sorbet, sherbet, lemonade, sodas, mint juleps (not to mention marmalade) are children of the medieval summer syrups and sharbats of the Muslim world. Even the modern instant drinks that I mixed up from spoonfuls of powders in the suburban California summers of my childhood date back 500 years, through the street vendors of early Victorian London, all the way to the street sellers of sixteenth-century Turkey and Persia.

Something beautiful was created as saltpeter and snow, sherbet and salt, were passed along and extended from the Chinese to the Arabs to the Mughals to the Neapolitans, to create the sweet lusciousness of ice cream. And it's a nice thought that saltpeter, applied earlier to war, became the key hundreds of years later to inventing something that makes us all smile on a hot summer day.

On the way home from Dolores Park last summer, Janet and I stopped at a neighbor's to get a glass of lemonade from the stand their kids had set up in front of the garage. I guess we still sell sharbats on the street here too.

Twelve

Does This Name Make Me Sound Fat?

Why Ice Cream and Crackers Have Different Names

SO FAR, WE'VE seen a lot hidden in the language of food. The Chinese history of ketchup and the Muslim histories of sherbet, macaroons, and escabeche tell us about the crucial role of the East in the creation of the West. The way we use words like *heirloom*, *a la*, *delicious*, or *exotic* on menus tells us about how we think about social class and about the nature of food advertising. But although we've talked about food words in terms of their history and the adjectives we use to describe them, I've said nothing so far about the sound of the food words themselves.

Why would the sound of a food word tell us anything? It's not obvious why the sounds in the name of a word might be suggestive of, say, the taste or smell of the food. Shakespeare expressed this skepticism most beautifully in *Romeo and Juliet*:

> *What's in a name? that which we call a rose*
> *By any other name would smell as sweet;*

Juliet is expressing the theory we call *conventionalism*: that a name for something is just an agreed upon convention. English uses the word *egg*, but Cantonese calls it *daan*, and Italian *uovo*, but if accidentally it had evolved the other way around, it would be fine as long as everyone agreed. The alternative view, that there is something about a name that fits the object naturally, that some names might naturally "sound more sweet" than others, is called *naturalism*.

Conventionalism is the norm in modern linguistics, because we have found that the sounds that make up a word don't generally tell you what the word means. Linguists phrase this by saying that the relation between sound and meaning is "arbitrary," a word first used by political philosopher John Locke in *An Essay Concerning Human Understanding*. Locke pointed out that if there were a necessary relationship between sound and meaning, all languages would have the same words for everything, and the word for egg in English and Italian would be the same as the Chinese word.

A moment's thought suggests another reason that conventionalism makes more sense than naturalism, at least for spoken (as opposed to signed) languages: spoken languages only have around 50 or so distinct "phones" (the distinct sounds that make up the sound structure of a language) and obviously have a lot more ideas to express than 50.

But 2500 years ago in the *Cratylus*, Plato points out that there are reasonable arguments for naturalism as well as conventionalism. Socrates first agrees with Cratylus's position that there is an "inherently correct" name for everything for "both Greeks and barbarians." One way to be natural or "inherently correct" is to use letters consistent with the meaning of the word. For example the letter o (omicron) is round, and "therefore there is plenty of omicron mixed up in the word *goggulon* (round)." Similarly, words with the sound r (Greek rho, ρ, which was pronounced as a rolling trilled r like modern Spanish) often mean something related to motion (*rhein* [flow], *rhoe* [current], *tromos* [trembling]).

But then Socrates turns right around and argues for the conventionalist position of Hermogenes by noting, for example, that even in different dialects of Greek words are pronounced differently, suggesting that convention is needed after all.

Linguistics as a discipline followed this latter line of reasoning, and

Ferdinand de Saussure, the Geneva professor who is one of the fathers of modern linguistics, made the principle of the "arbitrariness of the sign" a foundation of our field. But research in the last few decades, following the earlier lead of giants of linguistics from the past century like Otto Jespersen and Roman Jakobson, has shown us that there was something to naturalism after all: sometimes the sounds of a name are in fact associated with the tastes of food.

We call the phenomenon of sounds carrying meaning *sound symbolism*. Sound symbolism has ramifications beyond its deep philosophical and linguistic interest. Like other linguistic cues to marketing strategies sounds are crucial to food marketing and branding.

Sound symbolism has been most deeply studied with vowels, and in particular the difference between two classes of vowels, *front vowels* and *back vowels*, which are named depending on the position of the tongue when articulating the vowels.

The vowels i (the vowel in the words *cheese* or *teeny*) and ɪ (pronounced as in *mint* or *thin*) are front vowels. Front vowels, roughly speaking, are made by holding the tongue high up in the front part of the mouth. The figure below left shows a very schematic cutaway of the head, with the lips and teeth on the left, and the tongue high up toward the front of the mouth.

By contrast, the vowel ɑ (as in *large*, *pod*, or *on*) is a low back vowel;

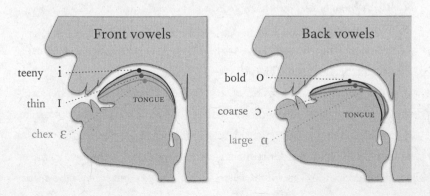

this sound is made by holding the tongue lower in the back part of the mouth; other back vowels are o (as in *bold*) and ɔ (as in the word *coarse* or my mother's New York pronunciation of *caught*). The figure at right on the preceding page shows a very schematic tongue position for these vowels; lower in general, and more toward the back of the throat.

A number of studies over the last 100 years or so have shown that front vowels in many languages tend to be used in words that refer to small, thin, light things, and back vowels in words that refer to big, fat, heavy things. It's not always true—there are certainly exceptions— but it's a tendency that you can see in any of the stressed vowels in words like *little*, *teeny*, or *itsy-bitsy* (all front vowels) versus *humongous* or *enormous* (back vowels). Or the i vowel in Spanish *chico* (front vowel, meaning "small") versus the ɔ in *gordo* (back vowel, meaning "fat"). Or French *petit* (front vowel) versus *grand* (back vowel).

In one marketing study, for example, Richard Klink created pairs of made-up product brand names that were identical except for having front vowels (*detal*) or back vowels (*dutal*) and asked participants to answer:

> *Which brand of laptop seems bigger, Detal or Dutal?*
> *Which brand of vacuum cleaner seems heavier, Keffi or Kuffi?*
> *Which brand of ketchup seems thicker, Nellen or Nullen?*
> *Which brand of beer seems darker, Esab or Usab?*

In each case, the product named with back vowels (Dutal, Nullen) was chosen as the larger, heavier, thicker product.

Since ice cream is a product whose whole purpose is to be rich, creamy, and heavy, it is not surprising that people seem to prefer ice creams that are named with back vowels. Eric Yorkston and Geeta Menon at New York University asked participants to read a press release describing a new ice cream about to be released. For half, the ice cream was called "Frish" (front vowel) while for the other half it was called "Frosh" (back vowel). Asked their opinions, the "Frosh" people rated this hypothetical ice cream as smoother, creamier, and richer than other participants rated "Frish," and were more likely to say they would buy it.

In a final twist, Yorkston and Menon distracted some participants by having them perform another task simultaneously, so they couldn't fully concentrate on reading about the ice cream. The distracted participants were even more influenced by the vowels, suggesting that the response to the vowels was automatic, at a subconscious level.

I wondered whether commercial ice creams make use of this subconscious association of ice cream names with back vowels as richer and creamier. To find out, I ran what University of Pennsylvania linguist Mark Liberman calls a Breakfast Experiment. Liberman—a tenacious advocate for bringing linguistics to bear on public affairs—often runs a quick experiment on a linguistic tip in the news before breakfast, posting the results on *Language Log*, the "blog of record" in linguistics. He is legendary for his ability to run complex linguistic statistical analyses in minutes, which he says comes from his days as a piano tuner.

My hypothesis was that we would see more back vowels in names of

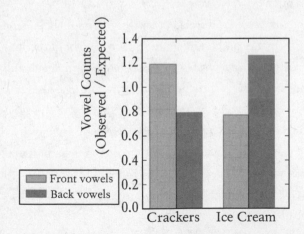

Front versus back vowels in cracker names and ice cream flavors (normalized by dividing by the expected count of front and back vowels computed from a large dictionary of English)

ice cream brands or flavors, and conversely that thin, light foods like crackers would have more front vowels.

I tested the hypothesis on two lists of food names from the web, the 81 ice cream flavors sold by either Haagen Dazs or Ben & Jerry's, and a list of 592 cracker brands from a dieting website. For each list, I counted the total number of front vowels (i, ɪ, ɛ, e, æ) and the total number of back vowels.

The result? As shown in the chart on the preceding page, I found more back vowels in ice cream names like Rocky Road, Jamoca Almond Fudge, Chocolate, Caramel, Cookie Dough, Coconut and front vowels in cracker names (note the extraordinary number of ɪ vowels) like Cheese Nips, Cheez It, Wheat Thins, Pretzel Thins, Ritz, Krispy, Triscuit, Thin Crisps, Cheese Crisps, Chicken in a Biskit, Snack Sticks, Ritz bits.

Of course there are exceptions: vanilla (the orange blossom of our day), has an ɪ. But most of the front vowels in ice cream flavors tend to be the names of small, thin ingredients in the ice cream (thin mint, chip, peanut brittle).

Sound symbolism is thus an important device in the toolbox of modern advertisers and designers of brand names, and in fact branding companies often get their insights from linguists.

While our ice cream and cracker connections might be subconscious, they are systematic, and linguists have theories about the underlying cause: about why front vowels are associated with small, thin, light things, and back vowels with big, solid, heavy things.

The most widely accepted theory, the *frequency code*, suggests that low frequencies (sounds with low pitch) and high frequencies (sounds with high pitch) are associated with particular meanings. The frequency code was developed by linguist John Ohala (my phonetics professor as an undergraduate at Berkeley) by extending work by Eugene Morton of the Smithsonian.

Morton noticed that mammals and birds tend to use low-frequency (deeper) sounds when they are aggressive or hostile, but use higher-frequency (higher-pitched) sounds when frightened, appeasing, or friendly. Because larger animals naturally make deeper sounds (the roar of lions) and smaller animals naturally make high-pitched sounds (the tweet of birds), Morton's idea is that animals try to appear larger when they are competing or aggressive, but smaller and less threatening otherwise.

Morton and Ohala thus suggest that humans instinctively associate the pitch of sounds with size. All vowels are composed of different frequency resonances. When the tongue is high and in the front of the mouth, it creates a small cavity in front. Small cavities cause higher-pitched resonances (the smaller the space for vibration, the shorter the wavelength, hence the higher the frequency). One particular resonance (called the second formant) is much higher for front vowels and lower for back vowels.

Thus the frequency code suggests that front vowels like ɪ and i are associated with small, thin, things, and back vowels like a and o with big heavy things because front vowels have higher-pitched resonances, and we instinctively associate higher pitch with smaller animals, and by extension smaller things in general.

Researchers have extended this idea to show that raising pitch or "fronting" vowels (moving the tongue a bit toward the front of mouth to make all vowels have a slightly higher second formant pitch) are both especially associated with babies or children. In an early paper I examined more than 60 languages around the world and proposed that the word endings used in many languages to indicate smallness or lightness come historically from a word originally meaning "child" or associated with names of children, like the *y* in pet names Barbie and Robby. My linguistics colleague Penny Eckert shows that front vowels are associated with positive affect, and that preadolescent girls sometimes use vowel fronting to subtly imbue their speech with sweetness or childhood innocence. Linguist Katherine Rose Geenberg found that speakers of American English move their vowels toward the front when using baby talk, and psychologist Anne Fernald shows that, across languages, talk to babies tends to have high pitch.

The frequency code isn't the only kind of sound symbolism in food. To see why, we'll need a brief digression. Consider these two pictures:

Suppose I told you that in the Martian language one of these two was called bouba and the other was called kiki and you had to guess which was which. Think for a second. Which picture is bouba? Which kiki? How about maluma versus takete?

If you're like most people, you called the jagged picture on the left *kiki* (or *takete*) and the round one on the right *bouba* (or *maluma*). This test was invented by German psychologist Wolfgang Köhler, one of the founders of Gestalt psychology, in 1929. Linguists and psychologists have repeated this experiment using all sorts of made-up words with sounds like bouba and kiki, and no matter what language they study, from Swedish to Swahili to a remote nomadic population of northern Namibia, and even in toddlers two and a half years old, the results are astonishingly consistent. There seems to be something about jagged shapes that makes people call them *kiki* and rounder curvy shapes that is somehow naturally *bouba*.

The link to food comes from the lab of Oxford psychologist Charles Spence, one of the world's foremost researchers in sensory perception. In a number of recent papers, Spence and his colleagues have studied the link between the taste of different foods, the curved and jagged pictures, and words like *maluma/takete*.

In one paper, for example, Spence, Mary Kim Ngo, and Reeva Misra asked people to eat a piece of chocolate and say whether the taste better matched the words *maluma* or *takete*. People eating milk chocolate (Lindt extra creamy 30 percent cocoa) said the taste fit the word *maluma* (and also matched the curvier figure). People eating dark chocolate (Lindt 70 percent and 90 percent cocoa) instead chose the word *takete* (and matched the jagged figure). In another paper they found similar results for carbonation; carbonated water was perceived as more "kiki" (and spiky) and still water was perceived as more "bouba" (and curvy). In other words, words with m and l sounds like *maluma* were associated with creamier or gentler tastes and words with t and k sounds like *takete* were associated with bitter or carbonated tastes.

These associations are very similar to what I also found with consonants in ice cream and cracker names. I found that l and m occurred more often in ice cream names, while t and d occurred more often in cracker names.

So what is it about bouba and maluma that people associate with visual images of round and curvy, or tastes of creamy and smooth, while kiki and takete are associated with jagged visual images and sharp, bitter, and sour tastes? Recent work by a number of linguists studied exactly which sounds seem to be causing the effects.

One reasonable proposal for what's going on has to do with continuity and smoothness. Sounds like m, l, and r, called *continuants* because they are continuous and smooth acoustically (the sound is pretty consistent across its whole length), are more closely associated with smoother figures. By contrast, *strident* sounds that abruptly start and stop, like t and k, are associated with the spiky figures. The consonant t has the most distinct jagged burst of energy of any consonant in English.

To help you visualize this, look at the display on the following page of the sound waves from a recording that I made of myself saying "maluma" followed by "takete." Note the relatively smooth wave for maluma, which has a relatively smooth flow of air. By contrast, the three sharp discontinuities in takete on the right occurred when I said the sounds t

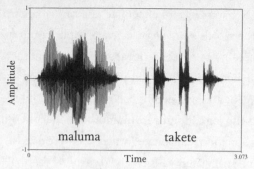

The waveform (sound waves) of me saying "maluma"
and "takete"

and k; for each of these consonants, the airflow is briefly blocked by the tongue in the mouth, and then a little burst of air explodes out.

What I call the synesthetic hypothesis suggests that the perception of acoustic smoothness by one of our five senses, hearing, is somehow linked to the perception of smoothness by two other senses: vision (seeing a curvy figure instead of a jagged one) and taste (tasting a creamy instead of sharp taste).

Synesthesia is the general name for the phenomenon of strong associations between the different senses. Some people, like Dan Slobin, a Berkeley professor of psychology and linguistics, are very strong synesthetes. For Slobin, each musical key is associated with a color: C major is pink, C minor is dark red tinged with black. But the bouba/kiki results suggest that, to at least some extent, we are all a little bit synesthetic. Something about our senses of taste/smell, vision, and hearing are linked at least enough so that what is smooth in one is associated with being smooth in another, so that we feel the similarity between sharpness detected by smell (as in cheddar), sharpness detected by touch or vision (like acute angles), and sharpness detected by hearing (abrupt changes in sound).

We can see this link between the senses even in our daily vocabulary. The words *sharp* and *pungent* both originally meant something tactile and visual: something that feels pointy or subtends a small visual angle, but both words can be applied to tastes and smells as well.

It's not clear to what extent these synesthetic links are innate or genetic, and to what extent they are cultural. For example, nomadic tribes in Namibia do associate takete with spiky pictures, but, unlike speakers of many other languages, they don't associate either the word or the pictures with the bitterness of dark chocolate or with carbonation. This suggests that the fact that we perceive bitter chocolate as "sharper" than milk chocolate or carbonated water as "sharper" than flat water is a metaphor that we learn culturally to associate with these foods. But we really don't know yet, because we are just at the beginning of understanding these aspects of perception.

There are, however, some evolutionary implications of the synesthetic smoothness hypothesis and of the frequency code.

John Ohala suggests that the link of high pitch with deference or friendliness may explain the origin of the smile, which is similarly associated with appeasing or friendly behavior. The way we make a smile is by retracting the corners of the mouth. Animals like monkeys also retract the corners of their mouths to express submission, and use the opposite facial expression (Ohala calls it the "o-face"), in which the corners of the mouth are drawn forward with the lips possibly protruding, to indicate aggression.

Retracting the corners of the mouth shrinks the size of the front cavity in the mouth, just like the vowels I or i. In fact, the similarity in mouth position between smiling and the vowel i explains why we say "cheese" when we take pictures; i is the smiling vowel.

Ohala's theory is thus that smiling was originally an appeasement gesture, meaning something like "don't hurt little old me." It evolved when mammals were in competitive situations as a way to make the voice sound more high pitched and the smiler appear smaller and less aggressive, and hence friendlier.

Both the frequency code and the synesthetic smoothness hypothesis may also be related to the origin of language. If some kinds of meaning are iconically related to sounds in the way that these hypotheses suggest, it might have been a way for speakers to get across concepts to hearers early on in the evolution of language. The origins of language remain a deep mystery. We do, however, have some hypotheses, like the "bow-wow" theory of language evolution, the idea that language emerged at least partly by copying nature, naming dogs after their bark and cats after their meow and so on. The frequency code suggests that perhaps one of the earliest words created by some cavewoman had high pitched i sounds that meant "baby," or low pitched α sounds that meant "big," or perhaps was an acoustically abrupt *kikiki* meaning "sharp." Such iconic concepts are only a small part of the vast number of things we talk about using language, but iconicity still may help us understand some of these crucial early bootstrappings of human language.

Whatever their early origins, vowels and consonants have become part of a rich and beautiful system for expressing complex meanings by combining sounds into words, just as smiling has evolved into a means of expressing many shades of happiness, love, and much else.

Whatever hidden meanings words and smiles may have, in the end there is always ice cream, as a much later bard, Wallace Stevens, told us:

> *Let be be finale of seem.*
> *The only emperor is the emperor of ice-cream.*

Thirteen

Why the Chinese Don't Have Dessert

IN TRENDY SAN FRANCISCO, the latest hip dessert is ice cream made with unusual flavors, like the banana-bacon ice cream served at Humphry Slocombe down on Twenty-Fourth Street. Bacon has been appearing on all sorts of desserts for some time now: bacon brownies, candied bacon, bacon peanut brittle. The donut shop down the street even has bacon-maple donuts. Now I'm sympathetic to the argument, made most persuasively by Janet, that bacon makes everything better. But I think that's not the only reason for bacon's dessert popularity: there's something else going on that's causing the hipster trend for all these bacon desserts. To solve the mystery, let's begin by tracing dessert back to its early origins.

First of all, dessert doesn't just mean "sweet food." A donut on the way to the gym is not dessert; it's just a lack of willpower. A dessert is a sweet course that's part of a meal, and eaten at the end.

The placement at the end of the meal is expressed in the etymology: the word *dessert* comes from French, where it is the participle of *desservir*, "to de-serve," that is, "to remove what has been served." The word was first used in France in 1539 and meant what you ate after the meal had been cleared away; spiced wine called *hippocras* accompanied by fresh or dried fruit, crisp thin wafers, or candied spices or nuts called *comfits* or *dragées*. Such dessert courses under various names have a long medieval tradition, occurring in the very first menu we still have for an English feast, from around 1285, where after "the table is taken away" the guests are served dragées and "plenty of wafers." (*Dragée* is still the technical term for a confection with a hard candied shell like Jordan almonds or M&Ms.)

But the word *dragée* and the tradition of eating light sweets with wine after dinner dates back far earlier than the Middle Ages. Dragée comes from the Greek word *tragemata*, which historian Andrew Dalby tells us was the name for the snacks eaten with wine in classical Greece after the table was cleared after a meal. A "second table" was set with wine and tragemata: cakes, fresh and dried fruits, nuts, sweets, and chickpeas and other beans.

Like comfits or dragées, their medieval descendants, however, tragemata were really snacks rather than what we now call dessert. In fact, Herodotus remarked in the fifth century BCE in his *Histories* that the dessert-loving Persians mocked the Greeks for not really having any proper desserts at all:

> *[The Persians] have few solid dishes, but many served up after as dessert ["epiphorēmata"], and these not in a single course; and for this reason the Persians say that the Hellenes leave off dinner hungry, because after dinner they have nothing worth mentioning served up as dessert, whereas if any good dessert were served up they would not stop eating so soon.*

It was the Persians whose love of desserts was the impetus that eventually changed these simple wafers and nuts into our modern desserts. Baghdad was established in a formerly Persian part of Mesopotamia, and a culinary new wave developed, as the great chefs of the Caliphs borrowed and enriched Persian desserts like the sweet almond pastry lauzīnaj and starch candy *fālūdhaj*, sour dishes like sikbāj, and the many sweet stews.

From the earliest menus we have, these sweet dishes tended to congregate roughly toward the end of the meal, a property likely derived from their origin in Baghdad. The ordering probably comes from medieval models of health and digestion; sweets were believed to help digest heavy food. Baghdad cookbooks from the very first one, the al-Warrāq's *Kitab al-Tabikh*, written in Baghdad c. 950–1000, place all the sweet puddings and fritters, lauzīnaj, and crepes at the end of the meal. This is most mouthwatering to see in the fabulous meals of medieval Arabic literature like *One Thousand and One Nights*, which end in dessert after dessert, like the meal from the "Tale of Judar and His Brothers" of

> *roasted chicken, roast meat, rice with honey, pilaf, sausages, stuffed lamb breast, nutty kunāfa swimming in bee's honey, ẓulābiyya "donuts," qatā'if pancakes folded around a sweet nut filling, and baklava.*

In "The Tale of the Sixth Brother," after serving meat porridge, goose stew in vinegar, and marinated chicken fattened on pistachio nuts, the host presses his guest to take dessert. "Take this dish away and bring the sweets," he says, offering almond conserve and fritters flavored with musk and "dripping with syrup" and almond jelly.

In medieval Muslim al-Andalus the man who was credited for bringing these things west from Baghdad was Ziryab, a musician who arrived in 822 at the court of Abd-al-rahman II of Cordoba. Ziryab was the inventor of the Andalusian musical form. Legend says that he memorized tens of thousands of songs and that he stayed up all night discussing composition with the Jinns. Ziryab was said to have first proposed that meals be served in courses, starting with a lamb soup he invented called *tafaya* made with almonds and cilantro. The eleventh-century Córdoba historian Ibn Hayyan tells us that people even credited Ziryab with "inventing" many of the fabled desserts of al-Andalus like lauzīnaj and qatayif that came from Baghdad. Ziryab seems to have personified in these legends both the glories of Al-Andalus and the rich foods of the eastern court at Baghdad.

A few hundred years later, a thirteenth-century Andalusian cookbook specifies that meals be served in seven courses, beginning with this tafaya (because it was particularly "healthy") and ending with three courses of desserts and egg dishes. And the first Spanish cookbook published after the Reconquista, Roberto de Nola's 1525 *Libro de Coʒina*, says that meals at court still begin with soup and end with sweets and fruit.

These fabulous foods spread to Europe, mainly through Muslim Andalusia and Sicily. The *Manuscrito Anonimo*, a medieval cookbook from Muslim Andalusia, gives recipes for dishes like *ʒirbaja*, an originally sweet-and-sour chicken stew, *jullabiyya*, chicken made with rose-syrup (*sharâb al-jullâb*, from the Persian word for rose), or lamb stewed with quince, vinegar, saffron, and coriander. These dishes were copied across Europe, first in Sicily, Naples, and England (all run by the Normans) and what we think of as "medieval" food developed: meat dishes seasoned with dried fruits, ginger, rosewater, and other Middle Eastern spices. The very first cookbook in English, the *Forme of Cury*, has recipes for rabbits in sugar, ginger, and raisins, or with honey and saffron; ground pork or chicken with dates in wine and sugar; and dishes like *mawmanee* and *blankmaunger* (savory puddings of sweetened boiled rice and almond milk with capon or fish that come from the medieval Arab dish *ma'muniyya*).

Throughout Europe, however, the tendency of sweet dishes to be served toward the end of the meal was not yet a strict requirement in the Middle Ages. Many sweet dishes were served in the middle of the meal, and savories like capon pie or venison at the end. In fact the drop in the price of sugar around the turn of the sixteenth century led to an increase in sweet recipes throughout the meal (as well as linguistic consequences—"sweet" was one of Shakespeare's favorite adjectives). Savory and sweet were intermingled, and a leg of mutton might be simmered with lemons, currants, and sugar, or chicken might be served with sorrel, cinnamon, and sugar, as in the following recipe for "Chekyns upon soppes" (basically chicken on cinnamon toast) from the 1545 early Tudor cookbook *A Propre Newe Booke of Cokerye*:

Chekyns upon soppes.

Take sorel sauce a good quantitie
and put in Sinamon and suger
and lette it boyle
and poure it upon the soppes
then laie on the chekyns.

From their medieval position scattered throughout the latter half of the meal, however, sweet foods began to move slowly toward their modern place at the very end of the meal. Culinary historian Jean-Louis Flandrin carefully annotated the presence of sugar in French recipes over time, and found a sharp drop in the use of sugar in meat and fish dishes as French cuisine developed from the fourteenth to the eighteenth century, corresponding to a rise in sweet desserts. The use of sugar and fruits with meat, still prevalent in Moroccan, Persian, Central Asian, and even parts of Eastern European cuisine, slowly began to die out in France.

The year 1600 marks about the halfway point in this transition toward a modern meal; at this time, French meat dishes were still often sweetened and *dessert* mainly still used to mean a light after-dinner snack or nuts, especially fruit or nuts. We know this from the first mention of dessert in 1612 in English, where it is described as a foreign "French" word in an early health and dietetics manual, William Vaughan's *Natvrall and Artificial Directions for Health*: "such eating, which the French call desert, is vnnaturall, being contrary to Physicke or Dyet."

You might applaud Vaughan's early warning about fat and sugar in rich "foreign" desserts, but in fact dessert still didn't yet mean all those rich foods. Vaughan was referring to fresh fruit, and expressing concern about how hard it was to digest fruit at the end of the meal unless it was thoroughly cooked. This is an opinion that my Grandma Anna would have thoroughly agreed with; dinner at her apartment in the Bronx meant boiled chicken or boiled fish with boiled potatoes, and boiled fruit for dessert. When she visited us in California in the 1970s she would pick luscious ripe apricots and peaches from the trees and promptly boil them for compote.

By a hundred years later, in the eighteenth century, the word *dessert* was borrowed into both British and American English. In British English the word retained its meaning of a light after-course. Given the American attitude toward food (something on the order of "Why eat an apple when you can eat an entire plate of cake and ice cream with whipped cream and chocolate syrup instead?"), you will not be shocked to know that by the time of our revolution, the word had shifted here to include more substantial sweet fare like cakes, pies, and ice cream. We know this because George and Martha Washington threw a party after Washington's New York City inauguration of 1789, at their Manhattan mansion on Cherry Street, and Pennsylvania Senator William Maclay put down the menu in his diary: "The dessert was, first apple pies, puddings, etc.; then iced creams, jellies, etc.; then water-melons, musk-melons, apples, peaches, nuts."

By the nineteenth and twentieth century, the idea that sweet things belong only in the dessert course became relatively strict in the classical French cuisine represented by Escoffier. There were exceptions, but they were specific, like Escoffier's *canard a l'orange*, and the vogue, especially after the rise of Nouvelle Cuisine, for duck magret with cherries or pan-seared foie gras with grapes or fruit conserves.

In American food the boundary is a bit less rigid, as Catalan super-chef Ferran Adrià once observed ("A hamburger with ketchup and Coca-Cola? That's the most intense symbiosis of sweet and savory imaginable"). And there are further remnants of medieval tastes in meats, what historian Ken Albala calls "throwbacks"—sweet-and-sour in barbecue, brown sugar and cloves for hams, fruit sauces with duck, or meats with cranberry sauce, apple sauce, and candied yams—preserved mainly in old-fashioned meals like Christmas and Thanksgiving. The great anthropologist Sidney W. Mintz, who pioneered the modern anthropology of food, notes that these fragments "demonstrate what anthropologists have long contended—that holidays often preserve what the everyday loses."

Besides these exceptional cases, however, we generally eat the savory things earlier in the meal and the sweet things for dessert.

Tracing the history of dessert demonstrated that a procession of the meal through savory courses with a sweet course at the end is a recent development in European cuisine. In other words, this particular sequence, and the idea of dessert, is something that some cuisines have (modern American, ancient Persian) and some don't (classical Greek and, as we will see, Chinese).

To explain how and in what way cuisines are different or similar, and how they change over time, I propose a theory called the "grammar of cuisine," which suggests that a cuisine is like a language. The metaphor comes from linguistic grammar. The grammar of English, for example, consists of implicit rules that specify that adjectives tend to come before nouns (we say "hot fudge," not "fudge hot"), or objects come after verbs ("eat chocolate" not "chocolate eat"). A grammar defines how linguistic parts are structured into a linguistic whole.

Just as a language has an implicit grammar that native speakers know even if they can't explain, a cuisine has an implicit structure, a set of rules about which foods go together, what constitutes a "grammatical" dish or meal in that cuisine. This implicit structure of cuisine consists of rules about how dishes are structured out of ingredients, meals are structured out of dishes, and entire cuisines out of particular flavor combinations and required cooking techniques. Each of these kinds of structuring helps explain the nature of cuisines and their similarities and differences.

We've already seen one aspect of the grammar of cuisine: the ordering of meals. One constraint of American and European cuisine is "dessert comes at the end" and another, related to entrée, the default ordering of the American dinner, which we might represent as a kind of "rule" with sequence of dishes (using parentheses to indicate optional dishes):

American dinner = (salad or appetizer)   main/entrée   (dessert)

This rule states that an American dinner consists of a main course, preceded by an optional salad or appetizer (or both), and possibly followed by dessert.

By contrast, French cuisine makes use of a cheese course, and a light green salad is often eaten after the main rather than before (and of course dessert at the end or, as the French say, *salé puis sucré*);

French dinner = (entrée)   plat   (salade)   (fromage)   (dessert)

Even moving one country over in Europe things change again; Italian cuisine has a distinct course (*primo*) that often consists of pasta or risotto:

Italian dinner = (antipasto) primo secondo (insalata) (formaggi) (dolce)

Some shifts in the ordering of the American meal are even more recent. Americans used to eat salad later in the meal, much as the French still do. The late MFK Fisher, one of America's greatest prose stylists and my favorite food writer, suggests that the modern custom of eating salad before the main course arose in California in the early twentieth century. Fisher grew up in Whittier, just east of Los Angeles, around the First World War, eating fresh lettuce salad before the meal, and writes that her "Western" custom of starting a meal with salad shocked her friends from the East Coast who all ate salad after. (Meals on the East Coast in the first half of the twentieth century might instead begin with grapefruit, a custom that my other New York grandmother, Grandma Bessie, kept to all her life.)

Despite the differences outlined above, the American and Western European meal sequences are pretty similar. By contrast, in Chinese cuisine a dessert course is not part of a meal at all. There was traditionally no exact Chinese word for dessert. The most frequently used modern translation, *tihm ban* 甜品 in Cantonese, or *tian dian* 甜点 in Mandarin, is most likely an extension, via borrowing from the West, of a word originally just referring to sweet snacks, not to dessert. The end of a traditional Cantonese meal, for example, is instead often marked by a serving of savory soup, or only occasionally (after the table is cleared) by fresh fruit.

This explains why the tradition of fortune cookies developed in America as dessert. Jennifer 8. Lee's *The Fortune Cookie Chronicles* tells us that little snacks stuffed with fortunes have been eaten in Japan since the nineteenth century. But only in the twentieth century in California did they begin to be served in Japanese and then Chinese restaurants as a dessert. The grammar of cuisine explains why: Chinese cuisine traditionally had no dessert course, and fortune cookies filled a kind of evolutionary niche for the final sweet cravings of American diners.

The lack of dessert also explains why baking and hence ovens have a much smaller role in Chinese cuisine; there were no ovens in my kitchens in China, and even now Janet's mom uses the oven in her kitchen in the San Gabriel Valley as a convenient place to store pots.

Of course Chinese cuisine does have sweet foods, like the lovely sweet soups called *tong sui* 糖水 (literally "sugar waters"), which *can* now be served as desserts, but more often act like snacks or small late-night meals. Janet and I often enjoy a one a.m. snack at my favorite sweet soup restaurant, Kowloon Tong out on Geary: the peanut soup called *fa seng wu* (花生糊) with rice dumplings (*tongyun* 汤圆), tofu curds with honey, red bean soup, tortoise jelly, although I'm not quite as fond of the Chinese red dates with frog fallopian tubes (don't ask).

While Chinese meals don't have the concept of a final sweet course, they do have structure of a different sort: constraints on the ingredients and their combination. A Cantonese meal, for example, consists of starch (rice, noodles, porridge) and nonstarch portions (the vegetables, meat, tofu, and so on). These can be mixed together in one dish (to form chow mein, chow fen, fried rice, and so on) or a meal can use plain white rice with the nonstarch served as separate dishes that each eater serves over their own portion of rice. Describing this in English requires the awkward word "nonstarch"; Cantonese has a word for this, *sung* 餸. The word for "grocery shopping" in Cantonese is *mai sung*: "buying sung" (since the starch is a staple that would already be in the house). Thus a typical Cantonese meal consists of a starch plus a *sung* 餸, or, to write a different kind of grammar rule, we might say:

meal = starch + sung

The grammar of cuisine does more than define the structure of a meal. Each cuisine also has implicit rules about the flavors that make up individual dishes. I like to think of dishes as words, and particular ingredients or flavor elements as the sounds (the "phones") that make up a word or dish.

Sounds differ from language to language, but they are also surprisingly similar. For example, every language seems to have a sound that's something like English *t* or English *p*. Why should this be? The late linguist Ken Stevens (in his *Quantal Theory of Speech*) explained that humans all have the same tongue and mouth physiology, and sounds like *t* result from certain configurations of the tongue (and lips, and vocal cords) that are easy for speakers to make reliably and also result in sounds that are easy for listeners to distinguish reliably.

Nonetheless, each language pronounces the universal *t* or *p* in a slightly different way. English *t* is different from Italian *t* or Cantonese *t*, French *p* is different from Spanish *p*. That's the main cause of our accents in foreign languages: we become expert at saying a *t* in the English way and it's hard to unlearn that and make a Japanese or a French *t*.

Similarly, based on a different aspect of the very same human tongues, the ability to perceive flavor elements like sweet, sour, bitter, salty, and umami are universal. But each cuisine may express these universal flavor elements using ingredients that add their own culturally specific flavors.

Each cuisine, for example, seems to have its own flavor element for sweet. My favorite is Malaysian *gula melaka*, a coconut palm sugar with a lightly smoky, caramelized taste. It's easy to find palm sugar here, but not good gula melaka, so I have to bring it back the rare times I'm there, or rely on generous visitors from Asia.

By contrast, the sweet taste of American food comes from refined white cane sugar or corn syrup, or, in special cases, maple syrup. In the gold rush days, San Franciscans instead used molasses for everything, pouring it on their food like ketchup. British and Commonwealth desserts often use golden syrup, Mexican cuisine raw piloncillo sugar, and Thai cuisine palmyra palm sugar.

The flavor elements for sour tend to be rice vinegars in China, tamarind in Southeast Asia, lemon juice or grain vinegar in the United States, sour orange or key lime in Central America, and wine vinegars in France (hence the name *vin-aigre* [sour wine]). Yiddish food is soured by crystals of citric acid called sour salt. This is what gives the sweet-and-sour flavor to my mom's cabbage stuffed with rice, beef, and tomatoes (a dish I love but that my father refers to as "beef in shrouds"). Other universal flavor elements include salt or umami (from sea salt, salted olives, capers, soy sauce, fish sauce, fermented shrimp paste, anchovies, and so on).

Not all flavor elements are universal. Combining different specific combinations of flavors is definitive of a cuisine, an idea that the late food scholar Elisabeth Rozin called the "flavor principle." She pointed out that a dish made with soy sauce, rice wine, and ginger tastes Chinese; the same ingredients flavored with sour orange, garlic, and achiote tastes Yucatecan. Add instead onion, chicken fat, and white pepper (or for baking, butter, cream cheese, and sour cream) and you've got my mother and grandmother's Yiddish recipes.

Recent work has used computational techniques on online databases of recipes to test cross-cuisine generalizations of Rozin's flavor principle at the molecular level. Y. Y. Ahn at Indiana University and his colleagues examined 60,000 online recipes to test the "food pairing hypothesis," a recent theory proposing that tasty recipes are more likely to combine ingredients that share flavor compounds. For example tomatoes and mozzarella share the compound 4-methylpentanoic acid. Ahn and his colleagues found an interesting difference between North American and Western European recipes, which do indeed tend to pair ingredients that share flavor compounds, and East Asian recipes, which combine ingredients (like beef, ginger, cayenne, pork, and onions) that don't have overlapping compounds. The difference suggests that preference for similar or different compounds may be part of what makes up a cuisine.

Interestingly, the East Asian lack of dessert seems to have played an important role in their results. They found that the North American ingredients with the most shared compounds are dessert ingredients like milk, butter, cocoa, vanilla, eggs, cream cheese, strawberries, and peanut butter. Thus it's possible that the difference in food pairing tendencies between East Asia and North America is caused by the fact that North America has dessert.

One last aspect of the grammar of cuisine has to do with cooking techniques rather than flavors. In Chinese cuisine, for example, ingredients need to be cooked before eating; a raw dish like a green salad just violates the structure of the cuisine. We might say that salad is "ungrammatical" in Chinese. Although salad is naturally now available in foreign restaurants (called *sa leut* in Cantonese), traditionally it would have been as bizarre in China to see someone munch on raw carrots or celery or bell peppers as it seems to most Americans to eat duck brains.

In early China cooking was associated with the concept of being civilized; neighboring cultures who ate their food raw were considered less civilized than those who cooked their food. The anthropologist Claude Lévi-Strauss suggested that this opposition between the raw and cooked is probably universal across cultures: that cooking is everywhere associated with civilization and with socializing and controlling nature.

But health is probably the most significant cause of the Chinese taboo on raw food, as suggested by the fact that even water is never consumed raw; it is always boiled before drinking. Drinking boiled water (and tea, with its antiseptic properties) presumably helped protect China from some of the water-transmitted epidemics suffered by the West. Americans and Europeans traditionally drank water raw, and partly as a consequence suffered epidemics of diseases like cholera until the nineteenth century when municipal water supplies began to be treated.

The Chinese cultural constraint against raw water runs very deep. Despite the fact that the municipal water in modern Hong Kong or Taipei is treated and perfectly safe and drinkable, people like my friend Fia who grew up in those very sophisticated cities still boil all their water, even keeping pitchers of preboiled water in the fridge.

The implicit cultural norms that make us think that desserts should be sweet, or that knishes should taste like chicken fat instead of butter, run just as deep. The discomfort of Fia in Taipei at the thought of drinking raw water, the shock of MFK Fisher's friends at salad occurring at the wrong place in a meal, the disgust at frog fallopian tubes or raw carrots come from the fact that a cuisine is a richly structured cultural object, with its component flavor elements and its set of combinatory grammatical principles, learned early and deeply.

I suspect that it is the grammar of cuisine that underlies the recent fad for pork in dessert. Bacon ice cream violates an implicit rule of American cuisine, the rule that says desserts should be sweet and not meaty and savory. We delight in bacon ice cream not because this is necessarily the most delicious way to serve bacon but, at least in part, because it breaks the rules, it's fun, it's rebellious, it's even . . . ungrammatical!

In fact, rebelling against these norms is one way that innovation happens. This is most evident with modernist cuisine ("molecular gastronomy" or "deconstructivist" cooking), which often uses ungrammatical dishes (popcorn soup, toffee of white chocolate and duck liver, caramelized tomato with hot raspberry jelly) as a creative tool. But consider as well the global borrowings that became our day-to-day foods like ketchup or ice cream or macaroons, borrowings that begin as an exotic import for the rich, and slowly became nativized. We haven't yet explained what drives this nativization, what causes the specific changes in each of these foods as they adapt to their new cuisine. The grammar of cuisine is the explanation: exotic imported luxury foods became everyday dishes by changing to fit the implicit structures of

cuisine. As medieval spices lost their centrality in the flavor principles of the food of Western Europe, macaroons and marmalades lost
their medieval rosewater and musk. As tomatoes with sugar became
one of Americas flavor principles (think ketchup, tomato soup, pasta
sauce), the sweet-and-sour tomatoey version of a former fish sauce
rocketed in popularity. Meanwhile in China, the grammar (remember
starch+sung) led the dominant use of tomatoes to be, not ketchup or
pasta sauce, but a stir-fry dish of tomatoes and eggs. The importance
in European cuisine of milk and cream led to Eastern sharbats becoming Western ice creams and American sherbets. Because of the Lenten
fasts central to the religion, culture, and diet of medieval Christianity,
sweet-and-sour meat sikbāj became fish and chips. Finally, as dessert
became an integral part of our cuisine, newly imported ingredients
led to new desserts like the macaroons, coconut cake, and ambrosia
from newly imported coconut, or the pecan pie from native American
foods like pecans. The grammar of cuisine even explains why fortune
cookies, originally a small Japanese temple snack, grew into a standard
dessert in American Chinese restaurants, filling the dessert gap in that
cuisine for American eaters.

Dessert is more than just a sensual pleasure (even one that causes us
to give higher restaurant review scores). It's a reflection of the implicit
cultural structures, the language of food hidden in plain sight, that
underlie every bite we take.

Epilogue

ON ANY GIVEN Friday night there's usually someone cooking with us at the sunny blue house on Bernal Hill; friends and family drop in to help make dinner, work our way through a new cuisine, or attempt recipes from the latest cookbook. Over the years many couples have met and eventually married while chopping garlic and ginger at our various houses and apartments, and their subsequent offspring have built gingerbread houses and stamped out cookies on the counters. The couples include Janet and yours truly; we met throwing a breakfast-for-dinner-themed cooking party and celebrate our anniversary now by cooking breakfast for dinner for everyone (having morning foods at night makes it an enjoyable violation of the grammar of cuisine).

Group cooking happens all over the world. In the Basque-speaking country of Spain where I spent sabbatical time, the private cooking clubs called *txoko* in Basque are a central part of the culture. (Basque, unrelated to any other languages of Europe, was illegal to speak during the Franco period, but like the Catalan language is undergoing a flowering among the younger generation.) The txoko (or in Spanish, *sociedad gastronómica*) was first created in the nineteenth century when members (originally only men) would get together to cook and eat at a communally organized kitchen. The clubs began in the Basque city of Donostia, San Sebastián in Spanish, but are now common throughout the Basque-speaking region. San Sebastián is set on a lovely curve of beach on the Bay of Biscay, between lush foggy green hills, and reminded me of home. Long a fishermen's town, the city is now a brilliant center of culinary innovation, full of Michelin-star restaurants and innovative tapas (*pintxos* in Basque).

We were in San Sebastián a few years ago during the harvest moon. At home we celebrate the Chinese harvest moon Mid-Autumn Festival the traditional way: by inviting people over to wander outside with a drink and look at the full moon (given the tiny backyards in San Francisco, "outside" means "on the roof," which can be a bit perilous because of the wine). In San Sebastián professor Eneko Agirre instead took us walking through the old city where we stopped at each bar for a glass of cider or the dry sparkling white wine called *txakolin* and a single seafood tapa: grilled squid, boquerones in vinegar, an innovative rose made out of grilled lobster in a blanket of dry-ice fog.

The food was superb everywhere, testifying to the Basques' long obsession with seafood. As Mark Kurlansky notes in his wonderful book *Cod*, the Basques accidentally happened upon North America while chasing cod across the Atlantic, but didn't bother to tell anyone because they wanted to keep the continent as a large private cod-drying rack. Food is not just an obsession of a few clubs or restaurants. Even outside of the formal txoko, there are many public kitchens available in San Sebastián for rent and group cooking is a common part of the culture.

What makes group cooking special, whether in San Sebastián or San Francisco, is that the meal benefits from what everyone brings, quite literally, to the table: their favorite ingredients, their culinary techniques, their family spices. I'll leave you with the thought that this "stone soup" metaphor is exactly what underlies the foods created by the great meetings of civilizations that also created our modern world. Ketchup, syrup, aspic, turkey, macaron, sherbet, and arrack are linguistic fossils of the high-class meals of Persian shahs, Baghdadi caliphs, Provençal princes, New York Astors, but also of Fujianese sailors, Egyptian pharmacists, Mexican nuns, Portuguese merchants, Sicilian pasta-makers, Amherst poets, and New York bakers, as each food passed along and changed to comply with the implicit structures of the borrowing cuisine: macaroons and marmalades losing their medieval rosewater and musk, fruit sharbats becoming luscious ice cream, vinegary meat sikbāj becoming Christian fish dishes suitable for Lent. Although the foods change, the words remain behind, mementos of our deep debt to each other from our shared past, just as the word *turkey* reminds us of tiny Portugal's obsession with naval secrets 600 years ago and *toast* and *supper* remind us of medieval pottages and toasty wassails.

How we talk about food also reflects human aspirations: our desire to live a healthy, natural, authentic life, to identify with our family and culture, and our deep strains of optimism and positivity. And it reflects our cognition: the link between vowel perception and the evolution of the human smile, the Gricean maxims that answer Katie's question about what we implicate when we say too much, advertising "tomato" ketchup, overmentioning fresh or tasty on aspirational menus or health on junk-food packages.

In other words, the linguistic and culinary habits of our own tribe or nation are not the habits of all tribes and nations. Yet all languages and cultures share a deep commonality, the social and cognitive traits that make us human. These facets—respect for our differences, and faith in our shared humanity—are the ingredients in the recipe for compassion. That's the final lesson of the language of food.

Notes

Note: The *Oxford English Dictionary* (OED Online, September 2013, Oxford University Press) is herein referred to as *OED*.

Introduction

4 **speed dates:** McFarland, Jurafsky, and Rawlings (2013).
4 **an author's covert biases:** Recasens, Danescu-Niculescu-Mizil, and Jurafsky (2013).
4 **how polite different people are on the web:** Danescu-Niculescu-Mizil et al. (2013).

One: How to Read a Menu

7 *La Maison de la Casa House, Continental Cuisine:* Trillin (1974), Chapter 1: The Travelling Man's Burden, 13.
7 **"continentalize your menu":** Seaberg (1973).
8 **Le crabmeat cocktail:** Zwicky and Zwicky (1980).
8 **online menu collection:** See Lesy and Stoffer (2013) for a beautiful sample from the collection.
8 **"tiny, unostentatious, literary-looking lady":** *The New York Times*, June 3, 1906.
8 **Astor House's breakfast menu:** The Astor House menu is available on the New York Public Library's website, http://digitalgallery.nypl.org/nypldigital/id?ps_rbk_701.
8 **five times more than cheap restaurants:** This result is based on software I wrote to analyze all 10,000 menus, using the menu prices to distinguish expensive restaurants and then examine their linguistic strategies; we'll introduce these methods in detail a few pages from now. For more on the social role of macaronic French, see Haley (2011), 33.
10 **We used a very large dataset:** Jurafsky et al. (2013).
11 **linguist Robin Lakoff pointed out:** Lakoff (2006).
12 **first discovered by Sibawayhi:** Al-Nassir (1993), Carter (2004).
13 **spent the rest of his life studying linguistics:** Carter (2004), 10.
13 **linguist George Zipf suggested:** Zipf (1934).

15 Zwicky calls "appealing adjectives": Zwicky and Zwicky (1980).
16 Steven Levitt and Stephen Dubner in *Freakonomics* show: Levitt and Dubner (2006), Levitt and Syverson (2005).
18 Grice pointed out: Grice (1989). Grice actually used the word *cooperative* rather than *rational*, but that term can be confusing because he gave cooperative a technical definition, not of being "helpful," but of participating in a particular agreed-upon communicative process.
18 Mark Liberman suggests: Liberman (2004).
20 Jane Ziegelman tells us: Ziegelman (2010).

Two: Entrée

22 "A couple of French terms": Davidson (1999), 281.
22 "We might . . . follow fashion in food": Braudel (1981), 189.
23 modern French definition: Rey (2011), entry for *entrée*.
24 "Cest que fault pour faire": Flandrin (2007), 182. Menus drawn from *Livre fort excellent de cuysine tres-utile & profitable contenant en soy la maniere dabiller toutes viandes. Avec la maniere deservir es banquets & festins. Le tout veu & corrige oultre la premiere impression par le grant Escuyer de Cuysine du Roy* (Lyon: Olivier Arnoullet, 1555).
24 Beef Palate with Gooseberries, etc.: Flandrin (2007), 66–68.
25 "Ducks in Ragout," etc.: Scully (2006).
26 *The Compleat Housewife*: Smith (1758), appendix. Figure © The British Library Board. 1037.g.9, f.415
26 a newly borrowed foreign word: The *OED* entry for *entrée* gives this quote from Verral: "Roasted ham. For this *entrée* is generally provided a new Westphalia or Bayonne ham."
26 It was called a *menu*: *OED* entry for *menu*.
28 This service à la Russe took over: Flandrin (2007), 94–95; Colquhoun (2007), 251–56.
28 hors d'oeuvres began to be served earlier: Flandrin (2007), 76, 101.
28 menu . . . is from 1907: Image courtesy of the New York Public Library. Miss Frank E. Buttolph Menu Collection.
28 the newly built Blanco's: Edwords (1914).
28 beloved fan dancer Sally Rand: Shteir (2004).
30 "insidious concoction": Wondrich (2007), 73.
30 here at the old Bank Exchange: Toro-Lira (2010).
30 Alioto's on Fisherman's Wharf: Miss Frank E. Buttolph Menu Collection, New York Public Library.
31 small 14-paged roast section: Escoffier (1921), 257–456, 469–75.
31 the modern *Larousse Gastronomique*: *Larousse Gastronomique* (2001).
31 "*Ce mot ne signifie pas du tout*": Montagné and Gottschalk (1938).
33 sociologists call *cultural omnivorousness*: Peterson (1992); (2005). Haley (2011) suggests that this movement began as early as the turn of the twentieth century and was led by the middle class rather than the elite.
33 find the best kind of fish sauce: Johnston and Bauman (2007).

33 **Google Ngram corpus:** The Google Ngram corpus is at http://books.goo gle.com/ngrams. The original paper describing it is Michel et al. (2011).

Three: From Sikbāj to Fish and Chips

35 **Chinese fishing villages:** "Chinese Fisheries in California," *Chamber's Journal of Popular Literature, Science, and Arts*, Vol. I (January 21, 1954), 48.
35 **Croatian methods:** Briscoe (2002), 65.
35 **Chilean and Peruvian miners introduced techniques:** For the history of Chileans and Peruvians in the gold rush, see Chan (2000).
36 *Diccionario de la lengua española*: Real Academia Española, *Diccionario de la lengua española, vigésima segunda edición*.
37 **King Khosrau and Borzūya:** Library of Congress image LC-USZ62-58235.
38 **an extensive canal system:** The famous canals of Baghdad are described in Campopiano (2012) and Adams (1965).
38 **Persia was at the center of the global economy:** For more on the Sasanian period, see Yarshater (2000), Eilers (2000), and Watson (2000).
38 **In one story, Khosrau sent a great number of cooks:** The legend comes from Baghdad, 400 years after Khosrau's time, in Nasrallah (2007), chapter 49.
39 **from Nawal Nasrallah's translation:** Nasrallah (2007).
39 **Meat Stew with Vinegar (sikbāj):** Here I've simplified and shortened Khosrau's sixth-century Persian recipe as given by Al-Warruq, based on Nasrallah (2007), 248–49, Laudan (2013).
40 **acetic acid is a potent antimicrobial:** Entani et al. (1998).
40 **Recipes for meat stews on these clay slabs:** Bottéro (2004), 85–86; Zaouali (2007), 23.
40 **Caliph al-Mutawakkil was once sitting:** Waines (2003).
40 *The Book of the Wonders of India*: Freeman-Grenville (1981).
40 **of fish made out of gold, with ruby eyes:** Freeman-Grenville (1981), story 41: The History of Ishaq, 62–64.
40 *The Treasury of Useful Advice*: Marin and Waines (1993). Translations from Zaouali (2007).
41 *Medieval Cuisine of the Islamic World*: Zaouali (2007).
41 **Fish sikbāj, Egypt, 13th century:** Zaouali (2007), 98.
42 **in southwestern France for *scabeg*, written in Occitan:** Lambert (2002). The recipe is from a cookbook written in Occitan and Latin, *Modus Viaticorum Preparandarum et Salsarum* (How to Prepare Foods and Sauces), from the last decades of the fourteenth century.
42 **dialects from Sicilian (*schibbeci*), to Neapolitan (*scapece*):** Michel (1996), 41; D'Ancoli (1972), 97; Aprosio (2003), 405. These sources and others suggest that the Catalan is the likely source.
42 **a Catalan cookbook from the first half of the 1300s:** Santanach (2008), 68–69.
42 **In Muslim regions like Baghdad or Spain, by contrast:** Perry (2005).
42 **Medieval Christians had very strict dietary restrictions:** Bynum (1987), 323; Albala (2011), 15–16.

42 **Melitta Adamson estimates:** Adamson (2004), 188.

42 *The French Cook,* **is divided into three sections:** Scully (2006).

43 *al-sikbāj* **began to be transcribed as** *assicpicium:* Martellotti (2001).

43 **bringing words for many seafood and other gastronomic terms:** See, for example, Prat Sabater (2003).

43 **"dusted fish":** *Mu'affar* (dusted fish), which appears in the thirteenth century in an Arabic cookbook written in Andalusia. Perry (2004).

44 **Gutiérrez de Santa Clara:** Santa Clara (1905).

44 **Peruvian historian Juan José Vega:** Vega (1993), 158.

44 *Diccionario de la lengua española:* The *Diccionario de la lengua española, 22.ᵃ edición,* the Royal Spanish Academy, gives the etymology for *cebiche* as "Quizá del ár. hisp. *assukkabáğ,* y este del ár. *sikbáğ."*

45 *Southern Barbarian Cookbook:* "Southern Barbarian" was the term used at the time in Japan for Europeans. The Southern Barbarians cookbook, called in Japanese 南蛮料理書 *Nanban ryórisho,* is described in Chapter 4: "The Barbarian's Cookbook" of Rath (2010).

45 **Fish dish:** Rath (2010), 106.

46 *tenporari,* **the name of a related dish:** Rath (2010), 106.

46 **This word is likely a borrowing of the Portuguese noun** *tempero:* Irwin (2011), 34–35, and also the *OED* entry for *tempura.*

46 **Manuel Brudo, a Portuguese crypto-Jewish doctor:** On Manuel Brudo, the Portuguese crypto-Jew who had lived in England, see Roth (1960). The origin of the pescado frito variant seems to have been a fish dish called *mu'affar* in Muslim Spain, which appears in the thirteenth century in an Arabic cookbook written in Andalusia. Charles Perry (2004) tells us that the name *mu'affar* originally meant "dusted fish." Further details on the relationship to Jewish food are in Marks (2010), "Peshkado Frito," 454–56.

46 **her recipe for battered and fried fish:** Glasse (1774), 378.

46 **The Jews Way of preserving Salmon:** Image courtesy Department of Special Collections, Stanford University Library.

47 **"Confined as the limits of Field Lane":** Charles Dickens, *Oliver Twist,* Chapter 26, "In which a mysterious character appears upon the scene," paragraph 2.

47 **"impregnated with the scents of fried fish":** Endelman (2002), 152.

47 **1846** *A Jewish Manual:* Montefiore (1846).

47 **"Jewish" fried fish, by contrast:** In her recipe for "escobeche," this same cold, fried, battered fish is simply soaked in vinegar with onions and spices.

47 **"This is another excellent way of frying fish":** Soyer (1855), 28.

48 **Ashkenazi Jewish proprietor Joseph Malin:** Shaftesley (1975), 393; Roden (1996), 113; Marks (2010), "Peshkado Frito," 454–56.

Four: Ketchup, Cocktails, and Pirates

49 **the large German contribution to American cuisine:** For more on the influence of German food on American, see Ziegelman (2010).

49 **Fujianese immigration to the United States has increased:** See, for example, Keefe (2009).

50 **traces of their languages in the old names of many rivers:** Norman and Mei (1976), Bauer Matthews (2006).

50 **layering local fish in jars with cooked rice and salt:** The hypothesis that these rice-based fermented fish products were first developed in rice paddies along the Mekong was formulated in a number of papers by Naomichi Ishige, including some with his colleague Kenneth Ruddle. See Ruddle and Ishige (2010) and Ishige (1986).

50 **"a Parma ham," with a "distinct sourness":** Hilton (1993).

51 **When the Han emperor Wu chased:** This legend about the origins of fish paste come from the "Important Arts for the People's Welfare" (齐民要术 *Qimin Yaoshu*), written in 544 CE. The English translation, not to mention an enormous amount of further information, is from Huang (2000), 382–83. This 741-page book is the definitive work on Chinese food science and food history, and is a masterpiece drawing from Huang Hsing-tsung's lifetime of work on food biochemistry. Huang was Joseph Needham's secretary in Chongqing in the 1940s. For more stories about H. T. Huang and Needham, see Winchester (2008).

52 **Fujian Red Rice Wine Chicken:** Adapted from Carolyn Phillip's terrific blog *Madame Huang's Kitchen.*

53 **Babylonians had a fish sauce called *siqqu*:** Curtis (1991); Bottero (2004), 61.

53 **Anchovies from the gulf were mixed with salt:** A very comprehensive survey of fermented fish products is Ruddle and Ishige (2005).

54 **Fujianese traders and seamen saw some of the same factories:** The hypothesis that fish sauce was a later innovation in Southeast Asia was proposed by Ishige; see Ishige (1993), 30. Huang (2000, 392, 297) gives further linguistic evidence about fish sauce's migration up the South China coast, pointing out that the Chinese name for fish sauce, *yulu* (fish dew), is an innovation and not related to the names of any of the traditional Chinese fermented fish products.

54 **Hokkien, Cantonese, and Mandarin are as linguistically different:** Hokkien is a subdialect of Southern Min, a Chinese dialect of 46 million speakers spoken in Fujian and Guangdong provinces, Taiwan, and throughout Southeast Asia. Southern Min variants and subdialects are called Hokkien, Taiwanese, Teochiu, and Amoy, among other names. I use the traditional word "dialect" to describe the regional spoken varieties of Chinese although, as mentioned, they are actually as different from each other as languages.

54 **A Chinese oceangoing junk:** From Needham (1971), 405. Image courtesy of Cambridge University Press.

55 **missionary dictionaries from the nineteenth century:** Penny Silva of the *Oxford English Dictionary* tells me that it was James Murray, the founder of the dictionary, who first figured out this etymology when he wrote the entry for this word in the Scriptorium in his back garden in 1889. Murray relied on an old dictionary, the 1873 *Dictionary of the Vernacular or Spoken*

Language of Amoy, a Hokkien to English dictionary compiled by missionaries in 1873, which listed ke-tchup (written 鮭汁) as the "brine of pickled fish." A modern Chinese dictionary, the 1992 *Putonghua Minnanhua Fangyan Cidian* (Mandarin-Southern Min Dictionary), says this word (written 鮭) has become archaic, and the Chinese character is often now used to describe completely unrelated fish. For more on Murray, I recommend Winchester (1998; 2003).

55 **Chinese sauce-making factories:** Anita van Velzen's ethnographic research shows that until the 1950s, all these kinds of kecap were made only by ethnic Chinese families; Velzen (1990; 1992).

56 **Edmund Scott, an English trader on Java:** Scott's memoirs make somewhat difficult reading, for the fierce xenophobia and ubiquitous violence (including torture). But also on account of his evil spelling. Scott (1606). *An exact discourse of the subtilties, fashishions [sic], pollicies, religion, and ceremonies of the East Indians as well Chyneses as Iauans, there abyding and dweling.* LONDON, Printed by W.W. for Walter Burre. 1606.

57 **"the original monarch of mixed drinks":** Wondrich (2010).

57 **"common drink":** By 1704 Charles Lockyer called punch the "common drink" of all Europeans in Asia.

58 **The cover of Charles Lockyer's:** Image courtesy Department of Special Collections, Stanford University Libraries.

59 **"Soy comes in tubs from Jappan":** Lockyer (1711).

59 **Lockyer would buy tubs of ketchup:** Lockyer advised anyone who wanted to make money on soy or ketchup to bring on the outbound trip to Asia as many reusable bottles as he could save. Nice to think of bottle recycling in the time of Queen Anne.

59 **imitating the taste of the expensive imported original:** Ketchup consumers were aware of the Asian origins of ketchup; the 1785 sixth edition of Johnson's Dictionary calls catsup "A kind of Indian pickle, imitated by pickled mushrooms," and Hannah Glasse's 1774 *The Art of Cookery*, in a recipe for mushroom ketchup on page 309, promises that the result "will taste like foreign catchup." Worcestershire sauce, a vinegar and anchovy sauce flavored with molasses, garlic, and tamarind, was developed in the 1830s by chemists Lea and Perrin from a recipe they advertised was brought back from Bengal.

59 **To Make KATCH-UP that will keep good Twenty Years:** Eales (1742).

60 **the household book:** Hickman (1977).

60 **Tomata Catsup:** Recipe 443 from Kitchner (1817).

61 **adding even more sugar and also lots of vinegar:** Smith (1996); Wilson (2008), 204–10.

61 **Heinz originally chose the spelling "ketchup":** See Harris (2013). You can see for yourself the recent rise in popularity of the spelling "ketchup" by using the Google Ngram viewer, which allows you to count the frequency of both words in British versus American sources over time.

61 **bans were repeatedly rescinded:** See, for example, Frank (1998), Pomerantz (2000), Allen et al. (2011).

62 **China dominated the world economy until the Industrial Revolution:** Frank (1998), 171–73.

Five: A Toast to Toast

65 **Rakia is the generic name:** Although of course spelled and pronounced differently in each language.

66 **The original meaning of the word *toast*:** *OED* entry for *toast*.

67 **"sinfull, and utterly unlawfull unto Christians":** Prynne (1628).

67 **toasts were made to the health of a lady:** Colquhoun (2007), 221.

67 **A report from the time:** Richard Steele, *The Tatler* 31 (1709): 8: "Then, said he, Why do you call live People Toasts? I answered, That was a new Name found out by the Wits to make a Lady have the same Effect as Burridge in the Glass when a Man is drinking."

67 **"A Beauty, whose Health is drank":** Richard Steele, *The Tatler* 71 (1709).

67 *A Carol for a Wassail Bowl:* image from page 67 in Henry Vizetelly, *Christmas with the Poets: A Collection of Songs, Carols, and Descriptive Verses*, 6th edition (London: Ward, Lock, & Tyler, 1872).

68 **in the apple-growing west of England:** Robert Herrick's 1648 *Hesperides* has the line "Wassaile the Trees, that they may beare You many a Plum, and many a Peare."

68 **a piece of toast soaked in cider in the trees:** Brears (1993).

68 **Wassail:** Recipe adapted from the always instructive Alton Brown and from Jenn Dowds, The Churchill, and Rosie Schaap, from *The New York Times*. December 12, 2012.

69 **slices of toast soaked in wine, water, or broth, called *sops*:** Hieatt and Butler (1985), 215: sops were "generally toasted pieces of bread."

69 **one-pot stews called *pottages*:** Wilson (1993), 3–19.

69 **"wel loved he by the morwe a sop in wyn":** Chaucer's *Canterbury Tales*, "The Franklin's Tale."

70 *Sowpes in galyngale:* Recipe 133 in Hieatt and Butler (1985).

70 *Soupes dorye:* Austin (1964), 11.

70 **the word *sop*, perhaps via its:** *OED* entry for *sop*.

70 **come our words *supper* and *soup*:** *OED* entry for *soup* and *supper*.

70 *waes hael* **(be healthy):** See the *OED* entries for *wassail, hale*, and *healthy*.

71 **in Paris at the fancy new "university":** Although I'm cheating here a bit since the word "university" only became common to describe the University of Paris a few decades later around 1200. See Mozely (1963) and Longchamps (1960).

71 **in this same Caucasian region of modern Georgia:** The hypothesis that wine was first developed in the Caucasus was first proposed by Russian botanist Nikolai Vavilov. McGovern (2009), 19.

71 **the "Noah hypothesis":** For a summary of these arguments, see McGovern (2003; 2009).

72 **"And the ark rested":** King James translation of Genesis 8 and 9.

72 **as early as Homer:** Burkert (1985), 374, note 37: "The formula appears in the Illiad 9.177 and six times in the Odyssey."

72 **a libation from the first *krater* of wine:** Burkert (1985), 70–72.

72 **The root **g'heu* (*pour*):** Benveniste (1969), 470–80.

72 **A 2400 to 2600 BCE carving:** http://www.britishmuseum.org/explore/highlights/highlight_objects/me/s/shell_plaque.aspx.

72 **Similar images of libations:** Matthews (1997).

73 **A hymn to Ninkasi:** Civil (1964).

73 **sheker similarly meant beer:** Homan (2004).

74 **infused with antioxidant herbs:** McGovern et al. (2010); McGovern, Mirzoian, and Hall (2009).

74 **the evil eye:** Dundes (1981), Foster (1972).

75 **An alembic of the Middle Ages:** Figure from Louis Figuier, *Les merveilles de l'industrie. Volume 4: Industries agricoles et alimentaires* (Paris, France: Furne Jouvet, c. 1880).

75 ***sicera*, which he defined as beer, mead:** St. Jerome, Letter 52, *To Nepotian: Ep. 52, Ad Nepotianum de vita clericorum et monachorum.* http://www.synaxis.org/cf/volume29/ECF00005.htm.

75 **in France the word *sicera*, now pronounced *sidre*:** *OED* entry for *cider*.

75 **the technology of distillation was perfected:** Wilson (2006).

76 **Other descendants of the word '*araq*:** *Arajhi*, a Turkic word for distilled liquor borrowed, presumably via Persian, from Arabic, is mentioned in Chinese documents as early as 1330. See Buell and Anderson (2010), 109, 115.

77 **found on pottery from 7000 to 6600 BCE:** McGovern (2009), 28–59.

Six: Who Are You Calling a Turkey?

78 **"introduces a full chorus of turkeys":** Edgar Allan Poe, *The Works of Edgar Allan Poe in Eight Volumes. Vol. VI. Miscellaneous Essays, Marginalia, etc.* (Philadelphia: J. B. Lippincott, 1895), 162.

79 **the species that Native Americans domesticated:** Thornton et al. (2012); Schorger (1966); Smith (2006), 8. A different species of wild turkey was independently domesticated by the ancient Pueblo peoples who built the cliff dwellings in the southern United States (Speller et al. 2010).

79 **Cortés described the streets:** Schorger (1966), 12.

79 **8000 turkeys were sold every five days:** Coe (1994), 96, quoting from Motolinía, *Memorales*, (Mexico City, 1903) 332.

80 **Turkey in stews:** Image used by permission of the Biblioteca Medicea Laurenziana, Florence, ms. Med. Palat. 218, c. 312v. On concession of the Italian Ministry for Goods, Cultural Activities and Tourism. Further reproduction by any means is prohibited.

80 **the Aztec feast in honor of a newborn child:** Sahagún (1957), 121–25.

80 **turkey moles made with chile:** Sahagún (1954), 37; Barros (2004), 20.

80 **1650 description of a Oaxacan turkey mole:** Barros (2004), 22.

81 **recipes for guisos and moles in early Mexican manuscripts:** Monteagudo (2004), Laudan and Pilcher (1999).

81 **an 1817 cookbook, whose recipe for mole de guajolote:** The 1817 recipe appears in the anonymous *Libro de Cocina de la Gesta de Independencia:* Monteagudo (2002), 58. See also Coe and Coe (1996), 214–16, and Monteagudo (2004), 34.

81 **Modern recipes are even more spectacular:** Berdan and Anawalt (1997), 169.

81 **the role of nuns in convents:** Monteagudo (2004).

82 **Ingredients from Rick Bayless's Recipe:** Bayless (2007), 198.

83 **all domesticated in the New World:** Smith (1997), Matsuoka et al. (2002), Austin (1988). Beans were likely independently domesticated in the Andes as well as Mesoamerica: Pickersgill and Debouck (2005).

83 **The turkey's trip to Europe:** Schorger (1966), 4.

84 **turkey from the mid-Atlantic trade islands:** Other New World products, for example potatoes, were known to have first reached Europe in this way from the Canaries rather than directly from the Americas. Ríos et al. (2007), Heywood (2012).

84 **The trader would bring goods:** Gelderblom (2004).

85 **The Antwerp Bourse:** Image courtesy Werner Wittersheim.

85 **enabled common pricings to be established:** Kohn (2003), 55.

85 *galine de Turquie* **(Turkish chicken):** Jacques Coeur, the fabulously wealthy French financier and trader with the Levant, sent his nephew Jean de Village to Alexandria in 1447 for an audience with the Mamluk sultan. Jean returned with *gallinas turcicas* (Turkish chickens). Clément (1863), 141 (footnote).

85 **Europeans in the 1400s:** Renaissance princes like Good King René of Provence bought the birds to populate their parks and menageries. And in 1491, guinea fowl were received at Marseille for Anne de Beaujeu, the sister and regent for King Charles VIII of France. See Antoine (1917), 35–50.

86 **Portuguese globes and nautical charts:** Harley (1988), Kimble (1933).

86 **confused in Dutch:** J. Reygersbergen, *Dye chronijcke van Zeelandt*, 1551: "Dese schipper . . . hadde in een nieu Landt gheweest in Africa, ghenaemt caput Viride, daer noyt eenighe schepen uyt dese Landen inne geweest hadden. . . . Dit schip brochte [1528] die eerste Kalkoensche hoenderen in Zeelandt."

87 **French naturalist Pierre Belon's drawing:** Image courtesy Department of Special Collections, Stanford University Libraries.

87 **Artemis turned them into guinea fowl,** *Meleagrides:* A less melodramatic but more plausible etymology for *meleagris* is that it is a borrowing from a Phoenician word related to the god Melqart (from the Semitic *melek*, "king"), because of early Phoenician ships trading in exotic birds along with olives and wine while they spread the alphabet around the Mediterranean. But that's a story for another day. See Thompson (1936), 114.

88 **"turkey well drest":** Tusser (1573).

88 **compared the "wilde Turkies" to "our English Turky":** Smith and Bradley (1910), 60; Forbush and Job (1912), 489.

88 **owes more to the autumn harvest festivals:** Baker (2009), Chapter 1; Smith (2006), 73; Ott (2012), ix.

88 **Thanksgiving was linked in schools and newspapers with the Pilgrims:** Smith (2006), 67–82.

89 **By 1658 an English pumpkin pie recipe:** Brook (1658).

89 **Pompkin. One quart stewed and strained:** Simmons (1796), 28. For a very engaging and comprehensive history of the pumpkin, see Ott (2012).

89 **Texas Pecan Pie. One cup of sugar:** *Ladies Home Journal* 15, no. 8(July 1898), 32. http://books.google.com/books?id=LKwiAQAAMAAJ&pg=PA36-IA36.

89 **pie crust filled with egg yolks, cream:** Recipe for "Pasteis de leite" in Newman (1964), 16; Austin (1964), 53.

90 **Two pecan maps:** Based on the research of Bert Vaux and Joshua Katz: Katz (2013), Vaux (2003).

91 **African American chef and food writer Edna Lewis:** Lewis (1976), 159.

91 **archaeological evidence of pots from early slave settlements:** Yentsch (1994; 1995).

Seven: Sex, Drugs, and Sushi Rolls

92 **pails of hot chicken tamales:** Peters (2013), 32.

92 **sample from a positive restaurant review:** I've subtly modified the wording in both reviews to preserve anonymity as much as possible.

93 **my colleagues on the menu study:** Jurafsky et al. (2014).

93 **With computer scientists Julian McAuley and Jure Leskovec:** McAuley, Leskovec, and Jurafsky (2012).

94 **how much more often a word occurs in good reviews:** The method we use, the weighted log odds ratio with informative Dirichlet prior (Monroe, Colaresi, and Quinn [2008]) involves a few other statistical tricks, like accounting for variance and controlling for how often we expect the words to occur by chance given their general frequency in English.

95 **Linguist and lexicographer Erin McKean notes:** Erin McKean quoted in Teddy Wayne, "Obsessed? You're Not Alone," *The New York Times*, March 22, 2013.

95 **"The girls nowadays indulge in such exaggerated statements":** Montgomery (1915), 95.

96 **more adjectives to describe pain than pleasure:** Rozin and Royzman (2001), 311.

96 **vocabulary to describe people we dislike:** Leising, Ostrovski, and Borkenau (2012).

96 **smaller vocabulary for smell:** Ankerstein and Pereira (2013).

96 **richer olfactory vocabularies:** Another olfactory rich language is Aslian, spoken on the Malay peninsula: Majid and Burenhult (2014).

97 **Cantonese is particularly rich in words for negative smells:** The word list and definitions are adapted from de Sousa (2011).

97 **"perhaps the world's oldest extant gastronomic treatise":** Dunlop (2008), 106; Knoblock and Riegel (2000), 308–9.

98 **"the variety of olfactory sensations experienced by their ancestors":** de Sousa (2011).

98 **genes coding for the detection of specific odors:** Gilad, Przeworski, and Lancet (2004).

98 **grassy smell of sauvignon blanc:** McRae et al. (2012).

98 **ability to detect the sulfurous smell of asparagus:** Pelchat et al. (2011).

98 biased to be especially aware of negative situations: Rozin and Royzman (2001), 311.

98 Linguist Douglas Biber has shown: Biber (1988; 1995).

99 the pioneering work of Texas psychology professor James Pennebaker: See Pennebaker (2011) and Pennebaker, Booth, and Francis (2007).

99 Pennebaker and his colleagues identified: Stone and Pennebaker (2002); Gortner and Pennebaker (2003); Cohn, Mehl, and Pennebaker (2004).

100 there are a lot of ways for things to go wrong in life: Peeters (1971); Unkelbach et al. (2008).

100 Robert Parker began to emphasize the sensual pleasure: McCoy (2005).

100 Literature professor Sean Shesgreen says: Shesgreen (2003).

102 link between junk-food cravings and drug addiction: Rozin and Stoess (1993); Rozin, Levine, and Stoess (1991); Hormes and Rozin (2010); Johnson and Kenny (2010); Ziauddeen, Farooqi, and Fletcher (2012); Stice et al. (2013).

102 Adam Gopnik: Gopnik (2011), 254.

102 occur more frequently: Have a higher log odds ratio.

103 Strauss found that Korean food commercials: Strauss (2005).

103 The link between dessert and sex: See, for example, Hines (1999).

104 Chris Potts has shown that this skew: Potts (2011), Pang and Lee (2008).

105 the *Pollyanna effect*: Boucher and Osgood (1969).

105 positive words are (on average) more frequent than negative words: Rozin, Berman, and Royzman (2010); Augustine, Mehl, and Larsen (2011).

105 unmarked form is much more likely to be positive: Zimmer (1964), 83.

106 When people forward news stories: Berger and Milkman (2012).

Eight: Potato Chips and the Nature of the Self

108 "one of the most marvelously constructed foods on the planet": Moss (2013).

111 *craft authenticity*: Carroll and Wheaton (2009). See also Beverland (2006); Beverland, Lindgreen, and Vink (2008); and Johnston and Bauman, (2007).

113 Pierre Bourdieu, whose famous book *Distinction*: Bourdieu (1984).

114 *traditional authenticity*: "Design Notebook: Peter Buchanan-Smith and the Urban Ax," *The New York Times*, June 30, 2010. See also Gilmore and Pine (2007) and Potter (2010).

114 ordering a plate of ketchup as his entire meal: Roman (2010), 6.

115 "threw forty-seven raw eggs across the kitchen at my head": Ogilvy (1963), 35–38.

115 "Don't use highfalutin language": Ogilvy (1963), 141.

115 "not just who they are, but who they want to be": Peters (2012), xiv.

115 working-class *–in'* suffix: Labov (1966).

115 appealing to more upscale voters: Lisa Miller, "Divided We Eat," *Newsweek*, November 22, 2010. http://www.newsweek.com/2010/11/22/what-food-says-about-class-in-america.html; Torjusen et al. (2001).

116 What they call the *interdependent self*: Markus and Conner (2013).

Nine: Salad, Salsa, and the Flour of Chivalry

117 the Russian word for hospitality: Smith and Christian (1984).

118 thousands of years of salt taxes: Kurlansky (2002).

118 a grinding stone from Syria: One of the British Museum's quern stones from Abu Hureyra, Syria: http://www.britishmuseum.org/explore/highlights/highlight_objects/pe/q/quern_stone_for_making_flour.aspx.

118 Anglo-Saxon *hlaf-dige* (loaf-kneader): *OED* entries for *lord* and *lady*.

119 bolting cloths: David (1977).

120 "White was his face as payndemayn": Chaucer, *Tale of Sir Thopas*, line 35.

120 Payn purdyeu: Hieatt (1988), 79.

121 "receive the flower of all, and leave me but the bran": Shakespeare's *Tragedy of Coriolanus*, Act I, Scene I.

121 brown bread was looked down upon even by the poor: David (1977), 48–49. See also the Worshipful Company of Bakers website, http://www.bakers.co.uk/A-Brief-History.aspx.

122 *samidu* (high-quality meal): The exact definition of *samidu* and *semidalis* are still not clear; scholars disagree whether they both meant a finely ground flour or conversely one that was high quality by being dense and nourishing. See, for example, Sallares (1991), 323.

122 Yale Culinary Tablets: Bottéro (2004).

122 Yiddish word *zeml*: Marks (2010), 632.

123 "à la meunière": *OED* entry for *meunière*.

123 borrowed from Provençal *salada*: *OED* entry for *salad*.

123 Salat (c. 1390): From the *Forme of Cury*, in Hieatt and Butler (1985), 115.

124 "If you eat it [cabbage] chopped": Cato (1934).

124 *cookie, cruller, pancake, waffle,* and *brandy*: Van der Sijs (2009).

124 "has a very pleasing flavor and tastes better than one can imagine": Benson (1987), 609.

124 *Apicius*, a fourth-century Latin collection of recipes: Grocock and Grainger (2006).

125 and scholar Charles Perry tells us: Perry (1987), 501.

125 French *saulce vert* was made of parsley: Scully (1988), 223.

125 *Le Menagier de Paris*: Greco and Rose (2009), 322.

125 Escoffier's French *sauce verte*: Escoffier (1921), 31.

126 Green Goddess Dressing: Phillip Roemer, the Palace Hotel, San Francisco.

127 in a volume written over 800 years ago in 1190: Wright (1857), 102.

127 Westphalian hams from formerly Celtic regions of what is now Germany: Martial talks about the hams of the Menapians, a people in Flanders not far from the famous ham-producing region of modern Westphalia in Germany.

127 *sausage,* which we got from French, from late Latin *salsicia*: Dalby (1996), 181.

127 *corn* in Old English originally meant a "particle" or "grain": *OED* entry for *corn*.

128 Salt cod was a huge staple of the Middle Ages: Kurlansky (1997).

128 a book explaining how to preserve soups and stews: The book was called *L'art de Conserver, Pendant Plusieurs Années, Toutes les Substances Animales*

et Végétales, and is available at http://gallicadossiers.bnf.fr/Anthologie/notices/01500.htm.

128 **pastrami:** According to the *OED* entry for *pastrami*, the word comes from Romanian *pastramă* (pressed and preserved meat), from the Ottoman Turkish *başdirma* (something pressed, forced down). See Dalby (1996), 201.

128 **"Bacon serves no real purpose in a refrigerated age":** Wilson (2012), 216.

129 **metal roller mills that completely removed bran:** David (1977), 31.

Ten: Macaroon, Macaron, Macaroni

130 **macaron delivery:** See http://www.lartisanmacaron.com/#!from-our-kitchen-to-yours.

131 **borrowed lauzīnaj from the Sassanid kings of Persia:** Called *lauẓēnag* in Middle Persian; see MacKenzie (1971), 53. See Ullmann (2000), 1758, for *lauẓinagun*.

131 **the "best and finest" pastry:** *Husrav i Kavātān U Rētak Ē: The Pahlavi Text "King Husrav and His Boy." Published with Its Transcription, Translation and Copious Notes. Being an English Version of the Thesis for the Degree of "Doctor of Philosophy" of the University of Heidelberg, Germany. With an Appendix and a Complete Glossary by Jamshedji Maneckji Unvala.* Paul Geuthner, 1921. Available online at http://catalog.hathitrust.org/Record/001357845.

131 **Charles Perry's translation:** Perry (2005).

131 **Some recipes for lauzīnaj:** Nasrallah (2007), 411.

132 **Roger II, from a mosaic:** Image courtesy Matthias Süßen.

132 **the rule of Roger I and Roger II of Sicily:** Johns (2002), Houben (2002).

132 *Marzapane* **. . . comes from the Arabic word** *mauthaban*: Ballerini (2005), 87, footnote 10.

133 **Marzipan. Peel the almonds well and crush:** Ballerini (2005), 87.

133 **caliscioni comes from the word for stocking:** The word *caliscioni* comes from medieval Latin *calisone*, attested in Padua about 1170, which Battisti and Alessio's *Diẓionario Etimologico Italiano* 1, page 695, says was a flour and almond sweet.

133 **How to Make Caliscioni:** Ballerini (2005), 88.

134 **Francesco Datini, a fourteenth-century merchant:** Simeti (1991), 227.

134 **The Greeks ate a dish made from sheets of fried dough called** *laganum*: Perry (1981); Serventi and Sabban (2000), 14–15.

134 **in the eastern Mediterranean that true dried pasta existed:** Perry (1981).

134 **the fifth-century Jerusalem Talmud:** Talmud Yerushalmi, Beitza I:9 and Challah I:4.

134 *itriyah* **was an Arabic word for dried noodles:** Perry (1981).

134 **It was thus in Sicily:** For the history of the Arab invention of pasta and its European spread, see Serventi and Sabban (2000), 14–15, Wright (2007), and Verde (2013).

134 **Muhammad al-Idrisi, the Moroccan-born geographer:** Perry (1981).

135 **the eleventh-century French scholar Rashi:** Silvano and Sabban (2002), 30–31.

135　**modern Yiddish word *chremsel*:** For a modern recipe for *chremslach* (the plural of *chremsel*), see Schwartz (2008), 178.

135　**the seer Nostradamus:** Redon, Sabban, and Serventi (1998), 205; de Nostredame (1555), 202.

136　***calzone*:** There were ravioli-like versions of this recipe too, some of them described by Jews who had emigrated north from Italy as well. For example, in the fourteenth century R. Moses Parnas of Rotenberg, Germany, wrote in the *Sefer haParnas* of "*calsinos* which are called *kreplins*," referring to the dumplings now called *kreplakh* in Yiddish. See Weingarten (2010), 55.

136　**We don't know whether *maccarruni* came from Arabic:** For two proposals for Arabic etymologies see Wright (1996) and Nasrallah (2013), 268.

136　**or even comes from the Greek *makaria*:** *OED* entries for *macaroni* and *macaroon*.

136　**the origin of the phrase "macaronic verse":** The *OED* entry for *macaronic* says that Teofilo Folengo described his 1517 macaronic poem *Liber Macaronices* as named for macaroni which was a "course, crude, rustic dish of flour, butter, and cheese."

136　**Sicilian maccherone was made of:** Ballerini (2005), 70.

136　**a list of fantastical desserts in Rabelais' *Gargantua and Pantagruel*:** Book 4, Chapter 59; the long list includes "Beuignetz. Tourtes de seize facons. Guauffres. Crespes. Patez de Coings. Caillebotes. Neige de Crème. Myrobalans confictz. Gelee. Hippocras rouge & vermeil. Poupelins. Macarons. Tartres vingt sortes. Crème. Confictures seiches & liquids soixante & dix-huyt especes. Dragee, cent couleurs."

137　***Martha Washington's Booke of Cookery*:** Hess (1996).

137　**probably written in the early 1600s:** Hess (1996), 462, concludes that this manuscript was written either in the 1650s or somewhat earlier, but was in any case a fair copy of an earlier manuscript.

137　**To Make Mackroons:** Hess (1996), 341.

137　**the turning point in this transition:** Albala (2007), 57.

138　**Macaron ("La maniere de faire du macaron"):** Scully (2006), 369.

138　**food writer Cindy Meyers writes:** Meyers (2009).

138　**A macaron in the style:** Image from Albert Seigneurie, *Dictionnaire Encyclopédique de l'épicerie et des industries amexes* (Paris: L'épicier, 1898).

138　**what the *Larousse Gastronomique* calls:** *Larousse Gastronomique* (2001), 706.

139　**Name mixups persisted in English:** For example, S. Williams' 1834 "The Parterê of Poetry and Historical Romance," page 227, has *macaronies* to mean "macaroons."

139　**use of coconut increased greatly:** Zizumbo-Villarreal (1996), Dixon (1985). There is a recipe for "Cocoa-Nut Cakes" in the 1833 (twelfth) edition of Lydia M. Child's *The American Frugal Housewife*. Available free online at http://www.gutenberg.org/ebooks/13493.

139　**on the back of another recipe for the cake:** Emily Dickinson museum. http://www.emilydickinsonmuseum.org/cooking.

139　**Dickinson's own recipe:** Food writer Tori Avey gives a nice explanation of how to make it on her blog *The History Kitchen*.

139 *Cocoanut Cake:* Recipe from a photograph of Dickinson's original, from *The History Kitchen* blog and then courtesy of Poet's House c/o President and Fellows of Harvard College.

140 **Emily Dickinson:** Image courtesy of The Emily Dickinson Collection, Amherst College Archives and Special Collections.

140 **ambrosia:** For example, there is an ambrosia recipe in Mary Newton Foote Henderson's *Practical Cooking and Dinner Giving* (New York: Harper & Brothers, 1877), 286.

140 **coconut macaroons, also appear first quite early:** The earliest recipe I have found with the full name is "Cocoa-nut Maccaroons" in Leslie (1840). But there is a coconut macaroon recipe labeled "Cocoa-nut cakes" in her earlier 1830 book *Seventy-five Receipts for Pastry, Cakes, and Sweetmeats*; this book also has what may be the very first recipe for cupcakes.

140 **matzo manufacturers like Streit's:** Personal communication from Alan Adler of Aron Streit, Inc.

140 **Esther Levy's 1871 *Jewish Cookery Book*:** Levy (1871), 78.

141 **A Parisian baker, Pierre Desfontaines:** The Ladurée website credits Desfontaines: www.laduree.com. The Gerbet family is mentioned in an article by Frédéric Levent, "Pour l'Honneur Retrouvé du Macaron Gerbet," *L'Echo Républicain*, August 24, 2010. http://web.archive.org/web/20100825182837/http://www.lechorepublicain.fr/pour-l-honneur-retrouve-du-macaron-gerbet-,697.html.

142 *The Macaroni:* Image courtesy of the Walpole Library, Yale University.

143 **the Persians probably got the almond pastry:** Perry (2005), 99; Nasrallah (2013), 59.

143 **the ideas of sociologists Georg Simmel and Thorstein Veblen:** Veblen (1899), Simmel (1904). See also Laudan (2013), 55.

143 **trickle down to the masses:** See also Goody (1982), Mintz (1985), and Anderson (2005).

Eleven: Sherbet, Fireworks, and Mint Juleps

144 **Ice cream was invented:** Two superb books on the history of ice cream and ices are David (1995) and Quinzio (2009).

145 **One day in the daily flavors:** Image courtesy of Janet Yu and Mr. and Mrs. Miscellaneous.

145 **handwritten in Grace Countess Granville's Receipt Book:** David (1979), 27.

146 **Neige de Fleur D'orange:** David (1979), 28. From Francois Pierre La Varenne, *Nouveau Confiturier*, later edition ca. 1696.

146 **by 1700 other ice cream flavors:** Quinzio (2009), 15.

146 **medieval cookbooks give recipes for cooking quince:** Lewicka (2011), 276, 461.

146 **appears in a thirteenth-century cookbook manuscript:** Miranda (1966), 300: Pasta de Membrillo. English translation by Charles Perry available at http://www.daviddfriedman.com/Medieval/Cookbooks/Andalusian/andalusian10.htm#Heading521.

147 To make Marmalade: Simmons (1796), 40.
147 To Make Orange Marmalade: Wilson (2010), 145.
148 Rhubarb syrup. Opens liver obstruction: Chipman and Lev (2006).
148 In medieval Persia: Batmanglij (2011), 503.
148 even mentioned in the Bible: David (1995), xi.
148 Claudia Roden talks nostalgically of the sharbat: Roden (2000), 484.
149 Lime Syrup (Sharbat-e ablimu): Recipe from Batmanglij (2011), 509. Courtesy Mage Publishers, www.mage.com.
149 the French naturalist Pierre Belon in 1553: http://books.google.com/books?id=VYcsgAYyIZcC&q=cherbet. Mysteriously, Belon used two words, *cherbet* and *sorbet*, and French traveler Nicolay also used *sorbet*. It's not clear why both were mentioned (perhaps different pronunciations by different ethnic groups in Istanbul?) or why the form "sorbet" caught on in Romance languages.
149 Thirsty passersby would buy a glass of syrup: Belon (1553), 418.
149 Jean Chardin, a seventeenth-century French traveler: Chardin (1673–1677).
150 *lohusa şerbet* served to new mothers: Isin (2003), 80.
150 "sherbets made in Turkie of Lemons, Roses, and Violets perfumed": David (1995), 156.
150 the guild of limonadiers: Spary (2012), 103.
150 The Arabs had earlier brought lemons: The word comes from Arabic *laymun* and Persian *līmūn*. Sweetened lemon juice had been a common trade commodity in medieval Egypt.
150 Pour faire de bonne Limonade: Audiger (1692), 291.
150 To make good lemonade: Translation from Quinzio (2009), 20.
151 potassium nitrate was called "Chinese snow": Butler and Feelisch (2008).
151 the physician Ibn Abī Uşaybi'a: Partington (1960), 311. Also al-Hassan (2001), 113.
152 An intimate character study: Image © The British Library Board. Add.r.1039.
153 "Saltpetre, which in gunpowder produces the explosive heat": The Ain-I-Akbari (Constitution of Akbar) is an administrative survey of the reign of Akbar. An English translation is available on the web: http://persian.packhum.org/persian/main?url=pf%3Ffile=00702051%26ct=47.
153 A goglet and bucket: Bayerische Staatsbibliothek München, Signatur: 4 Oecon. 1550.
154 "Wine may freeze in Glasses": From Porta (1658), Book 14, Chapter 11.
155 Robert Boyle said that "a Mixture of Snow and Salt": Boyle (1665), 111.
155 Raspberry Shrub (1834): *Thomsonian Botanic Watchman*, Vol. 1, No. 1 (1834), 63.
156 the FDA requires that sherbet: http://www.accessdata.fda.gov/scripts/cdrh/cfdocs/cfcfr/CFRSearch.cfm?fr=135.140.
156 what Mayhew called an "effervescing draught": Mayhew (1851).
157 "cola" comes from the kola nut: Kiple and Ornelas (2000), 684–92; Lovejoy (1980).

Twelve: Does This Name Make Me Sound Fat? Why Ice Cream and
Crackers Have Different Names

161 **Roman Jakobson:** Jakobson and Waugh (2002).
162 **Richard Klink created pairs:** Klink (2000).
162 **Eric Yorkston and Geeta Menon at New York University:** Yorkston and
Menon (2004).
164 **cracker brands from a dieting website:** The URL is http://www.calorie
king.com/foods/calories-in-crackers-crispbreads-rice-cakes_c-
Y2lkPTk1.html?bid=-1&sid=37084.
164 **I found more back vowels:** Experimental details: I counted only the stressed
syllables, and I normalized each count by the expected count of that vowel,
computed by counting all stressed syllables in the CMU Pronouncing Dictionary of English. Since the vowel æ is the most low and back of the front
vowels, I also ran the analysis again considering æ as a back vowel and got
the same results. Finally, in addition to looking at all front vowels versus
all back vowels, I also tried comparing the counts of just one front vowel
i and one back vowel ɑ as Yorkston and Menon did. Once again, I found a
tendency for ice creams to use back vowels and crackers to use front vowels.
164 **insights from linguists:** Will Leben, the Chair of Linguistics at Lexicon
Branding, has a nice blog on linguistic issues in branding: blog.lexicon-
branding.com/tag/will-leben.
164 **the *frequency code*:** Ohala (1994).
164 **Eugene Morton:** Morton (1977).
165 **associated with babies or children:** Eckert (2010), Geenberg (ms), Fernald
et al. (1989), Jurafsky (1996).
166 **something about jagged shapes:** For the pair bouba/kiki, psychologists
Ramachandran and Hubbard found that 95 percent of people associated
bouba with the rounder figure. Swedish: Ahlner and Zlatev (2010). Swahili:
Davis (1961). Otjiherero in Namibia: Bremner et al. (2013). Tamil: Ramachandran and Hubbard (2001). In children: Maurer, Pathman, and Mondloch (2006).
167 **Recent work by a number of linguists:** D'Onofrio (2013), Ahlner and
Zlatev (2010), Westbury (2005), Nielsen and Rendall (2011).
169 **nomadic tribes in Namibia:** Bremner et al. (2013).

Thirteen: Why the Chinese Don't Have Dessert

171 **first used in France:** *Le Grand Robert de la Langue Française*, entry for
dessert.
171 **dessert courses under various names:** Names like "issue" or "voidee" or
sometimes just as a numbered course.
172 **English feast, from around 1285:** From the *Treatise of Walter of Bibbesworth*,
cited and translated in Hieatt and Butler (1985), 3.
172 **Dragée comes from the Greek word *tragemata*:** *OED* entry for *dragée*.

172 A "second table" was set: Dalby (1996), 23. See also Athenaeus's *The Deipnosophists*, Book 14, §§ 46–85 in the Yonge translation.

172 Herodotus remarked in the fifth century BCE: Macaulay (1890), Book 1 (Clio), § 133.

172 a culinary new wave developed: Waines (1989), 8.

173 sweets were believed to help digest: Nasrallah (2007), 43.

173 "roasted chicken, roast meat, rice with honey": Lewicka (2011), 56; Perry (2001), 491.

173 fritters flavored with musk and "dripping with syrup": Haddawy and Mahdi (1995), 290.

173 the man who was credited for bringing these things: Makki and Corriente (2001), 202–6.

173 people even credited Ziryab with "inventing" many of the fabled desserts: Makki and Corriente (2001), 202–6.

174 Ziryab seems to have personified in these legends: Reynolds (2008).

174 meals be served in seven courses: Miranda (1966), 120. Available in English translation by Charles Perry at http://www.daviddfriedman.com/Medieval/Cookbooks/Andalusian/andalusian3.htm#Heading125.

174 Roberto de Nola's 1525 *Libro de Cozina*: Nola (1525), 37.

174 *mawmanee*: Rodinson (2001).

175 Chekyns upon soppes: *A Propre Newe Booke of Cokerye*. c. 1557. John Kynge and Thomas Marche, Crede Lane, London.

175 Flandrin carefully annotated the presence of sugar: Flandrin (2007).

176 In British English the word retained its meaning: We can see this from the definition first written in the 1895 edition of the *Oxford English Dictionary*:
   a. A course of fruit, sweetmeats, etc. served after a dinner or supper; "the last course at an entertainment"
   b. "In the United States often used to include pies, puddings, and other sweet dishes." Now also in British usage.

176 William Maclay put down the menu in his diary: Baker (1897), 192.

177 "A hamburger with ketchup" Gopnik (2011), 269.

177 historian Ken Albala calls "throwbacks": Albala (2007), 57.

177 "holidays often preserve what the everyday loses": Mintz (1985), 87.

180 While Chinese meals don't have the concept of a final sweet course: For more on the structure of Chinese cuisine, go straight to Anderson (1988) and Chang (1977). For more on the general idea of the structures of cuisines, see Anderson (2005).

181 linguist Ken Stevens (in his *Quantal Theory of Speech*): Stevens (1972).

181 generous visitors from Asia: For example, I'm still grateful to Robyn Eckhardt of the *EatingAsia* blog, who once brought me some just as I was running out.

181 gold rush days: Natural leavening was used in the earliest San Francisco bakeries like Boudin, but the loaves were just called "French bread"; not until after 1900 did the term "sourdough" become associated with French and Italian bread in San Francisco, likely borrowed from the Klondike Gold Rush in Alaska (Peters 2013, Carl Nolte, p.c.).

181 San Franciscans instead used molasses for everything: Peters (2013), 6; Kamiya (2013), 175.

182 Elisabeth Rozin called the "flavor principle": Rozin (1973).
182 Y. Y. Ahn at Indiana University and his colleagues: Ahn et al. (2011), Drahl (2012).
183 In early China: Fiskesjö (1999).
183 Claude Lévi-Strauss: Lévi-Strauss (1969).

References

Adams, Robert McCormick. 1965. *Land behind Baghdad: A History of Settlement on the Diyala Plains*. University of Chicago Press.

Adamson, Melitta Weiss. 2004. *Food in Medieval Times*. Greenwood Press.

Ahlner, F., and J. Zlatev. 2010. "Cross-Modal Iconicity: A Cognitive Semiotic Approach to Sound Symbolism." *Sign Systems Studies* 38(1): 298–348.

Ahn, Yong-Yeol, Sebastian E. Ahnert, James P. Bagrow, and Albert-László Barabási. 2011. "Flavor Network and the Principles of Food Pairing. *Scientific Reports* 1: 196.

al-Hassan, Ahmad Y. 2001. "Military Fires, Gunpowder and Firearms." Chapter 4.4 in *Science and Technology in Islam. Part II: Technology and Applied Sciences*, edited by Ahmad Y. al-Hassan, Maqbul Ahmed and Albert Zaki Iskandar. UNESCO. http://books.google.com/books?id=h2g1qte4iegC&q=ibn+bakhtawayh.

Al-Nassir, A. A. 1993. *Sibawayh the Phonologist*. Kegan Paul.

Albala, Ken. 2007. *The Banquet: Dining in the Great Courts of Late Renaissance Europe*. University of Illinois Press.

———. 2011. "Historical Background to Food and Christianity." In *Food and Faith in Christian Culture*, edited by Ken Albala and Trudy Eden, 7–200. Columbia University Press.

Albala, Ken, and Trudy Eden, eds. 2011. *Food and Faith in Christian Culture*. Columbia University Press.

Allen, Robert C., Jean-Pascal Bassino, Debin Ma, Christine Moll-Murata, and Jan Luiten Van Zanden. 2011. "Wages, Prices, and Living Standards in China, 1738–1925: In comparison with Europe, Japan, and India." *The Economic History Review* 64(S1): 8–38.

Amerine, Maynard Andrew, and Edward Biffer Roessler. 1976. *Wines: Their Sensory Evaluation*. New York: W.H. Freeman.

Anderson, Eugene N. 1988. *The Food of China*. New Haven: Yale University Press.

———. 2005. *Everyone Eats*. New York University Press.

Ankerstein, Carrie A., and Gerardine M. Pereira. 2013. "Talking about Taste: Starved for words." In *Culinary Linguistics: The Chef's Special*. Edited by Cornelia Gerhardt, Maximiliane Frobenius and Susanne Ley. Benjamins.

Antoine, Thomas. 1917. "La Pintade (poule d'Inde) dans les Textes du Moyen Âge."*Comptes-Rendus des Séances de l'Académie des Inscriptions et Belles-Lettres* 61(1): 35–50.

Aprosio, Sergio. 2003. *Vocabolario Ligure Storico Bibliografico. II.2*. Società Savonese di Storia Patria.

Audiger, Nicolas. 1692. *La Maison Reglée*. Paris.

Augustine, Adam A., Matthias R. Mehl, and Randy J. Larsen. 2011. "A Positivity Bias in Written and Spoken English and Its Moderation by Personality and Gender." *Social Psychological and Personality Science* 2(5): 508–15.

Austin, Daniel F. 1988. "The taxonomy, evolution and genetic diversity of sweet potatoes and related wild species." In *Exploration, Maintenance and Utilization of Sweet Potato Genetic Resources: Report of the First Sweet Potato Planning Conference 1987*. Lima, Peru; International Potato Center, 27–59. Available at http://cipotato.org/ library/pdfdocs/SW19066.pdf.

Austin, Thomas, ed. 1964. *Two Fifteenth-century Cookery-books*. Published for the Early English Text Society by the Oxford University Press. Available online at University of Michigan Humanities Text Initiative.

Baker, James W. 2009. *Thanksgiving: The Biography of an American Holiday*. Hanover: University Press of New England.

Baker, William Spohn. 1897. *Washington after the Revolution: 1784–1799*. Philadelphia.

Ballerini, Luigi, ed. 2005. *The Art of Cooking: The First Modern Cookery Book. By The Eminent Maestro Martino of Como*. Translated and annotated by Jeremy Parzen. University of California Press.

Barros, Cristina. 2004. "Los Moles. Aportaciones Prehispánicas." In *Patrimonio Cultural y Turismo. Cuadernos 12. El mole en la ruta de los dioses: 6° Congreso sobre Patrimonio Gastronómico y Turísmo Cultural. Memorias (Cultural Heritage and Tourism, Volume 12: Mole on the Route of the Gods. Proceedings of the 6th Congress on Gastronomic Heritage and Cultural Tourism)*, 19–28. Puebla: Consejo Nacional para la Cultura y las Artes.

Batmanglij, Najmieh. 2011. *Food of Life: Ancient Persian and Modern Iranian Cooking and Ceremonies*. Mage.

Bauer, Robert S. 1996. "Identifying the Tai substratum in Cantonese," in *The Fourth International Symposium on Language and Linguistics*, Thailand, pp. 1806–1844. Institute of Language and Culture for Rural Development, Mahidol University.

Bayless, Rick. 2007. *Authentic Mexican*. William Morrow.

Belon, Pierre. 1553. *Les Observations de Plusieurs Singularitez et Choses Memorables Trouvées en Grèce, Asie, Judée, Egypte, Arabie et Autres Pays Étrangèrs*. http:// books.google.com/books?id=VYcsgAYyIZcC.

Benson, Adolph Burnett. 1987. *Peter Kalm's Travels in North America: The English Version of 1770*. New York: Dover.

Benveniste, Emile. 1969. *Indo-European Language and Society*. University of Miami Press.

Berdan, Frances F., and Patricia Rieff Anawalt. 1997. *The Essential Codex Mendoza*. Vol. 2. University of California Press.

Berger, Jonah, and Katherine L. Milkman. 2012. "What Makes Online Content Viral?" *Journal of Marketing Research* 49(2): 192–205.

Beverland, Michael B. 2006. "The 'Real Thing': Branding Authenticity in the Luxury Wine Trade." *Journal of Business Research* 59: 251–58.

Beverland, Michael B., Adam Lindgreen, and Michiel W. Vink. 2008. "Projecting Authenticity Through Advertising." *Journal of Advertising* 37(1): 5–15.

Biber, Douglas. 1988. *Variation Across Speech and Writing*. Cambridge: Cambridge University Press.

Biber, Douglas. 1995. *Dimensions of Register Variation: A Cross-Linguistic Comparison*. Cambridge: Cambridge University Press.

Bottéro, Jean. 2004. *The Oldest Cuisine in the World: Cooking in Mesopotamia*. University of Chicago Press.

Boucher, Jerry, and Charles E. Osgood. 1969. "The Pollyanna Hypothesis." *Journal of Verbal Learning and Verbal Behavior* 8(1): 1–8.

Bourdieu, Pierre. 1984. *Distinction: A Social Critique of the Judgement of Taste*. Translated by Richard Nice from the 1979 French original. Harvard University Press.

Boyle, Robert. 1665. *New Experiments and Observations Touching Cold, or an Experimental History of Cold, Begun*. London: John Crook. http://quod.lib.umich.edu/e/eebo/A29001.0001.001.

Braudel, Fernand. 1981. *The Structures of Everyday Life. Volume 1 of Civilization and Capitalism 15th–18th Century*. New York: Harper & Row.

Brears, Peter. 1993. "Wassail! Celebrations in Hot Ale." In *Liquid Nourishment*, edited by C. Anne Wilson, 106–41. Edinburgh University Press.

Bremner, Andrew J., Serge Caparos, Jules Davidoff, Jan de Fockert, Karina J. Linnell, and Charles Spence. 2013. " 'Bouba' and 'Kiki' in Namibia? A Remote Culture Make Similar Shape–Sound Matches, But Different Shape–Taste Matches to Westerners." *Cognition* 126: 165–72.

Briscoe, John. 2002. *Tadich Grill*. Ten Speed Press.

Brook, Nath. 1658. *The Compleat Cook*. Printed by E.B. for Nath. Brook, at the Angel in Cornhill. London.

Buell, Paul D., and Eugene N. Anderson. 2010. *A Soup for the Qan: Chinese Dietary Medicine of the Mongol Era as Seen in Hu Sihui's Yinshan Zhengyao*. Leiden: Brill.

Burenhult, Niclas, and Asifa Majid. 2011. "Olfaction in Aslian Ideology and Language." *The Senses and Society* 6(1): 19–29.

Burkert, Walter. 1985. *Greek Religion*. Translated by John Raffan from the 1977 German original. Harvard University Press.

Butler, Anthony R., and Martin Feelisch. 2008. "Therapeutic Uses of Inorganic Nitrite and Nitrate: From the Past to the Future." *Circulation* 117: 2151–59.

Bynum, Caroline Walker. 1987. *Holy Feast and Holy Fast: The Religious Significance of Food to Medieval Women*. Berkeley: University of California Press.

Campopiano, Michele. 2012. "State, Land Tax and Agriculture in Iraq from the Arab Conquest to the Crisis of the Abbasid Caliphate (Seventh–Tenth Centuries)." *Studia Islamica, nouvelle édition/new series* 3: 5–50.

Carroll, Glenn R., and Dennis Ray Wheaton. 2009. "The Organizational Construction of Authenticity: An Examination of Contemporary Food and Dining in the U.S." *Research in Organizational Behavior* 29: 255–82.

Carter, M. G. 2004. *Sibawayhi*. Oxford: I. B. Tauris.

Cato. 1934. *De Agricultura*. Loeb Classical Library edition, Bill Thayer's Web Site, University of Chicago. http://penelope.uchicago.edu/Thayer/E/Roman/Texts/Cato/De_Agricultura/K*.html.

Chan, Sucheng. 2000. "A People of Exceptional Character: Ethnic Diversity, Nativism, and Racism in the California Gold Rush." Chapter 3 in *Rooted in Barbarous Soil: People, Culture, and Community in Gold Rush California*, edited by Kevin Starr and Richard J. Orsi, 44–85. California Historical Society.

Chang, K. C., ed. 1977. *Food in Chinese Culture: Anthropological and Historical Perspectives*. Yale University Press.

Chardin, Sir John. 1673–1677. *Travels in Persia, 1673–1677*. Vol. 2. From Chapter 15, "Concerning the Food of the Persians." http://www.iras.ucalgary .ca/~volk/sylvia/Chardin15.htm.

Chipman, Leigh N., and Efraim Lev. 2006. "Syrups from the Apothecary's Shop: A Genizah Fragment Containing One of the Earliest Manuscripts of Minhaj al-Dukkan." *Journal of Semitic Studies* LI/1: 137–68.

Civil, Miguel. 1964. "A Hymn to the Beer Goddess and a Drinking Song." In *Studies Presented to A. Leo Oppenheim, June 7, 1964*, 67–89. The Oriental Institute of the University of Chicago.

Clément, Pierre. 1863. *Jacques Coeur et Charles VII*. Deuxieme edition. Paris: Didier et Cie.

Coe, Sophie D. 1994. *America's First Cuisines*. University of Texas Press.

Coe, Sophie D., and Michael D. Coe. 1996. *The True History of Chocolate*. Thames and Hudson.

Cohn, Michael A., Matthias R. Mehl, and James W. Pennebaker. 2004. "Linguistic Markers of Psychological Change Surrounding September 11, 2001." *Psychological Science* 15(10): 687–93.

Colquhoun, Kate. 2007. *Taste: The Story of Britain through its Cooking*. Bloomsbury.

Cowen, Tyler. 2012. *An Economist Gets Lunch*. Dutton.

Curtis, Robert I. 1991. *Garum and Salsamenta*. E. J. Brill.

D'Ancoli, Francesco. 1972. *Lingua Spagnuola E Dialetto Napoletano*. Napoli: Libreria Scientifica Editrice.

D'Onofrio, Annette. 2013. "Phonetic Detail and Dimensionality in Sound-Shape Correspondences: Refining the *Bouba-Kiki* Paradigm." *Language and Speech*. Published online November 15, 2013.

Dalby, Andrew. 1996. *Siren Feasts: A History of Food and Gastronomy in Greece*. Routledge.

Danescu-Niculescu-Mizil, Cristian, Moritz Sudhof, Dan Jurafsky, Jure Leskovec, and Christopher Potts. 2013. "A Computational Approach to Politeness with Application to Social Factors." *Proceedings of the 51st Annual Meeting of the Association for Computational Linguistics*. Stroudsburg, PA: Association for Computational Linguistics.

Danescu-Niculescu-Mizil, Cristian, Robert West, Dan Jurafsky, Jure Leskovec, and Christopher Potts. 2013. "No Country for Old Members: User Lifecycle and Linguistic Change in Online Communities." *Proceedings of the International World Wide Web Conference*.

David, Elizabeth. 1977. *English Bread and Yeast Cookery*. Allen Lane.

———. 1979. "Fromages Glacés and Iced Creams." *Petits Propos Culinaire* 2: 23–35.

———. 1995. *Harvest of the Cold Months: The Social History of Ice and Ices*. Viking.

Davidson, Alan. 1999. *The Oxford Companion to Food*. Oxford University Press.

Davis, R. 1961. "The Fitness of Names to Drawings: A Cross-Cultural Study in Tanganyika." *British Journal of Psychology* 52: 259–68.

de Sousa, Hilário. 2011. "Changes in the Language of Perception in Cantonese." *The Senses and Society* 6(1): 38–47.

Dixon, Clifton V. 1985. "Coconuts and Man on the North Coast of Honduras." In *Yearbook. Conference of Latin Americanist Geographers*, Vol. 11, 17–21.

Drahl, Carmen. 2012. "Molecular Gastronomy Cooks Up Strange Plate-Fellows." *Chemical & Engineering News* 90(25): 37–40.

Dundes, Alan. 1981. "Wet and Dry, the Evil Eye: An Essay in Indo-European and Semitic Worldview." In *The Evil Eye: A Folklore Casebook*, 257–312.

Dunlop, Fuchsia. 2008. *Shark's Fin and Sichuan Pepper: A Sweet-Sour Memoir of Eating in China*. Norton.

Eales, Mrs. 1742. *The Art of Candying and Preserving in Its Utmost Perfection*. London: R. Montagu. http://books.google.com/books?ei=T3awT7zRHuaJ iALYltXWAw.

Eckert, Penelope. 2010. "Affect, Sound Symbolism, and Variation." *Penn Working Papers in Linguistics* 16.1. University of Pennsylvania.

Edwords, Clarence Edgar. 1914. *Bohemian San Francisco: Its Restaurants and Their Most Famous Recipes; The Elegant Art of Dining*. P. Elder and Company.

Eilers, Wilhelm. 2000. "Chapter 11: Iran and Mesopotamia." In *The Cambridge History of Iran*. Volume 3, Part 1: *The Seleucid, Parthian and Sasanian Periods*. Cambridge University Press.

Endelman, Todd M. 2002. *The Jews of Britain: 1656 to 2000*. University of California Press.

Entani, E., M. Asai, S. Tsujihata, Y. Tsukamoto, and M. Ohta. 1998. "Antibacterial Action of Vinegar Against Food-Borne Pathogenic Bacteria Including *Escherichia coli* O157:H7." *Journal of Food Protection* 61(8): 953–59.

Escoffier, Auguste. 1921. *The Complete Guide to the Art of Modern Cookery: The First Translation into English in Its Entirety of Le Guide Culinaire*. Translated by H. L. Cracknell and R. J. Kaufmann. John Wiley, 1979.

Fernald, A., T. Taeschner, J. Dunn, M. Papousek, B. Boysson-Bardies, and I. Fukui. 1989. "A Cross-Language Study of Prosodic Modifications in Mothers' and Fathers' Speech to Preverbal Infants." *Journal of Child Language* 16: 477–501.

Fiskesjö, Magnus. 1999. "On the Raw and the Cooked Barbarians of Imperial China." *Inner Asia* 1(2): 139–68.

Flandrin, Jean-Louis. 2007. *Arranging the Meal: A History of Table Service in France*. Vol. 19. University of California Press.

Forbush, Edward Howe, and Herbert Keightley Job. 1912. *A History of the Game Birds, Wild-Fowl and Shore Birds of Massachussetts and Adjacent States: With Observations on Their . . . Recent Decrease in Numbers; Also the Means for Conserving Those Still in Existence*. Wright & Potter printing company, state printers.

Foster, George. 1972. "The Anatomy of Envy: A Study in Symbolic Behavior." *Current Anthropology* 13(2): 165–202.

Frank, Andre Gunder. 1998. *ReOrient: Global Economy in the Asian Age*. University of California Press.

Freeman-Grenville, G.S.P., ed. and trans. 1981. *The Book of the Wonders of India, Kitab ajaib al-hind*. Written by Captain Buzurg ibn Shahriyar of Ramhormuz. Translation published by East-West Publications. London.

Geenberg, Katherine Rose. Under review. *Sound Symbolism in Adult Baby Talk (ABT): The Role of the Frequency Code in the Construction of Social Meaning*.

Gelderblom, Oscar. 2004. "The Decline of Fairs and Merchant Guilds in the Low Countries, 1250–1650." *Jaarboek voor Middeleeuwse Geschiedenis* 7: 199–238.

Gilad, Y., M. Przeworski, and D. Lancet. 2004. "Loss of Olfactory Receptor Genes Coincides with the Acquisition of Full Trichromatic Vision in Primates. *PLOS Biology* 2:E5.

Gilad, Y., O. Man, S. Pääbo, and D. Lancet. 2003. "Human Specific Loss of Olfactory Receptor Genes." *Proceedings of the National Academy of Sciences* 100: 3324–27.

Gilmore, James H., and B. Joseph Pine II. 2007. *Authenticity: What Consumers Really Want*. Boston: Harvard Business School Press.

Glasse, Hannah. 1774. *The Art of Cookery, Made Plain and Easy: Which Far Exceeds Any Thing of the Kind Yet Published* . . . Printed for W. Strahan, J. and F. Rivington, J. Hinton. http://books.google.com/books?id=xJdAAAAAIAAJ.

Goody, Jack. 1982. *Cooking, Cuisine, and Class*. Cambridge: Cambridge University Press.

Gopnik, Adam. 2011. *The Table Comes First: Family, France, and the Meaning of Food*. Random House.

Gortner, Eva-Maria, and James W. Pennebaker. 2003. "The Archival Anatomy of a Disaster: Media Coverage and Community-wide Health Effects of the Texas A&M Bonfire Tragedy." *Journal of Social and Clinical Psychology* 22: 580–60.

Greco, Gina L., and Christine M. Rose, trans. 2009. *The Good Wife's Guide. Le Menagier de Paris. A Medieval Household Book*. Cornell University Press.

Grice, H. P. 1989. *Studies in the Way of Words*. Harvard University Press.

Grocock, C. W., and Sally Grainger. 2006. *Apicius: A Critical Edition with an Introduction and an English Translation of the Latin Recipe Text Apicius*. Prospect Books.

Haddawy, Husain, and Muhsin Mahdi. 1995. *The Arabian Nights*. Norton.

Haley, Andrew. 2011. *Turning the Tables: Restaurants and the Rise of the American Middle Class, 1880–1920*. Chapel Hill: University of North Carolina Press.

Harley, J. B. 1988. "Silences and Secrecy: The Hidden Agenda of Cartography in Early Modern Europe." *Imago Mundi* 40: 57–76.

Harris, Aisha. 2013. "Is There a Difference between Ketchup and Catsup?" *Slate*, April 22.

Hess, Karen. 1996. *Martha Washington's Booke of Cookery: And Booke of Sweetmeats*. Columbia University Press.

Heywood, Vernon H. 2012. "The Role of New World Biodiversity in the Transformation of Mediterranean Landscapes and Culture." *Bocconea* 24: 69–93.

Hickman, Peggy. 1977. *A Jane Austen Household Book*. David & Charles.

Hieatt, Constance B., ed. 1988. *An Ordinance of Pottage: An Edition of the Fifteenth Century Culinary Recipes*. Beinecke MS 163. Yale University.

Hieatt, Constance B., and Sharon Butler, eds. 1985. *Curye on Inglysch: English Culinary Manuscripts of the Fourteenth Century (Including the Forme of Cury)*. Oxford University Press.

Hilton, Chris. 1993. " 'The Ultimate Anchovy' and Tea Soup: Brief Notes on the Foods of the Dong People of Guanxi Province, South China." In *The Wilder Shores of Gastronomy: Twenty Years of the Best Food Writing from the Journal Petits Propos Culinaires*, edited by Alan Davidson and Helen Saberi, 76–80. Berkeley: Ten Speed Press, 2002.

Hines, Caitlin. 1999. "Rebaking the Pie: The WOMAN AS DESSERT Metaphor." In *Reinventing Identities: The Gendered Self in Discourse*, edited by M. Bucholtz, A.C. Liang, and L.A. Sutton. Oxford University Press.

Homan, Michael M. 2004. "Beer, Barley, and שֵׁכָר in the Hebrew Bible." In *Biblical and Judaic Studies*, Vol. 9: *Le-David Maskil: A Birthday Tribute for David Noel Freedman*, edited by Richard Elliott Friedman and William H. C. Propp, 25–38. Eisenbrauns.

Hormes, Julia M., and Paul Rozin. 2010. "Does 'Craving' Carve Nature at the Joints? Absence of a Synonym for Craving in Many Languages." *Addictive Behaviors* 35(5): 459–63.

Houben, Hubert. 2002. "Religious Toleration in the South Italian Peninsula during the Norman and Staufen Periods." *The Society of Norman Italy* 38: 319.

Huang, H. T. 2000. *Fermentations and Food Science. Needham's Science and Civilization in China*, Vol. 5, 382–83. Cambridge University Press.

Irwin, Mark. 2011. *Loanwords in Japanese*. Amsterdam: John Benjamins.

Ishige, Naomichi. 1986. "Narezushi in Asia: A Study of Fermented Aquatic Products (2)." *Bulletin of the National Museum of Ethnology* 11(3): 603–68.

———. 1993. "Cultural Aspects of Fermented Foods in East Asia." In *Fish Fermentation Technology*, edited by Cherl-ho Lee, Keith H. Steinkraus, and P. J. Alan Reilly. United Nations University Press.

Isin, Mary. 2003. *Sherbet & Spice: The Complete Story of Turkish Sweets and Desserts*. I. B. Tauris.

Jakobson, Roman, and Linda R. Waugh. 2002. *The Sound Shape of Language*. Walter de Gruyter.

Johns, Jeremy. 2002. *Arabic Administration in Norman Sicily: The Royal Diwan*. Cambridge University Press.

Johnson, Paul M., and Paul J. Kenny. 2010. "Dopamine D2 Receptors in Addiction-like Reward Dysfunction and Compulsive Eating in Obese Rats." *Nature Neuroscience* 13(5): 635–41.

Johnson, Steven. 2006. *The Ghost Map: The Story of London's Most Terrifying Epidemic—and How It Changed Science, Cities and the Modern World*. Riverhead Books.

Johnston, J., and S. Bauman. 2007. "Democracy versus Distinction: A Study of Omnivorousness in Gourmet Food Writing." *American Journal of Sociology* 113(1): 165–204.

Jurafsky, Dan, Victor Chahuneau, Bryan R. Routledge, and Noah A. Smith. 2013. "Modest versus Ostentatious Language for Product Differentiation: A Case Study in Restaurant Menus." Submitted manuscript.

———. 2014. "Narrative Framing of Consumer Sentiment in Online Restaurant Reviews." *First Monday*, 19:4.

Jurafsky, Daniel. 1996. "Universal Tendencies in the Semantics of the Diminutive." *Language* 72(3): 533–78.

Kahneman, Daniel. 2011. *Thinking, Fast and Slow*. Farrar, Straus and Giroux.

Kamiya, Gary. 2013. *Cool Gray City of Love*. Bloomsbury.

Kao, Justine, and Dan Jurafsky. 2012. "A Computational Analysis of Style, Affect, and Imagery in Contemporary Poetry." *NAACL Workshop on Computational Linguistics for Literature*. Montréal, Canada. June 8, 2012. Stroudsburg, PA: Association for Computational Linguistics.

Katz, Joshua. 2013. "Beyond 'Soda, Pop, or Coke' Regional Dialect Variation in the Continental US." http://www4.ncsu.edu/~jakatz2/project-dialect.html.

Keefe, Patrick. 2009. *The Snakehead: An Epic Tale of the Chinatown Underworld and the American Dream*. Doubleday.

Kimble, George H. 1933. "Portuguese Policy and Its Influence on Fifteenth Century Cartography." *Geographical Review* 23(4): 653–59.

Kiple, Kenneth F., and Kriemhild Coneè Ornelas. 2000. *The Cambridge World History of Food*, 684–92. Cambridge University Press.

Kitchner, William. 1817. *Apicius Redivivus: Or, The Cook's Oracle*. London.

Klink, Richard R. 2000. "Creating Brand Names with Meaning: The Use of Sound Symbolism." *Marketing Letters* 11(1): 5–20.

Knoblock, John, and Jeffrey Riegel. 2000. *The Annals of Lu Buwei: A Complete Translation and Study*. Stanford University Press.

Kohn, Meir. 2003. "Organized Markets in Pre-Industrial Europe." Working Paper 03-12. Available at SSRN, http://ssrn.com/abstract=427764.

Kotthoff, Helga. 2010. "Comparing Drinking Toasts—Comparing ethnopragmatics." *Freiburger Arbeitspapiere zur Germanistischen Linguistik* 1.

Krumme, Coco. 2011. "Velvety Chocolate with a Silky Ruby Finish. Pair with Shellfish." *Slate*.

Kurlansky, Mark. 1997. *Cod: A Biography of the Fish That Changed the World*. Random House.

———. 2002. *Salt: A World History*. New York: Walker and Company.

Labov, William. 1966. *The Social Stratification of English in New York City*. Washington DC: The Center for Applied Linguistics.

Lakoff, Robin. 2006. "Identity a la Carte; or, You Are What You Eat." In *Discourse and Identity (Studies in Interactional Sociolinguistics)*, edited by Anna De Fina, Deborah Schiffrin, and Michael Bamberg, 147–65. Cambridge University Press.

Lambert, Carole. 2002. "Medieval France B. The South." In *Regional Cuisines of the Middle Ages: A Book of Essays*, edited by Melissa Weiss Adamson, 68–89. New York: Routledge.

Larousse Gastronomique. 2001. New York: Clarkson Potter.

Laudan, Rachel. 2013. *Cuisine and Empire*. University of California Press.

Laudan, Rachel, and Jeffrey M. Pilcher. 1999. "Chiles, Chocolate, and Race in New Spain: Glancing Backward to Spain or Looking Forward to Mexico?" *Eighteenth-Century Life* 23(2): 59–70.

Leising, Daniel, Olga Ostrovski, and Peter Borkenau. 2012. "Vocabulary for Describing Disliked Persons Is More Differentiated Than Vocabulary for Describing Liked Persons." *Journal of Research in Personality* 46: 393–96.

Lesy, Michael, and Lisa Stoffer. 2013. *Repast: Dining Out at the Dawn of the New American Century, 1900–1910*. New York: W. W. Norton.

Leslie, Eliza. 1840. *Directions for Cookery, in Its Various Branches*. 11th ed. Philadelphia: Carey and Hart.

Lévi-Strauss, Claude. 1969. *The Raw and the Cooked: Introduction to a Science of Mythology. Vol. I*. New York: Harper & Row.

Levitt, Steven D., and Stephen J. Dubner. 2006. *Freakonomics: A Rogue Economist Explores the Hidden Side of Everything*. William Morrow.

Levitt, Steven D., and Chad Syverson. 2005. "Market Distortions When Agents Are Better Informed: The Value of Information in Real Estate." Working Paper 11053, National Bureau of Economic Research.

Levy, Esther. 1871. *Jewish Cookery Book*. Philadephia: W.S. Turner.

Lewicka, Paulina B. 2011. *Food and Foodways of Medieval Cairenes*. Leiden: Brill.

Lewis, Edna. 1976. *The Taste of Country Cooking*. Knopf.

Liberman, Mark. 2004. "Modification as Social Anxiety." *Language Log*, May 16.

Lockyer, Charles. 1711. *An Account of the Trade in India*. Available online at http://books.google.com/books?id=CdATAAAAQAAJ.

Longchamps, Nigel de. 1960. *Speculum Stultorum*. Edited, with an Introduction and Notes, by John H. Mozley and Robert R. Raymo. Berkeley and Los Angeles: University of California Press.

Lovejoy, Paul E. 1980. "Kola in the History of West Africa (La kola dans l'histoire de l'Afrique occidentale)." *Cahiers d'études africaines* 20(112): 97–134.

Macaulay, G. C., ed. 1890. *The History of Herodotus*. English translation, London: Macmillan and Company.

MacKenzie, D. N. 1971. *A Concise Pahlavi Dictionary*. London: Oxford University Press.

Majid, Asifa, and Niclas Burenhult. 2014. "Odors are expressible in language, as long as you speak the right language." *Cognition* 130(2): 266–70.

Makki, Mahmud Ali, and Federico Corriente, trans. 2001. *Crónica de los emires Alhakam I y ʾAbdarrahman II entre los años 796 y 847 (Almuqtabis II-1)*. Translation of Ibn Hayyan, Abu Marwan Hayyan ibn Khalaf. Zaragoza, Spain: Instituto de Estudios Islamicos y del Oriente Próximo (Institute of Islamic and Near Eastern Studies).

Mann, Charles C. 2011. *1493: Uncovering the World that Columbus Created*. Knopf.

Marin, Manuela, and David Waines, eds. 1993. *Kanz Al-Fawa'id Fi Tanwiʾ Al-Mawaʾid* (Medieval Arab/Islamic Culinary Art). Wiesbaden and Beirut: Franz Steiner Verlag.

Marks, Gil. 2010. *Encylopedia of Jewish Food*. Wiley.

Markus, Hazel Rose, and Alana Conner. 2013. *Clash! 8 Cultural Conflicts That Make Us Who We Are*. Penguin.

Mars, Gerlad, and Yochanan Altman. 1987. "Alternative Mechanism of Distribution in a Soviet Economy." In *Constructive Drinking: Perspectives on Drink from Anthropology*, edited by Mary Douglas, 270–79. Cambridge University Press.

Martellotti, A. 2001. *Il Liber de Ferculis di Giambonino da Cremona: La Gastronimia Araba in Occidente Nella Trattatistica Dietetica*. Fasano, Italy: Schena Editore.

Matsuoka, Yoshihiro, Yves Vigouroux, Major M. Goodman, Jesus Sanchez, Edward Buckler, and John Doebley. 2002. "A Single Domestication for Maize Shown by Multilocus Microsatellite Genotyping." *Proceedings of the National Academy of Sciences* 99(9): 6080–84.

Matthews, Donald M. 1997. *The Early Glyptic of Tell Brak: Cylinder Seals of Third Millennium Syria*. Vol. 15. Ruprecht Gmbh & Company.

Matthews, Stephen. 2006. "Cantonese Grammar in Areal Perspective." In *Grammars in Contact: A Cross-Linguistic Typology*, edited by Alexandra Y. Aikhenvald and Robert M. W. Dixon, 220–36. Oxford: Oxford University Press.

Maurer, D., T. Pathman, and C. J. Mondloch. 2006. "The Shape of Boubas:

Sound-Shape Correspondences in Toddlers and Adults." *Developmental Science* 9: 316–22.

Mayhew, Henry. 1851. *London Labour and the London Poor.* London.

McAuley, Julian J., Jure Leskovec, and Dan Jurafsky. 2012. "Learning Attitudes and Attributes from Multi-Aspect Reviews." IEEE International Conference on Data Mining. Brussels, Belgium. December 10–13, 2012.

McCoy, Elin. 2005. *The Emperor of Wine: The Rise of Robert M. Parker, Jr. and the Reign of American Taste.* Ecco.

McFarland, Daniel A., Dan Jurafsky, and Craig M. Rawlings. 2013. "Making the Connection: Social Bonding in Courtship Situations." *American Journal of Sociology* 118(6): 1596–1649.

McGovern, Patrick E. 2003. *Ancient Wine: The Search for the Origins of Viniculture.* Princeton University Press.

———. 2009. *Uncorking the Past: The Quest for Wine, Beer, and Other Alcoholic Beverages.* University of California Press.

McGovern, Patrick E., Armen Mirzoian, and Gretchen R. Hall. 2009. *Ancient Egyptian Herbal Wines. Proceedings of the National Academy of Sciences* 106(18): 7361–66.

McGovern, Patrick E., M. Christofidou-Solomidou, W. Wang, F. Dukes, T. Davidson, and W. S. El-Deiry. 2010. "Anticancer Activity of Botanical Compounds in Ancient Fermented Beverages." *International Journal of Oncology* 37(1): 5–21.

McRae, Jeremy F., Joel D. Mainland, Sara R. Jaeger, Kaylin A. Adipietro, Hiroaki Matsunami, and Richard D. Newcomb. 2012. "Genetic Variation in the Odorant Receptor OR2J3 Is Associated with the Ability to Detect the 'Grassy' Smelling Odor, cis-3-hexen-1-ol." *Chemical Senses* 37(7): 585–93.

Meyers, Cindy. 2009. "The Macaron and Madame Blanchez." *Gastronomica: The Journal of Food and Culture* 9(2): 14–18.

Michel, Andreas. 1996. *Vocabolario Critico Degli Ispanismi Siciliani.* Palermo: Centro di Studi Filologici e Linguistici Siciliani.

Michel, Jean-Baptiste, Yuan Kui Shen, Aviva Presser Aiden, Adrian Veres, Matthew K. Gray, William Brockman, The Google Books Team, Joseph P. Pickett, Dale Hoiberg, Dan Clancy, Peter Norvig, Jon Orwant, Steven Pinker, Martin A. Nowak, and Erez Lieberman Aiden. 2011. "Quantitative Analysis of Culture Using Millions of Digitized Books." *Science* 331(6014): 176–82.

Mintz, Sidney W. 1985. *Sweetness and Power: The Place of Sugar in Modern History.* Penguin.

Miranda, Ambrosio Huici. 1966. *La Cocina Hispano-Magrebí Durante La Época Almohade.* Ediciones Trea, 2005 edition.

Monroe, Burt L., Michael P. Colaresi, and Kevin M. Quinn. 2008. "Fightin' Words: Lexical Feature Selection and Evaluation for Identifying the Content of Political Conflict." *Political Analysis* 16(4): 372–403.

Montagné, Prosper, and Alfred Gottschalk. 1938. *Larousse Gastronomique.* Larousse.

Monteagudo, José Luis Curiel. 2002. *Libro de cocina de la Gesta de Independencia: Nueva España, 1817/Anónimo.* Mexico: Conaculta.

———. 2004. "Construcción y Evolución del Mole Virreinal." In *Patrimonio Cultural y Turismo. Cuadernos 12. El mole en la ruta de los dioses. 6° Congreso sobre*

Patrimonio Gastronómico y Turismo Cultural (Puebla 2004). Memorias, 29–62. Puebla: Consejo Nacional para la Cultura y las Artes.

Montefiore, Judith Cohen. 1846. *The Jewish Manual*. London. Available at http://www.gutenberg.org/ebooks/12327.

Montgomery, L. M. 1915. *Anne of the Island*. Grosset and Dunlop.

Morton, Eugene S. 1977. "On the Occurrence and Significance of Motivation-Structural Rules in Some Bird and Mammal Sounds." *American Naturalist* 111(981): 855–69.

Moss, Michael. 2013. *Salt, Sugar, Fat: How the Food Giants Hooked Us*. Random House.

Mozely, J. H., trans. 1963. *A Mirror for Fools: The Book of Burnel the Ass*, written by Nigel Longchamp. University of Notre Dame Press.

Nasrallah, Nawal. 2007. *Annals of the Caliphs' Kitchens: Ibn Sayyār Al-Warrāq's Tenth-Century Baghdadi Cookbook*. Brill.

———. 2013. *Delights from the Garden of Eden*. Equinox.

Needham, Joseph. 1971. *Science and Civilisation in China*. Volume 4: *Physics and Physical Technology*. Part III: *Civil Engineering and Nautics*. Cambridge University Press.

New York Public Library. Miss Frank E Buttolph Menu Collection.

Newman, Elizabeth Thompson. 1964. *A Critical Edition of an Early Portuguese Cookbook*. University Microfilms International.

Nielsen, A., and D. Rendall. 2011. "The Sound of Round: Evaluating the Sound-Symbolic Role of Consonants in the Classic Takete-Maluma Phenomenon." *Canadian Journal of Experimental Psychology* 65(2): 115–24.

Noble, Ann C. 1984ff. The Wine Aroma Wheel. http://winearomawheel.com.

Nola, Roberto de. 1525. *Libro De Coçina*. Republished in 1969 by Taurus Ediciones Madrid.

Norman, Jerry, and Tsu-lin Mei. 1976. "The Austroasiatics in Ancient South China: Some Lexical Evidence." *Monumenta Serica* 32: 274–301.

Nostredame, Michel de. 1555. *Traité des fardemens et confitures*. Lyons.

Ogilvy, David. 1963. *Confessions of an Advertising Man*. Southbank Publishing, 2004 ed.

Ohala, John J. 1994. "The Frequency Codes Underlies the Sound Symbolic Use of Voice Pitch." In *Sound Symbolism*, edited by L. Hinton, J. Nichols, and J. J. Ohala, 325–47. Cambridge: Cambridge University Press.

Ott, Cindy. 2012. *Pumpkin: The Curious History of an American Icon*. University of Washington Press.

Pang, Bo, and Lillian Lee. 2008. "Opinion Mining and Sentiment Analysis." *Foundations and Trends in Information Retrieval* 2(1): 1–135.

Partington, James Riddick. 1960. *A History of Greek Fire and Gunpowder*. Cambridge: W. Heffer and Sons.

Peeters, Guido. 1971. "The Positive/Negative Asymmetry: On Cognitive Consistency and Positivity Bias." *European Journal of Social Psychology* 1(4): 455–74.

Pelchat, Marcia Levin, Cathy Bykowski, Fujiko F. Duke, and Danielle R. Reed. 2011. "Excretion and Perception of a Characteristic Odor in Urine after Asparagus Ingestion: A Psychophysical and Genetic Study." *Chemical Senses* 36(1): 9–17.

Pennebaker, James W. 2011. *The Secret Life of Pronouns*. Bloomsbury Press.

Pennebaker, James W., Roger J. Booth, and Martha E. Francis. 2007. LIWC2007 (Linguistic Inquiry and Word Count, software). Austin, TX.

Perry, Charles. 1981. "The Oldest Mediterranean Noodle: A Cautionary Tale." *Petits Propos Culinaires* 9: 42–44.

————. 1987. "The Sals of the Infidels, PPC 26." In *Medieval Arab Cookery*, edited by Maxime Rodinson, A. J. Arberry, and Charles Perry, 501. Prospect Books, 2006.

————. 2001. "A Thousand and One 'Fritters': The Food of the Arabian Nights." In *Medieval Arab Cookery*, edited by Maxime Rodinson, A. J. Arberry, and Charles Perry. Prospect Books, 2006.

————. 2004. "Through the Ages, a Fried Fish Triathlon." *Los Angeles Times*, October 27, http://articles.latimes.com/2004/oct/27/food/fo-fish27.

————, trans. 2005. *A Baghdad Cookery Book: The Book of Dishes (Kitāb al-Tabīkh)*. Prospect Books.

Peters, Erica J. 2012. *Appetites and Aspirations in Vietnam: Food and Drink in the Long Nineteenth Century*. Lanham, MD: AltaMira Press.

————. 2013. *San Francisco: A Food Biography*. Rowman & Littlefield.

Peterson, Richard A. 1992. "Understanding Audience Segmentation: From Elite and Mass to Omnivore and Univore." *Poetics* 21(4): 243–58.

————. 2005. "Problems in Comparative Research: The Example of Omnivorousness." *Poetics* 33(5/6): 257–82.

Pickersgill, B., and D. G. Debouck. 2005. "Domestication Patterns in Common Bean (*Phaseolus vulgaris L.*) and the origin of the Mesoamerican and Andean Cultivated Races." *Theoretical and Applied Genetics* 110(3): 432–44.

Pomerantz, Kenneth. 2000. *The Great Divergence: China, Europe, and the Making of the Modern World Economy*. Princeton University Press.

Porta, John Baptista. 1658. *Natural Magick*. English edition.

Potter, Andrew. 2010. *The Authenticity Hoax*. HarperCollins.

Potts, Christopher. 2011. "On the Negativity of Negation." In *Proceedings of SALT* 20: 636–59.

Prat Sabater, Marta. 2003. *Préstamos del Catalán en el Léxico Español (Lexical Borrowings from Catalan into Spanish)*. PhD Dissertation, Universitat Autònoma de Barcelona.

Prynne, William. 1628. *Healthes' Sicknesse. Or A Compendious and Briefe Discourse; Proving, the Drinking and Pledging of Healthes, to be Sinfull, and Utterly Unlawfull unto Christians*. Pamphlet. Available online at http://quod.lib.umich.edu/e/eebo/A10184.

Quinzio, Jeri. 2009. *Of Sugar and Snow*. University of California Press.

Ramachandran, V. S., and E. M. Hubbard. 2001. "Synaesthesia: A Window into Perception, Thought and Language." *Journal of Consciousness Studies* 8: 3–34.

Rath, Eric C. 2010. *Food and Fantasy in Early Modern Japan*. University of California Press.

Recasens, Marta, Cristian Danescu-Niculescu-Mizil, and Dan Jurafsky. 2013. "Linguistic Models for Analyzing and Detecting Biased Language." *Proceedings of the 51st Meeting of the Association for Computational Linguistics*. Stroudsburg, PA: Association for Computational Linguistics.

Redon, Odile, Francoise Sabban, and Silvano Serventi. 1998. *The Medieval Kitchen: Recipes from France and Italy*, 205. University of Chicago Press.

Rey, Alain, ed. 2011. *Le Grand Robert de la Langue Française, version électronique. Deuxième edition du Dictionnaire alphabetqiue et analogique de la Langue Française de Paul Robert.*

Reynolds, Dwight. 2008. "Al-Maqqarī's Ziryab: The Making of a Myth." *Middle Eastern Literatures* 11(2): 155–68.

Ríos, Domingo, Marc Ghislain, Flor Rodríguez, and David M. Spooner. 2007. "What Is the Origin of the European Potato? Evidence from Canary Island Landraces." *Crop Science* 47(3): 1271–80.

Roden, Claudia. 1996. *The Book of Jewish Food*. New York: Knopf.

———. 2000. *The New Book of Middle Eastern Food*. New York: Knopf.

Rodinson, Maxime. 2001. "Ma'muniyya East and West." In *Medieval Arab Cookery*, 183–97. Prospect Books.

Rodinson, Maxime, A. J. Arberry, and Charles Perry. 2006. *Medieval Arab Cookery*. Prospect Books.

Roman, Kenneth. 2010. *The King of Madison Avenue: David Ogilvy and the Making of Modern Advertising*. Palgrave Macmillan.

Roth, Cecil. 1960. "The Middle Period of Anglo-Jewish History 1290–1655, Reconsidered." *Transactions of the Jewish Historical Society of England* 19: 1–12.

Rozin, Elisabeth. 1973. *The Flavor-Principle Cookbook*. Hawthorn Books.

Rozin, Paul, Loren Berman, and Edward Royzman. 2010. "Biases in Use of Positive and Negative Words Across Twenty Languages." *Cognition & Emotion* 24: 536–48.

Rozin, Paul, Eleanor Levine, and Caryn Stoess. 1991. "Chocolate Craving and Liking." *Appetite* 17: 199–212.

Rozin, Paul, and Edward B. Royzman. 2001. "Negativity Bias, Negativity Dominance, and Contagion." *Personality and Social Psychology Review* 5(4): 296–320.

Rozin, Paul, and Caryn Stoess. 1993. "Is There a General Tendency to Become Addicted?" *Addictive Behaviors* 18: 81–87.

Ruddle, Kenneth, and Naomichi Ishige. 2005. *Fermented Fish Products in East Asia*. Hong Kong: International Resources Management Institute.

———. 2010. "On the Origins, Diffusion and Cultural Context of Fermented Fish Products in Southeast Asia." In *Globalization, Food and Social Identities in the Asia Pacific Region*, edited by James Farrer. Tokyo: Sophia University Institute of Comparative Culture.

Sahagún, Bernardino de. 1954. *Florentine Codex: General History of the Things of New Spain. Book 8: Kings and Lords*. Translated by Arthur J. O. Anderson and Charles E. Dibble. Santa Fe: School of American Research.

———. 1957. *Florentine Codex: General History of the Things of New Spain. Book 4: The Soothsayers*. Translated by Arthur J. O. Anderson and Charles E. Dibble. Santa Fe: School of American Research.

Sallares, Robert. 1991. *The Ecology of the Ancient Greek World*. Cornell University Press, 323.

Santa Clara, Pedro Gutiérrez de. 1905. *Historia de las Guerras Civiles del Perú (1544–1548) y de Otros Sucesos de las Indias*. Vol. 3. Chapter 40, 520. Madrid: Victorio Suarez. http://books.google.com/books?id=b6wTAAAAYAAJ&pg=PA520.

Santanach, Joan, ed. 2008. *The Book of Sent Soví: Medieval Recipes from Catalonia.* Translated by Robin Vogelzang. Barcino-Tamesis.

Schorger, A. W. 1966. *The Wild Turkey: Its History and Domestication.* University of Oklahoma Press.

Schwartz, Arthur. 2008. *Jewish Home Cooking.* Berkeley: Ten Speed Press.

Scott, Edmund. 1606. *An Exact Discourse of the Subtilties.* London: Printed by W.W. for Walter Burre.

Scully, Terence, ed. 1988. *The Viandier of Taillevent: An Edition of All Extant Manuscripts*, 223. University of Ottawa Press.

————. 2000. *The Neapolitan Recipe Collection.* Ann Arbor: University of Michigan Press.

————, trans. 2006. *La Varenne's Cookery: The French Cook; The French Pastry Chef; The French Confectioner.* Francois Pierre, Sieur de la Varenne. Totnes: Prospect Books, 369.

Seaberg, Albin G. 1973. *Menu Design-Merchandising and Marketing.* 2nd Ed. Boston: Cahners Books International.

Serventi, Silvano, and Françoise Sabban. 2002. *Pasta: The Story of a Universal Food.* New York: Columbia University Press.

Shaftesley, John M. 1975. "Culinary Aspects of Anglo-Jewry." In *Studies in the Cultural Life of Anglo-Jewry*, edited by Dov Noy and Issachar Ben-Ami. Jerusalem: Magnes Press.

Shesgreen, Sean. 2003. "Wet Dogs and Gushing Oranges: Winespeak for a New Millennium." *The Chronicle of Higher Education*, March 7.

Shteir, Rachel. 2004. *Striptease: The Untold History of the Girlie Show.* Oxford University Press.

Silverstein, Michael. 2003. "Indexical Order and the Dialectics of Sociolinguistic Life." *Language and Communication* 23: 193–229.

Simeti, Mary Taylor. 1991. *Pomp and Sustenance: Twenty-five Centuries of Sicilian Food.* New York: Henry Holt.

Simmel, Georg. 1904. "Fashion." *International Quarterly* 10: 130–50.

Simmons, Amelia. 1796. *American Cookery . . . A Facsimile of the Second Edition, Printed in Albany, 1796*, with an Introduction by Karen Hess. Bedford, MA: Applewood Books, 1996.

Smith, Andrew F. 1996. *Pure Ketchup.* University of South Carolina.

————. 2006. *The Turkey: An American Story.* University of Illinois Press.

Smith, Bruce D. 1997. "The Initial Domestication of Cucurbita Pepo in the Americas 10,000 Years Ago." *Science* 276(5314): 932–34.

Smith, Eliza. 1758. *The Compleat Housewife: or, Accomplished Gentlewoman's Companion.* 16th Ed. London: Printed for C. Hitch.

Smith, John, and Arthur Granville Bradley. 1910. *Travels and Works of Captain John Smith.* Vol. 1. Burt Franklin.

Smith, R.E.F., and David Christian. 1984. *Bread and Salt: A Social and Economic History of Food and Drink in Russia.* Cambridge University Press.

Soyer, Alexis. 1855. *A Shilling Cookery for the People.* London: Routledge.

Spary, E. C. 2012. *Eating the Enlightenment: Food and the Sciences in Paris, 1670–1760.* University of Chicago Press.

Speller, Camilla F., Brian M. Kemp, Scott D. Wyatt, Cara Monroe, William D.

Lipe, Ursula M. Arndt, and Dongya Y. Yang. 2010. "Ancient Mitochondrial DNA Analysis Reveals Complexity of Indigenous North American Turkey Domestication." *Proceedings of the National Academy of Sciences* 107(7): 2807–12.

Stevens, Kenneth N. 1972. "The Quantal Nature of Speech: Evidence from Articulatory-Acoustic Data." In *Human Communication: A Unified View*, edited by P. B. Denes and E. E. David Jr., 51–66. New York: McGraw Hill.

Stone, Lori D., and James W. Pennebaker. 2002. "Trauma in Real Time: Talking and Avoiding Online Conversations about the Death of Princess Diana." *Basic and Applied Social Psychology* 24(3): 173–83.

Strauss, Susan. 2005. "The Linguistic Aestheticization of Food: A Cross-Cultural Look at Food Commercials in Japan, Korea, and the United States." *Journal of Pragmatics* 37(9): 1427–55.

Stice, Eric, Kyle S. Burger, and Sonja Yokum. 2013. "Relative ability of fat and sugar tastes to activate reward, gustatory, and somatosensory regions." *American Journal of Clinical Nutrition* 98(6): 1377–1384.

Thompson, D'Arcy Wentworth. 1936. *A Glossary of Greek Birds*. Oxford University Press.

Thornton, Erin Kennedy, Kitty F. Emery, David W. Steadman, Camilla Speller, Ray Matheny, and Dongya Yang. 2012. "Earliest Mexican Turkeys (*Meleagris gallopavo*) in the Maya Region: Implications for Pre-Hispanic Animal Trade and the Timing of Turkey Domestication." *PLOS ONE* 7(8).

Torjusen, H., G. Lieblein, M. Wandel, and C. Francis. 2001. "Food System Orientation and Quality Perception Among Consumers and Producers of Organic Food in Hedmark County, Norway." *Food Quality and Preference* 12: 207–16.

Toro-Lira, Guillermo. 2010. *History of Pisco in San Francisco*. Lima, Peru: Libros GTL.

Trillin, Calvin. 1974. *American Fried: Adventures of a Happy Eater*. Doubleday.

Tusser, Thomas. 1573. *Five Hundreth Points of Good Husbandry*. London.

Ullman, Manfred. 2000. *Wörterbuch der klassischen arabischen Sprache*. Otto Harrassowitz Verlag.

Unkelbach, Christian, Klaus Fiedler, Myriam Bayer, Martin Stegmüller, and Daniel Danner. 2008. "Why Positive Information Is Processed Faster: The Density Hypothesis." *Journal of Personality and Social Psychology* 95(1): 36–49.

Van der Sijs, Nicoline. 2009. *Cookies, Coleslaw, and Stoops: The Influence of Dutch on the North American Languages*. Amsterdam University Press.

Vaux, Bert. 2003. "The Harvard Dialect Survey." http://dialect.redlog.net.

Veblen, Thorstein. 1899. *The Theory of the Leisure Class: An Economic Study in the Evolution of Institutions*. Macmillan & Company, Ltd.

Vega, Juan José. 1993. "La influencia morisca y mora: tres casos específicos." In *Cultura, identidad y cocina en el Perú*, edited by Rosario Olivas Weston. Lima: Universidad San Martín de Porres.

Velzen, Anita van. 1990. *The Taste of Indonesia: Producers of Kecap and Tauco in Cirebon and Cianjur*. Bandung: Institute of Social Studies.

———. 1992. *Small Scale Food Processing Industries in West Java: Potentialities and Constraints*. Bandung: Institute of Social Studies.

Verde, Tom. 2013. "Pasta's Winding Way West." *Saudi Aramco World* 64: 1.

Waines, David. 1989. *In a Caliph's Kitchen*. Riad el Rayyes Books.

————. 2003. " 'Luxury Foods' in Medieval Islamic Societies." *World Archaeology* 34(3): 571–80.

Watson, William. 2000. "Chapter 13: Iran and China." In *The Cambridge History of Iran*. Volume 3, Part 1: *The Seleucid, Parthian and Sasanian Periods*. Cambridge University Press.

Weingarten, Susan. 2010. "Medieval Hanukkah Traditions: Jewish Festive Foods in their European Contexts." *Food and History* 8(1): 41–62.

Westbury, C. 2005. "Implicit Sound Symbolism in Lexical Access: Evidence from an Interference Task." *Brain and Language* 93: 10–19.

Wilson, Bee. 2008. *Swindled*. Princeton University Press.

————. 2012. *Consider the Fork*. Basic Books.

Wilson, C. Anne. 1993. "Pottage and Soup as Nourishing Liquids." In *Liquid Nourishment*, edited by C. Anne Wilson, 3–19. Edinburgh University Press.

————. 2006. *Water of Life*. Prospect Books.

————. 2010. *The Book of Marmalade*. Prospect Books.

Winchester, Simon. 1998. *The Professor and the Madman: A Tale of Murder, Insanity, and the Making of the Oxford English Dictionary*. Harper Collins.

————. 2003. *The Meaning of Everything: The Story of the Oxford English Dictionary*. Oxford.

————. 2008. *The Man Who Loved China: The Fantastic Story of the Eccentric Scientist Who Unlocked the Secrets of the Middle Kingdom*. Harper.

Wondrich, David. 2007. *Imbibe!: From Absinthe Cocktail to Whiskey Smash, a Salute in Stories and Drinks to "Professor" Jerry Thomas, Pioneer of the American Bar*. Penguin.

————. 2010. *Punch: The Delights (and Dangers) of the Flowing Bowl*. Penguin.

Wright, Clifford A. 1996. "Cucina Arabo-Sicula and Maccharruni." *Al-Mashaq: Studia Arabo-Islamica Mediterranea*, 9: 151–77.

————. 2007. "The History of Macaroni." http://www.cliffordawright.com. Accessed November 24, 2013.

Wright, Thomas. 1857. *A Volume of Vocabularies*. Privately printed. Chapter 6, "The Treatise De Utensilibus of Alexander Neckam (of the Twelfth Century)." Available online at http://books.google.com/books?id=NXoKAAAAIAAJ.

Yarshater, Ehsan. 2000. "Iranian Historical Tradition." *The Seleucid, Parthian and Sasanian Periods*. Cambridge Histories Online. Cambridge University Press.

Yentsch, Anne E. 1994. *A Chesapeake Family and Their Slaves: A Study in Historical Archaeology*, 205. Cambridge University Press.

————. 1995. "Hot, Nourishing, and Culturally Potent: The Transfer of West African Cooking Traditions to the Chesapeake." *Sage* 9 (Summer): 2.

Yorkston, Eric, and Geeta Menon. 2004. "A Sound Idea: Phonetic Effects of Brand Names on Consumer Judgments." *Journal of Consumer Research* 31: 43–51.

Zaouali, Lilia. 2007. *Medieval Cuisine of the Islamic World*. Translated by M. B. DeBevoise. University of California Press.

Ziauddeen, Hisham, I. Sadaf Farooqi, and Paul C. Fletcher. 2012. "Obesity and the Brain: How Convincing Is the Addiction Model?" *Nature Reviews Neuroscience* 13(4): 279–86.

Ziegelman, Jane. 2010. *97 Orchard: An Edible History of Five Immigrant Families in One New York Tenement.* Harper.

Zimmer, Karl. 1964. *Affixal Negation in English and Other Languages.* Supplement to *Word* 20:2, Monograph 5.

Zipf, George Kingsley. 1934. *The Psycho-Biology of Language.* Houghton Mifflin.

Zizumbo-Villarreal, Daniel. 1996. "History of Coconut (*Cocos nucifera L.*) in Mexico: 1539–1810." *Genetic Resources and Crop Evolution* 43(6): 505–15.

Zwicky, Ann, and Arnold Zwicky. 1980. "America's National Dish: The Style of Restaurant Menus." *American Speech* 55: 83, 87–92.

Acknowledgments

This book has been surprisingly many years in the making and would never have been written without the support of many people. I am very happy to thank my incredible agent Howard Yoon, who encouraged me to write this book many years ago and kept on providing smart, calm guidance; my editor, the fabulous Maria Guarnaschelli, for her editing, wise advice, generosity, and contagious enthusiasm, my superb copy editor Carol Rose, and the rest of the fantastic team at Norton, including editorial assistant Mitchell Kohles, publicity director Louise Brockett, designer Kristen Bearse, production manager Anna Oler, and managing editor Nancy Palmquist; Stanford University for supporting me on the sabbatical and Stanford's Center for Advanced Study in the Behavioral Sciences for further support and for providing an intellectual home during the writing, along with the support of the wonderful staff there, particularly librarians Tricia Soto and Amanda Thomas; Eric and Elaine Hahn, who offered the use of their lovely house during other parts of the writing; the remarkable young students over the years who have taken my Stanford freshman linguistics seminar, The Language of Food, especially my collaborator Josh Freedman, who in addition to our joint work described in Chapter 8 read the manuscript and gave suggestions throughout; my amazing cousin and role model, sociologist Ron Breiger, who besides other advice pointed out the work of Andre Gunder Frank; Stephanie Shih for suggesting that I look at the history of macaroons and flour; Chia-Wei Woo, then running the Hong Kong University of Science and Technology, who first pointed out the Chinese origins of ketchup; my Mom and Dad for their support (and for the always wise editing suggestions of Dad, still an eagle-eyed reader in his nineties); John McWhorter, Lera Boroditsky, and Erin Dare for superb advice and suggestions throughout the project.

Some of the chapters grew out of pieces I wrote for *Slate*, *Gastronomica*, and the *Stanford Magazine*, where I am very lucky to have had great editors: Laura Anderson, Daniel Engber, Ginny McCormick, and especially Darra Goldstein and Juliet Lapidos.

Finally of course, this book would not have been possible without the ideas, edits, suggestions, and support of my wife, Janet.

Many people over the years gave me advice and ideas, answered questions, suggested resources or people, and spotted flaws; thanks to Alan Adler at Aron Streit, Inc., KT Albiston, Domenica Alioto, Mike Anderson, Mike Bauer, Pete Beatty, Leslie Berlin, Jay Bordeleau, Jason Brenier, Ramón Cáceres, Marine Carpuat, Alex Caviness, John Caviness, Victor Chahuneau, Karen Cheng, Paula Chesley, Fia Chiu, Shirley Chiu, Anna Colquohoun, Alana Conner, Erin Dare, Melody Dye, Penny Eckert, Paul Ehrlich, Eric Enderton, Jeannette Ferrary, Shannon Finch, Frank Flynn, Thomas Frank, Cynthia Gordon, Sam Gosling, Sara Grace Rimensnyder, Elaine Hahn, Eric Hahn, Lauren Hall-Lew, Ben Hemmens, Allan Horwitz, Chu-Ren Huang, Calvin Jan, Kim Keeton, Dacher Keltner, Faye Kleeman, Sarah Klein, Scott Klemmer, Steven Kosslyn, Robin Lakoff, Joshua Landy, Rachel Laudan, Adrienne Lehrer, Jure Leskovec, Beth Levin, Daniel Levitan, Mark Liberman, Martha Lincoln, Alon Lischinsky, Doris Loh, Jean Ma, Bill MacCartney, Michael Macovski, Madeleine Mahoney, Victor Mair, Pilar Manchón, Jim Martin, Katie Martin, Linda Martin, Jim Mayfield, Julian McAuley, Dan McFarland, Joe Menn, Lise Menn, Bob Moore, Petra Moser, Rob Munro, Steven Ngain, Carl Nolte, Lis Norcliffe, Barry O'Neill, Debra Pacio Yves Peirsman, James Pennebaker, Charles Perry, Erica Peters, Steven Pinker, Christopher Potts, Matt Purver, Michael Ramscar, Terry Regier, Cecilia Ridgeway, Sara Robinson, Deborah Ross at The Manischewitz Company, Kevin Sayama, Tyler Schnoebelen, Amin Sepehri, Ken Shan, Noah Smith, Peter Smith, Rebecca Starr, Mark Steedman, Janice Ta, Deborah Tannen, Paul Taylor, Peter Todd, Marisa Vigilante, Rob Voigt, Dora Wang, Linda Waugh, Bonnie Webber, Robb Willer, Dekai Wu, Mei Hing Yee, Courtney Young, Linda Yu, Samantha Zee, Katja Zelljadt, Daniel Ziblatt, and Arnold Zwicky.

Image Credits

Page 27. Image © The British Library Board. 1037.g.9, f.415
Page 29. Image courtesy of the New York Public Library
Page 37. Library of Congress image LC-USZ62-58235
Page 46. Image courtesy Department of Special Collections, Stanford University Libraries
Page 54. Image courtesy Cambridge University Press
Page 58. Image courtesy Department of Special Collections, Stanford University Libraries
Page 80. Image courtesy Florence, The Biblioteca Medicea Laurenziana, ms. Med. Palat. 218, c. 312v. On concession of the Ministry for Goods, Cultural Activities and Tourism. Further reproduction by any means is prohibited.
Page 85. Image courtesy Werner Wittersheim.
Page 87. Image courtesy Department of Special Collections, Stanford University Libraries
Page 114. Image © Bettmann/Corbis
Page 122. Image courtesy the Yale Babylonian Collection
Page 132. Image courtesy Matthias Süßen
Page 140. Image courtesy The Emily Dickinson Collection, Amherst College Archives & Special Collections
Page 142. Image courtesy of The Lewis Walpole Library, Yale University
Page 145. Image Courtesy Janet Yu and Mr. and Mrs. Miscellaneous
Page 152. Image © The British Library Board 1037.g.9, f.415
Page 153. Image courtesy Bayerische Staatsbibliothek München, Signatur: 4 Oecon. 1550 m

Index

Page numbers in *italics* refer to illustrations.
Page numbers beginning with 191 refer to notes.

Abbasid Dynasty, 12, 38–40, 131
Abd-al-rahman II, 173
Account of the Trade in India, An
  (Lockyer), 57–59, *58*
acetic acid, 40, 47
Adamson, Melitta, 42
adjectives, as linguistic status clues,
  17–18
Adrià, Ferran, 177
advertising techniques, 5, 159, 189
  customized for target audiences,
    114–15
  for junk foods, 108–16, 118
  TV, 103
Africa, culinary contributions from,
  84, 91, 157
African American food, 91, 143
Aga stove, sales manual for, 114–15
Agirre, Eneko, 188
Agra, 152–53
Ahn, Y. Y., 182
Ain-I-Akbari, 153, 206
Akbar the Great, Mughal Emperor,
  152–53, *152*
Akkadians, 72–73, 76, *122*
à la Française, 25–26
al-Andalus, 173–74
à l'Anglaise, 25
à la Russe, 26, 28
Albala, Ken, 177
ale, *see* beer, ale
alembic, 75, *75*
Alembic, 77
Alioto's, 30

Allen, Robert C., 61
almonds, almond paste, 131–34, 135,
  136–37, 139, 140, 141, 142, 143
amaretti, 139
America:
  culinary contributions of, 25, 26
  global culinary influence on, 49, 59,
    91
  New World cultural blending in,
    43 44, 79–83, 88–91
  slave trade in, 91, 128, 157
  see also United States
American Cookery (Simmons), 89, 147
anchovies, 53–54, 60
Andalusia, 4, 89, 136, 147, 173–174,
  194
Anglo-Saxon language, 118–19
Anna Karenina (Tolstoy), 96
Anne of Austria, 138
Anne of the Island (Montgomery), 95
Antwerp, as trading and financial hub,
  84–86
Antwerp Bourse, 85, *85*
Apicius, 124, 127
Appert, Nicolas, 128
appetizer course, 21, 23–25, 30
Arabs:
  and cooling technology, 151
  culinary contributions from, 3, 56,
    76, 89, 117, 125, 130–31, 134, 136,
    142, 146–47, 150, 157, 159, 173
  in trade, 52
  see also specific cultures
'*araq*, 76

"arbitrariness of the sign," 161
arbitrary relationships, 160
arrack, 2, 56–57, 59, 61, 76, 155, 188
*Arranging the Meal: A History of Table
   Service in France* (Flandrin), 24
*Art of Cookery, Made Plain and Easy,
   The* (Glasse), 46, 196
asparagus, in smell perception, 98
aspic, 3, 43, 48, 188
Audiger, Nicolas, 150, 155
Austen, Jane, 60
authenticity, marketing appeal to, 111,
   114
Aux Lyonnais, 23
Aztecs, 79–80, *80*

Babylon, 40, 48, 53, *122*
back vowels, 161–67, *161, 163*, 207
bacon, 18–19, 118, 128, 171, 184
bacteria, 117
Baghdad, 12, 38–39, 40, 42, 131, 142,
   172–74, 188
Bank Exchange, 30
banquets, 24–26
ba som (sour fish), 50
Basques, 187–88
Batmanglij, Najmieh, 148–49
Bayless, Rick, 82
Bay to Breakers race, 107
beer, ale, 19–20, 56, 64–65, 68–69,
   72–77
   reviews of, 93–96, 99, 104
BeerAdvocate, 93, 95
Belon, Pierre, *87*, 149, 206
Bernhardt, Sarah, 126
Biber, Douglas, 98
bin Yehuda, Isaac, 40
Bi-Rite Creamery, 144–45
Blanco's Restaurant, 28–29, *29*
blogs, bloggers, 99, 163, 208
Boccaccio, Giovanni, 136
bolting, bolting cloths, 119, 121, 129
Book of Sent Soví, The, 42
Book of the Wonders of India, The, 40
bouba/kiki (*maluma/takete*) experi-
   ment, 166–69, *168*, 207
Bourdieu, Pierre, 113
Borzūya the scholar, *37*, 38
Bottéro, Jean, 40

"bow-wow" theory, 170
Boyle, Robert, 155
bragget, 69
bran, 118, 121, 128
brandies, 76
Braudel, Fernand, 22
bread, linguistic history of, 117–23,
   120, 202
Breakfast Experiment, 163
British Museum, 118
Brown-Bakers guild, 121
Brudo, Manuel, 46, 194
Buch der weißhait, Das, *37*
Burning Man, 107
Buttolph, Miss Frank E., 8

cabbage, 124, 127
California gold rush, 35, 57, 64, 181
caliscioni, 132–36, 203
   recipe for, 133
calisson d'Aix, 135–36
Cambodia, 50, 51, 53
candy, 131
canning, 128
Canterbury Tales (Chaucer), 69, 120
Cantonese language, 55, 96–98, 180,
   195
carbonation, 156–57, 167, 169
Caribbean, 59, 128, 139, 142
Carnival, 107
Carol for a Wassail Bowl, A (Foster), 67
Caruso, Enrico, 126
Cato, 124
Celts, 127
ceviche, 3, 35–36, 48
   recipe for, 44–45
Chahuneau, Victor, 10, 93
Chamomile High Club, 65
champagne, 65
Chardin, Jean, 149–50
Charles II, King of England, 145
Chaucer, Geoffrey, 69, 118, 120, 133
cheese:
   macaroni and, 143
   in pastries, 135–36
   saying (when taking photos), 169
Cheetos, 107
Chekyns upon soppes, recipe for, 175
Cheung Hing, 92

chicken, red rice wine recipe for, 52
Child, Julia, 31
Chile, culinary contributions from, 35–36, 48, 62
chile sauces, 79–80
China:
  ancient languages of, 50
  cooking techniques in, 183
  culinary contributions from, 1–2, 3–4, 35, 49–63, 77, 90, 116, 121, 130, 148, 157, 159, 177, 182, 185, 195–96
  economic dominance by, 61–63
  gunpowder developed in, 151
  lack of dessert in, 179–80, 183
  languages of, 54–55, 97–98, 195
  toasting traditions of, 65, 74
  in trade, 38, 40, 54, 56–57, 61–62, 135
Chinese Mid-Autumn Festival, 188
Chinese New Year Parade, 107, 116
Chinese pot still, 56
chocolate, 167, 169
  as marketed to women, 103
  in *mole poblano*, 81–83
Christians, Christianity, 132
  culinary influence of, 42–43, 45–46, 48, 67, 82, 125, 135, 185
Christmas:
  carolling at, 68
  feasts, 35, 88, 177
Church of the Martorana, *132*
cider, 68
  linguistic roots of, 66, 74–76
cis-3-hexen 1-ol, 98
citric acid, 157, 182
citrus, 43–44, 57
Civil War, U.S., 60, 139
Clash! (Markus and Conner), 116
Cliff House, 30
cocktails, 2, 57, 65, 77, 155
Cocoanut Cake, Dickinson's recipe for, 139
coconuts, 139–41, 142, 143, 185
Cod (Kurlansky), 188
coffee, 21
cola, as term, 157
cold packs, 151
cole slaw, 124

Colquhoun, Anna, 48
Columbian exchange, 81, 83
Columbus, Christopher, 83
comfits, 171–72
comparison, language of, 112
Compleat Housewife, The: or, Accomplished Gentlewoman's Companion (E. Smith), 26, 27
Complete System of Cookery, A (Verral), 26
computational linguistics, 93–106
computers, linguistic tools of, 4, 13–14
Confessions of an Advertising Man (Ogilvy), 115
Conner, Alana, 116
Consider the Fork (Wilson), 128
consonants, in sound symbolism, 167–68, 170
continuant sounds, 167
conventionalism, 159–60
cookbooks, 25, 26, 39, 40–41, 47, 59, 89, 120, 123, 125, 131, 132, 136, 137, 142, 146, 194
  first American, 89, 147
  first American Jewish, 140–41
  first English language, 70, 174
  world's oldest, 40, 122, *122*, 173
  see also specific titles
Coriolanus (Shakespeare), 121
corned beef, 127
Cortes, Hernán, 79
cost:
  drug metaphor and, 101–2
  in real vs. fake substitutes, 18–20
  as reflected in menu language, 5, 7–20, 21
  sexual metaphor and, 100–101
  and short vs. long words, 13–14
  and vague vs. specific terms, 15–17
Costello, Elvis, 107
courses:
  order of, 3–4, 5, 21–34, *27*, 171–80
  see also specific courses
Cowen, Tyler, 10
crackers, sound symbolism in names of, *163*, 164, 167
craft authenticity, 111
Cratylus (Plato), 160

Croatia:
  culinary contributions from, 35
  toasting traditions of, 65, 70
Ctesiphon, Persia, 36–38
cuisine:
  culture and, 2, 4, 6, 184
  food pairing variations in, 182–83
  restaurant status and, 7–20
Cuisine and Empire (Laudan), 143
*Cuisinier François, Le (The French
  Cook)* (La Varenne), 25, 42,
  137–38, 146
cultural blending, foods borrowed
  through, 2, 4, 5, 43–45, 47–48, 79,
  81–83, 88–89, 91, 130–31, 142–43,
  152, 184–85, 187–89
cultural omnivorousness, 33–34, 192
cupcakes, 102, 205
custard pies, 89–90

Dalby, Andrew, 172
Datini, Francesco, 134
David, Elizabeth, 145
Davidson, Alan, 22
Dawe, Philip, *142*
Day of the Dead, 116
De Agricultura (Cato), 124
Decameron (Boccaccio), 136
Della Porta, Giambattista, 154
Democracy in America (Tocqueville),
  92
Desfontaines, Pierre, 141
de Sousa, Hilario, 98
dessert:
  craving for, 102
  etymology of term, 171, 176, 179
  history of, 171–85
  in music and songs, 103
  pastries, 133–36, 140
  sexual association of, 102–4
  Thanksgiving, 88–90
dessert course, at end of meal, 3–4, 5,
  21, 30, 171–78
Diana, Princess, death of, 99
Dianda's Italian American Pastry, 130
Diccionario de la Lengua Castellana, 44
Diccionario de la Lengua Española, 36,
  44
Dickens, Charles, 47

Dickinson, Emily, 139, *140*
dietary restrictions:
  Christian, 42, 135, 185
  Jewish, 140
  Muslim, 76
differentiation, language of, 112–13
dim sum, 90, 92, 116
dinde, 78, 86
dinner, as term, 70
distilling, of spirits, 56–57, 62, 65,
  75–76, *75*
Distinction (Bourdieu), 113
dragées, 171–72
Drake, Francis, 62
drink hael, 71
drugs:
  and guilt, 102
  as metaphor for foods, 94, 101–2,
  110, 112, 118
Dubner, Stephen, 16
Dunlop, Fuschia, 97
durum wheat, 134–35
Dutch culinary contributions, 123–24
Dutch East Indies Company, 62–63

Earle, Steve, 107
Easter, 130
East India Company, 57
East-West cultural sharing, 2, 4, 45,
  76, 81, 83
EATymology, 4
Eckert, Penny, 165
economics:
  linguistics and, 4–5, 11, 101
  and trade, 61–63
Economist Gets Lunch, An (Cowen), 10
Ecuador, 48
effervescence, 156–57, 167
egg tarts (*daan tat*), 90
Egypt, 40–41, 148, 149, 188
endosperm, 119, 121
endothermic reactions, 151, 154
England:
  in Asian trade, 56–57, 59, 61–62
  culinary contributions from, 25–26,
  28, 48, 49, 60–61, 69, 75, 87–88,
  89, 118–19, 122, 126, 136, 142, 147,
  154, 156, 172, 174, 176, 182
  imperialism of, 63

entrée course:
French vs. U.S. use of term, 21–25
linguistic history of, 21–34, 130, 143,
178
entrée de table, 24
entremets, 25
escabeche, 3, 36, 43–45, 48, 49, 159
linguistic evolution of, 42, 43, 44
Escoffier, Auguste, 30–31, 115, 125,
176–77
Essay Concerning Human Understanding, An (Locke), 160
Ethiopia, 79, 85
evil eye, 74
evolution:
negative differentiation in, 100
in origin of smiles, 169
of language, 170
exaggeration, 94–95
exogenous factors, 15

Fabrique de Macarons Blanchez bakery, 138
Falstaff, 66
fast food, 49
fat, 102, 176
chicken, 182, 184
feitoria, 84
fermentation, 1–2, 50, 52, 55, 62, 73,
77
Fernald, Anne, 165
Fernet Branca, 65
fireworks, 144, 151
fish:
fried, 42, 43–48, 123
Jewish recipes for, 46–48
salted, 47, 127–28
in *sikbāj*, 40–42, 189
fish and chips, 2–3, 49, 185
culinary roots of, 36, 48
fish course, 25, 28
Fisher, MFK, 179, 184
fish sauce, fermented, 1–2, 50–54, 127,
185, 195
ketchup and, 49–50, 54–55, 57,
59–60, 63
Fitzgerald, F. Scott, 115
Flandrin, Jean-Louis, 24, 175
flavor principle, 182

Flesch-Kincaid measure of language
complexity, 111
fleur de sel, 119
Florentine Codex, *80*
flour:
linguistic history of, 117–23, 128–29
salt and, 117–18
flower, use of term, 119, 121
food pairing hypothesis, 182–83
food words, sound and connotation in,
159–70
Forme of Cury, 70, 123, 174
Fortune, 114
Fortune Cookie Chronicles, The (Lee),
179
fortune cookies, 4, 179–80, 185
Foster, Myles Birket, *67*
4-methylpentanoic acid, 182
1493 (Mann), 63
Fourth of July, 144
France:
culinary contributions from, 21–25,
28, 30–32, 34, 42, 48, 70, 75, 78,
123, 129, 136, 137, 138, 141, 150,
155, 171, 175–79, 182
culinary status of, 7–8, 12, 20, 29,
33, 113, 118–19, 130, 143
Frances, 23–24
Frank, Andre G., 61
Freakonomics (Dubner and Levitt), 16
Freedman, Josh, 108
freezing, development of technology
for, 3, 146, 151–58
French Cook, The (*Le Cuisine François*;
La Varenne), 25, 42, 137–38, 146
French fries, 2–3, 36, 48, 49, 107
French revolution, 138
French toast, 120
frequency code, 164–66, 169–70
front vowels, 161–67, *161*, *163*, 207
fruit, fresh vs. cooked, 176
Fujian province, 49–54, 61–62
Fujian Red Rice Wine Chicken, recipe
for, 52

Gama, Vasco da, 84
ganache, 130, 141
Gargantua and Pantagruel (Rabelais),
136

garos, garum, 53, 128
Gay Pride parade, 116
Geenberg, Katherine Rose, 165
*General History of the Things of New
Spain* (Sahagún), 80
genetics, in smell perception, 98
Genghis Khan, 152
Gerbet, Claude, 141
Germany, culinary contributions from,
19–20, 49, 70, 87, 122, 124
gin, 56
Glasse, Hannah, 46, 47, 196
gnocchi, 136
Golden Gate Bakery, 90
Google Ngram corpus, 33–34, 105,
141, 193, 196
Gopnik, Adam, 102
Grace Countess Granville's Receipt
Book, 145
"grammar of cuisine" theory, 177–78,
180–85
grapes, for wine, 71–73
Great American Music Hall, 28–29
Greece, ancient, 53, 71–72, 74, 78, 122,
132, 134, 136, 146, 160, 172, 177
Green Goddess Dressing, recipe for, 126
green sauce, 124–27
Grice, H. Paul, 18–19, 110, 189, 192
group cooking, 187–88
gruel, 134
Guangdong province, 51–52
Guangxi province, 50
Guide Culinaire, Le (Escoffier), 31
guild of limonadiers, 150
guinea fowl, 85–87, 91, 199
gula melaka, 181
gunpowder, 151, 153
Gutíerrez de Santa Clara, Pedro, 44

Hale, Sarah Josepha, 88
ham, 127
Hardly Strictly Bluegrass, 107
Harris, Emmy Lou, 107
Harun al-Rashid, 39
health:
in Chinese cooking, 183
marketing appeal to, 5, 109–10, 114,
115, 118
toasting to, 65–67, 70–72, 74, 77

Heinz, 60–61
Hellman, Warren, 107, 116
Henry IV, Part I (Shakespeare), 86
Henry VII, King of England, 69
Henry VIII, King of England, 46
herbs, in beverages, 74, 76–77
Hermogenes, 160
Herodotus, 172
heung (smells good), 97
Hilton, Chris, 50
hiphop culture, 77
hippocras, 171
Histoire de la Nature des Oyseaux, L'
(Belon), 87
Histories (Herodotus), 172
History of Medicine (*Uyūn al-ānbā*; Ibn
Abī Usaybi'a), 151
hlaf-dige, 118
hlaf-weard, 118
Hmong-Mien, 50
Hokkien language, 54–55, 195
Holland:
in Asian trade, 56, 62
culinary contributions from, 123,
124
Homer, 72
Hong Kong, 97
hops, 64, 69
hors d'oeuvres, 25–26, 28
Huang Hsing-tsung, 195
Humphry Slocombe, 144, 171

Ibn Abī Usaybi'a, 151
Ibn Bakhtawayh, 151
Ibn Hayyan, 173
Ibn Shahriyar, Buzurg, 40
ice, in cooling, 148, 149, 151
ice cream, 3, 155, 176, 185, 189
evolving technology of, 144–58
fad for unusual flavors in, 144–45,
171, 184
recipes for, 145–46
sound symbolism in names of,
162–64, *163*, 167
ice creameries, 144–45
icehouses, 148
Idrisi, Muhammad al-, 134–35
Illinois language, 90
imitation foods, 19, 59, 196

independent self, 116
India, 78, 151–52
 trade with, 38, 40, 57, 61, 83–84
India Pale Ale, 65
Indo-Europeans, 71–72, 74
Indonesia, 55, 57
Industrial Revolution, 62
information theory, 13
interdependent self, 116
Internet, 8, 10, 13
 recipes on, 182
 restaurant reviews on, 92–106
 see also specific sites
isicia, 127
Islam, spread of, 38–42, 48, 130–32,
 146
issue de table, 24
Italy, culinary contributions from, 33,
 34, 35, 42, 65, 89, 123, 124–25, 131,
 136, 139, 142, 153–55, 178–79
itria, 134

Jakobson, Roman, 161
Japan, culinary contributions from, 36,
 45–46, 48, 49, 51, 63, 179
Java, 56–57, 62
Jerome, Saint, 74–75
Jesperson, Otto, 161
Jesuits, 45–46
Jewish Cookery Book (Levy), 140–41
Jewish Manual, A (Montefiore), 47
Jewish recipes for fish, 46–48
Jews, 36, 40, 65, 107, 117, 122, 132,
 148
 culinary contributions of, 46–48,
 73–74, 128, 130, 135, 140, 182, 194,
 204
John of Caput, 37
julep, as term, 157
junk foods:
 craving for, 102, 108, 118
 linguistics in marketing of, 107–16

Kalm, Pehr, 124
Kam tribe, 50–51
*Kanz Al-Fawa'id Fi Tanwi' Al
 Mawa'id, or The Treasury of Useful
 Advice for the Composition of a
 Varied Table*, 40–41

Katz, Joshua, 90
kasuzuke (Japanese dish), 52
Kelis, 103
kecap, 55
ketchup, 47, 57, 59–63, 79, 130, 143,
 159, 184, 185, 188, 189, 196
 and Chinese economic history,
 61–62
 linguistic roots of, 1–2, 49–50,
 54–55, 57, 60–61
 plate of, for dinner, 114
 recipes for, 59–60
 U.S. production of, 60–61
kettle corn, 107
Khosrau I Anushirvan, Shahanshah of
 Persia, 36–39, 37, 131
Kitāb al-Tabīkh (*Book of Cookery, The*;
 al-Warrāq), 39, 131, 173
Kitāb al-Tabīkh (*Book of Dishes, The*;
 al-Baghdadi), 131
Kitab al-Wusla, 125
Klein, Sarah, 117
Klink, Richard, 162
Köhler, Wolfgang, 166
Korea, food vocabulary of, 103
Kurlansky, Mark, 188

lactic acid, 50
Ladies' Home Journal, The, 89
Ladurée pastry shop, 141
La Fontaine, Jean de, 38
Lakoff, Robin, 11
language:
 change in, 31–33, 95
 cuisine compared to, 177–78, 181
 evolutionary origin of, 169–70
 pronunciation in, 90, 161–62, 165,
 181
Language Log, 163
La Oaxaqueña, 82
Laos, 50, 51
Larousse Gastronomique, 31, 33, 138–39
lasagne, as term, 134, 135
La Taqueria, 92
Latin, 43, 71, 120, 122, 123, 126, 127,
 132, 148
Laudan, Rachel, 143
lauzīnaj, 3, 131–34, 137, 143, 172, 173
 recipe for, 131

La Varenne, François Pierre de, 25, 42, 137–38, 146
leavening, 117, 208
Lee, Jennifer B., 179
Lehrer, Adrienne, 100
lemonade, 144, 156, 157, 158
  recipes for, 150–51, 156
lemons, 30, 43, 57, 149–50
  etymology of word, 206
Lent, 42, 135, 189
Leskovec, Jure, 93
Lévi-Strauss, Claude, 183
Levitt, Steven, 16
Levy, Esther, 140
Lewis, Edna, 91
libations, 72–73, 77
Liberman, Mark, 18, 163
Libro de Coȝina (de Nola), 174
Lime Syrup (*Sharbat-e ablimu*), recipe for, 148–49
Lincoln, Abraham, 88
"linguistic fillers," 15–17, 20
Linneaus, Carl, 87
liquid nitrogen, 151
Liuqiu Guo Shi Lue (*Account of the Ryukyu Islands*; Zhao Huang), 54
Livre Fort Excellent de Cuysine Tres-Utile et Profitable, 24
Llibre del Coch (Master Robert), 43
Lloyd, Martha, 60
locavores, 9–10
Locke, John, 160
Lockyer, Charles, 57–59, *58*, 61, 196
lohusa şerbet, 150
Louis XIV, King of France, 138
love, use of term, 95

Macao, 89–90
macaroni, 3, 7, 8, 204
  linguistic history of, 130–43
Macaroni, The (Dawe), *142*
macaroni and cheese, 143
macaronic French, 7–8, 20, 143, 191
macaronic verse, 7, 136, 204
Macaroni Journal, 135
Macaronis, 141–42, *142*
macarons, 3, 8, 130, 138–39, *138*, 141, 143, 188

macaroons, 3, 159, 184–85, 189, 205
  linguistic history of, 130–43
  recipes for, 137, 138, 140–41
Maclay, William, 176
Mad Men, 114
Magia Naturalis (Della Porta), 154
Mahabharata, 152
main course, as term, 34
Maison des Soeurs Macarons bakery, 138
Maison Reglée, La (Audiger), 150
makaria, 134, 136
malic acid, 157
Malin, Joseph, 48
maluma/takete (bouba/kiki) experiment, 166–69, *168*, 207
manchet, 121
Mandarin Chinese, 54, 55, 97, 179, 195
Manischewitz, 140
Mann, Charles, 63
Manuscrito Anonimo, 174
Marcus, Hazel Rose, 116
Maria Theresa, Infanta of Spain, 138
Maritime Silk Road, 53
marked words, 105–6
marketing:
  of junk foods, 107–16
  linguistic status clues in, 9, 110–16, 159
  to the masses, 113–15
  through sound symbolism, 161–67
  to wealthy clientele, 110–13
  see also advertising techniques
marmalade, 146–47, 157, 185, 189
  recipes for, 147
Martellotti, Anna, 43
Martha Washington's Booke of Cookery, 137
Martino, Maestro, 132–33, 136
marzipan, *marȝapane*, 132–34, 135, 142
  recipe for, 133
Mason Adam pâtisserie, 138
matzo, 48
Maven, 65, 77
"maxim of quantity," 18
"maxim of relevance," 18
Mayhew, Henry, 121, 156
mayonnaise, 126
McAuley, Julian, 93
McGovern, Patrick, 71

McKean, Erin, 95
meals, order of courses at, 3–4, 5,
21–34, *27*, 171–80
meats:
preserved, 127
savory and sweet, 174–75, 177
meat stew, 39, 42
medicine, food as, 148, 155, 157, 176
Meleager (Sophocles), 78, 87, 91
meleagris, 87, 199
membrillo, 146
Menagier de Paris, Le, 125
Menon, Geeta, 162–63, 207
menus:
author's linguistic study of, 10–20,
93, 112, 191
historical perspective of, 7–8,
19–20, 130, 172
linguistic status clues in, 5, 7–20,
111, 143, 159
modern, 20, 34
New York Public Library collection
of, 8
origin and etymology of, 26
for Washington's inauguration, 176
Merry Wives of Windsor, The (Shakespeare), 66
Mesopotamia, 36–41, 72–73, 148
*Methodus Refrigerandi ex Vocato Sale
Nitro Vinum Aquamque* (Villafranca), *153*
meunière, 123
Mexico, culinary contributions from,
3, 79–81, 112, 124, 182, 188
Meyers, Cindy, 138
michelada, recipe for, 64
Mill, 66
milling, 118, 123, 129
Ming dynasty, 61
mining, 35–36, 57, 62
salt, 118
Mintz, Sidney W., 177
miso, 51
Misra, Reeva, 166–67
Mitchell's, 145
Moche, 44, 48
modernist cuisine, 184
molasses, 181–82
mole, 80–83

molecular gastronomy, 144
mole poblano de guajolote (Turkey with
Puebla Mole), recipe for, 81–83,
91, 198
Mon-Khmer, 50–51
Montefiore, Judith Cohen, 47
Morat's, 150
Morton, Eugene, 164–65
Moss, Michael, 108
mouth feel, vocabulary for, 96, 103
Mr. and Mrs. Miscellaneous, 145, *145*
Mughals, 152, 157
mushrooms, in ketchup, 59–60
music, dessert association in, 103
Music Box, 28
Mutawakkil, al-, 40

Nahuatl, 79, 81
naming, sound connotation in, 159–70
nam pla, 53
narezushi, 51
Nasrallah, Nawal, 39
Native Americans, 79, 88, 90, 91
naturalism, 159
*Natvrall and Artificial Directions for
Health* (Vaughan), 176
Neckam, Alexander, 127
negative bias, 98, 99, 104
negative differentiation, 96, 99, 100,
112–13
negative emotional words, negative
sentiment words, 94–96
as expressed in stories, 98–99
Neige de Fleur D'orange, recipe for, 146
New World:
cultural sharing in, 43–44, 80–83,
88–89, 91
turkeys in, 79–83, 88–91
Ngo, Mary Kim, 166–67
*97 Orchard: An Edible History of Five
Immigrant Families* (Ziegleman),
20
Ninkasi, 73
Noah hypothesis, 71–72
Nola, Roberto de, 174
noodles, 134–35
Normans, 118–19, 126, 132, 142, 152,
174
Nostradamus, 135–36

nougats, 131, 143
Nouvelle Cuisine, 177
Nowrūʒ (Persian New Year), 130, 131
nuns, 81, 138, 188
nuoc mam, 2, 53
nuts, 60, 131–32, 157

Ogilvy, David, 114–15, *114*
Ogilvy and Mather, 114
Ohala, John, 164–65, 169
Ohlone, 35
Old Clam House, 35
Oliver Twist (Dickens), 47
omicron letters, 160
One Thousand and One Nights, 38, 39, 173
orange blossom ice cream, early recipes for, 145–46
oranges, in marmalade, 147
Ottomon Empire, 80–81, 148, 149, 154
ovens, China's lack of, 180
Ovid, 87
Oxford Companion to Food (Davidson), 22
Oxford English Dictionary, 26, 195

Pacio, Debra, 103
pain perdu, payn purdyeu, recipe for, 120
Palace Hotel, 126
Panchatantra, *37*, 38
Parker, Robert, 100
Passover, 130, 135, 140
pasta:
    linguistic history of, 134–36, 139, 141–43
    terms for, 135
pastel de nata, 89
pastries, 131–36
    and pasta, 135
    savory and sweet, 135–36
payndemayn, paindemain, 119–21
pecan, pronunciation of, 90, *90*
pecan pie, recipe for, 89
Pennebaker, James, 99
Perry, Charles, 125, 131, 194
Persia:
    culinary contributions from, 2–3, 12–13, 36–39, 48, 76, 79, 131, 142, 146, 148–49, 157, 172–74, 177, 188
    in trade, 53

Persian sherbet, 156
Peru, culinary contributions from, 35–36, 43, 48, 62
pescado frito, 43
    recipe for, 45
Peters, Erica J., 115
phones (language), 160, 181
phosphoric acid, 157
Phu Quoc, 53
pieces of eight, 36, 57, 62, 63
pies, 89–90
Pilgrims, and First Thanksgiving, 88, 91
pirates, 61–63
Pisco punch, 30, 36, 64, 76
pitch, 164–65, 169
Pizarro González, Francisco, 43–44
plat, 21, 34
Plato, 131, 160
Poe, Edgar Allan, 78
politicians, linguistic devices of, 114–15
Pollyanna effect, 5, 105–6
Polo, Marco, 53, 135
Pomerantz, Kenneth, 61
Pop Rocks, 156
Porter, Eleanor, 105
Portlandia, 9–10
Portugal:
    in Asian trade, 62
    culinary contributions from, 3, 43–46, 48, 89–90, 188
    New World exploration by, 79, 83–84, 86, 189
positive bias, 104–6
positive emotional words, positive sentiment words, 94, 95, 96, 104–5
potato chips, 33, 108–16, 118, 130
potatoes, fried, 2–3, 36, 48, 49, 107
pottages, 69
Potts, Chris, 104
preservatives, preservation:
    fermenting as, 50, 51, 55
    hops as, 65, 69
    salt as, 47, 50, 54, 55, 127–28
    vinegar as, 39–40, 46–47, 128
pronunciation:
    regional, 90, *90*
    tongue in, 161–62, *161*, 165, 181

Propre Newe Booke of Cokerye, 175
pumpkin pie, recipe for, 89
punch, 2, 30, 36, 57, 155
Puritans, 66–67
Purver, Matt, 48

Quantal Theory of Speech (K. Stevens),
    181
quince paste, 146–47
Qingming Festival, 130

Rabelais, François, 136
rakia, 65, 66, 76
Ramayana, 152
Rand, Sally, 28
Rashi, 135
Raspberry shrub, recipe for, 155–56
Rath, Eric C., 46
ravioli, 134, 204
recipes:
    world's oldest, 73, 76
    see also specific recipes
red rice wine, 49–50, 76
    chicken recipe for, 52
refined foods, 5, 117, 129
refrigeration, development of, 128,
    148, 151–55, *153*
regression (statistical tool), 101, 112
relevé (remove), 25–26
Republic (Plato), 130
resonance, 164–65
restaurant reviews:
    author's linguistic study of, 5,
        92–106
    negative, 95–100
    positive, 96, 100–106
restaurants:
    chain, 17
    ethnic and cultural variety in, 14,
        33–34, 48
    linguistic clues to status and cost of,
        7–20, 191
    linguistics in evaluation of, 92–106
    see also specific establishments
Rhubarb syrup, recipe for, 148
rice, fermented red, 55–56
Richard II, King of England, 70
roast course, 25–26, 31
Robert, Master, 43

Roden, Claudia, 148
Roger I, King of Sicily, 132
Roger II, King of Sicily, 132, *132*,
    134–35
Rome, ancient, 53, 72, 123, 148
Romeo and Juliet (Shakespeare), 159
Routledge, Bryan, 10, 93
Rozin, Elizabeth, 182
rum, 56, 57, 59, 155

Sahagún, Bernardino de, 80
sailors, culinary contribution of, 40,
    46–47, 54, 56, 57, 62, 188
Saison, 7, 11
saison, 129
salad, 5, 30, 183
    first recipe for, 123
    as term, 123–24
salad course, 179, 184
salsa, 5, 123, 124
salsa en polvo, 64
salsa verde, recipe for, 125
salt, 5, 181, 182
    and flour, 117–18
    in freezing, 146, 154–55, 157
    linguistic history of, 123–29
    as preservative, 47, 50, 54, 55,
        127–28
    sour, 182
    -sugar balance, 108
salt cod, 128
salting, salted, 47, 50, 54, 55, 127–28
    as term, 95, 123
saltpeter (potassium nitrate), 151,
    153–54, 157–58
Salt Sugar Fat (Moss), 107
sandwich cookies, 141
San Francisco, 62, 78
    celebrations and festivals in, 107,
        116, 130, 144, 188
    Chinese in, 49, 65, 107, 116, 130, 188
    culinary culture of, 7, 21, 23–24,
        28–30, 33, 35–36, 48, 64–65, 66,
        77, 82, 92, 93, 117, 126, 128, 171,
        181–82, 208
San Francisco earthquake (1906), 28,
    30, 126
San Sebastian, Spain, 187–88
Sassanid empire, 36–38, 131, 142

sauce, 5, 124–27
  linguistic roots of term, 55, 123, 124
sauerkraut, 124, 127
sausage, 127
Saussure, Ferdinand de, 161
Scheel, Mrs., 132–33
Scotland, 56, 147
Scott, Edmund, 56–57, 62, 196
seafood, 35–36, 44, 188
  see also fish
seasonings, 129
secondi, 34
semantic bleaching, 55, 94–95
semolina, 122
September 11th, 2001, terrorist attacks,
  99
sex, as metaphor for foods, 5, 94,
  100–104
"Shahnameh, The," 38
Shakespeare, William, 67, 86, 121, 159,
  175
Shakur, Tupac, 77
Shannon, Claude, 13
sharbat, 155, 158, 185, 189
  recipe for, 148–49
sheker, 73–75
sherbet, 143, 148–52, 154, 159, 185, 188
  powders and tablets, 149–50, 156–57
  roots of term, 148, 155, 156
Shesgreen, Sean, 100
shikaru, 73, 76
shikker, 65, 66, 75–76
Shilling Cookery for the People (Soyer),
  47–48
shrub (drink), 155–56
Sibawayhi, 12–13
Sicily, culinary contributions from,
  130–31, 134–36, 142, 152, 174, 188
sikbāj:
  culinary history of, 2–3, 35–48, 41,
    122, 130, 131, 143, 172, 185, 189
  recipes for, 39, 40–42
silver, 62
silver reals, 36, 57, 62, 63
Simmel, Georg, 143
Simmons, Amelia, 89, 147
simnel cake, 122
siqqu, 53
slave trade, 91, 128, 157

slivovitz, 65
Slobin, Dan, 168
smell perception:
  synesthesia in, 168
  vocabulary for, 96–98
smiles, origin of, 144, 169–70, 189
Smith, Eliza, 26, 27
Smith, Noah, 10, 93
Smitten, 144
Snickers bars, 131
snow, in cooling, 141, 148, 154, 157
"social stage model of coping," 99
sociedad gastronómica, 187
Socrates, 160
sodas, 144, 157
soft drinks, 3
sole meunière, 123
Sophocles, 78, 87
sops, 69–70, 120
sorbets, as term, 146, 155, 156, 157, 206
sound symbolism, 161–67
  visual experiment in, 166
soup course, 25, 28, 30
sourdough, 117, 129, 208
sourness, 156–57, 181
  cultural variations in, 182
Southern Barbarian Cookbook, 45–46, 194
soy, 53, 55, 59
  sauce, 51
Soyer, Alexis, 47
Spain:
  culinary contributions from, 3,
    42–43, 49, 53, 123, 131, 132, 146,
    152, 187–88
  New World conquest by, 43–44, 63,
    80–84, 91
Spence, Charles, 166–67
spice trade, 83–84
spirits, distilled, 56–57
status, markers of, 5, 7–20, 29, 33,
  110–16, 118–19, 134, 142, 143, 150,
  159
"status anxiety," 18
Stevens, Ken, 181
Stevens, Wallace, 170
Stevenson, Robert Louis, 63
stills, 56, 75, 75
stories, negative emotions expressed
  through, 98–99

Strabo, 127
Strauss, Susan, 103
Streit's, 140
strident sounds, 167
sugar, 2, 73, 77, 128, 134, 139, 155,
    174–76, 181–82
  craving for, 102
  palm, 181–82
  -salt balance, 108
Sumatra, 56–57
supper, linguistic roots of, 70, 189
sushi, 47, 51, 63
  sexual association of, 102
Sutro, Adolph, 30
Sutro baths, 30
sweet:
  in Chinese cooking, 180
  cultural variations in, 181–82
  and savory, 174–75, 177, 182, 185
  and sour, 38, 61, 182, 185
sweets, 131–34, 173–75, 181
  see also dessert
synesthesia, synesthesic hypothesis,
    168–70
syrups, 3, 147–49, 155, 157, 181, 188

Tadich Grill, 35
tafaya, 173–74
Tai-Kadai, 50–51
Tajín, 64
tamales, *80*, 82, 92, 116
Tang dynasty, 151
tapas, 188
taquerias, 92
Taqueria Vallarta, 92
tartaric acid, 157
Taste of Country Cooking, The (Lewis),
    91
taste perception:
  cultural variation in, 181–82
  synesthesia in, 168
  vocabulary for, 96
tempura, 36, 46, 48, 49
Texas Pecan Pie, 89
texture perception, vocabulary of,
    103
Tezcatlipoca (trickster god), 79
Thailand, 50, 51, 53, 182
Thanksgiving, 28, 35, 78, 88–91, 177

"Things That Can Never Come Back,
    Are Several, The" (Dickinson),
    139
Times of London, 47
toast (bread), 66, 69–70
toasting, 3, 6, 64–77, 189
  to "health" and "life," 65–67,
    70–71, 72, 74, 77
Tocqueville, Alexis de, 92
toi toi toi, 74
Tolstoy, Leo, 96
tomata catsup, recipe for, 60
tomatoes, in ketchup, 2, 55, 60, 185
  chemical compounds in, 182
tones, language, 97
tongue, in pronunciation, 161–62, *161*,
    165, 181
torrone, 131
totolmole, 80
trading, international, 2, 38, 40, 53, 54,
    56–58, 61–63, 83–84, 86
traditional authenticity, 114–15
tragemata, 172
Transamerica Pyramid, 30
trans fats, 110
trauma, linguistic symptoms of, 99,
    106
Treasure Island (Stevenson), 63
Trick Dog, 77
Trillin, Calvin, 7, 20, 33
Turkey, 72, 78, 85, 148, 149–50, 157
turkey cock, 85–86
turkeys, 3, 6, *87*, 130, 188, 189, 198
  linguistic history of, 78–91
  in *mole*, 80–83
Turkish Delight, 131
turtle soup, 19–20
txakolin, 188
txoko, 187

umami, 181, 182
United States:
  culinary contributions of, 28, 30, 32,
    60–61, 70, 88–91, 120, 131, 141,
    142, 155–56, 176, 177, 181–82
  order of courses in Europe vs.,
    178–79
  public opinion in, 92–93
unmarked words, 105–6

urbanization, 98
usquebagh, 56

van Oosten Batavia arrack, 56
Vaughan, William, 176
Vaux, Bert, 90
Veblen, Thorsten, 143
Vega, Juan José, 44
Venice, 80–81
Verral, William, 26
Viandier, Le, 125
Vietnam, 50, 51, 57
    culinary contributions from, 2, 53
Villafranca, Blas, 153–54, *153*
vinegar, 38–41, 43, 46–47, 50, 123, 124,
    128, 149, 155, 182
Visher, Mrs., 124
visual perception:
    synesthesia in, 168
    vocabulary for, 96
vowels, in sound symbolism, 161–67,
    161, *163*, 169, 189, 207
Vulgate Bible, 74

waes hael, 70–71
Warrāq, Ibn Sayyār al-, 39, 131, 173
Washington, George and Martha, 176
wassail, 68–71
    recipe for, 68–69
"wassail the trees," 68
water, disease and, 183–84
Watson, Doc, 107
weddings:
    culinary traditions in, 3, 6, 24
    toasting at, 65–66, 72, 76
wheat:
    kernel structure of, 119
    milling of, 118, 123, 129

for pasta, 134–35
    see also flour
wheat germ, 119, 129
Wilson, Bee, 128
Wilson, C. Anne, 147
wine, 56, 66, 69, 71, 98, 156, 157, 188,
    197
    freezing of, 154
    linguistic history of, 71–74
    red rice, 49–50, 56
    reviews of, 100
    spiced, 171–72
Wireker, Nigellus, 71
Witherly, Steven, 108
Wondrich, David, 30, 57, 155
Worchestershire sauce, 59, 196
word frequency, 104
word pairs, markedness in, 105
World War I, 28, 179
Wu, Emperor of China, 50–51

Yale Culinary Tablets, 40, 122, *122*
"Yankee Doodle," 142
yeast, 117
Yelp, 92–93, 104
Yi (Hundred Yue), 50–51
Yi Yin, 97
Yorkston, Eric, 162–63, 207
Yu, Janet, 53, 65, 66, 97, 107, 108, 125,
    126, 144, 158, 171, 180, 187
Yu, Linda, 103

Zheng Chenggong (Koxinga), 61–62
Zheng He, 53
Zhou Huang, *54*
Ziegleman, Jane, 20
Zipf, George, 13
Ziryab, 173–74